Vital Signs

Perspectives on the Health
of American Campaigning

David A. Dulio
Candice J. Nelson

Foreword by
James A. Thurber

BROOKINGS INSTITUTION PRESS
Washington, D.C.

Copyright © 2005
THE BROOKINGS INSTITUTION
1775 Massachusetts Avenue, N.W., Washington, D.C. 20036
www.brookings.edu

Library of Congress Cataloging-in-Publication data
Dulio, David A.
Vital signs : perspectives on the health of American campaigning /
David A. Dulio and Candice J. Nelson.
p.   cm.
Summary: "Through analysis of the 2004 presidential campaigns of George W. Bush and John F. Kerry, explores the strengths and weaknesses of the current U.S. campaign system and possible approaches to improving campaign conduct"—Provided by publisher.
Includes bibliographical references and index.
ISBN-13: 978-0-8157-1952-6 (cloth : alk. paper)
ISBN-10: 0-8157-1952-3 (cloth : alk. paper)
ISBN-13: 978-0-8157-1951-9 (paper : alk. paper)
ISBN-10: 0-8157-1951-5 (paper : alk. paper)
   1. Presidents—United States—Election—2004. 2. United States—Politics and government—2001–. 3. Political campaigns—United States—Case studies.
I. Nelson, Candice J., 1949– . II. Title.
E905.D85 2005
324.7'0973'090511—dc22   2005018130

9 8 7 6 5 4 3 2 1
The paper used in this publication meets minimum requirements of the American National Standard for Information Sciences—Permanence of Paper for Printed Library Materials: ANSI Z39.48-1992.

Typeset in Sabon

Composition by R. Lynn Rivenbark
Macon, Georgia

Printed by R. R. Donnelley
Harrisonburg, Virginia

For Adrianne

D.A.D.

For my mother, Jean R. Nelson,
and in memory of my father, Richard T. Nelson

C.J.N.

Contents

Foreword

Election campaigns are central events in American democratic life. An important function of campaigns is that they link citizens with government by providing a regular opportunity for the governed both to give their consent to their representatives and to hold those same representatives accountable for past performance. These political campaigns profoundly affect public officials and the policies they pursue, as they are democratic battles among candidates for the opportunity to serve in public office. Campaigns educate voters about candidates' policy positions and persuade the electorate to vote for one of those candidates based on their visions for the role of government as well as specific policy proposals.

Arguably, almost any consequential political development in American politics and government is closely connected with campaigns and the electoral process. Because of this, understanding the complexity and dynamics of election campaigns and the roles of the central actors in this process is essential to appreciating our democratic system. Recently, however, our democratic system has come under some scrutiny because of several problems that supposedly plague our campaigns. This list of ills includes, but is not limited to, negative campaigning, the high cost of campaigns, and a focus on personality over issues and substance. In short, the health of our system of campaigning has been called into doubt. This book is an evaluation of the health of campaigning in the United States.

This volume presents a careful examination and evaluation of the role of candidates, political consultants, party leaders, and the general public in American campaigns—some of the main players in our campaigns. The central purpose of this book is to address the question, What is the status of campaigning in America? *Vital Signs: Perspectives on the Health of American Campaigning* explores the well-being of our system of campaigning by analyzing modern campaign management over the past several years, culminating in the 2004 election. The book is structured around four questions: Who makes the key decisions about what is done in campaigns? What do the principal campaign actors think about specific aspects of our system? How do these electoral actors see the role of money in our system and what do they think of reform? Are campaigns being run ethically?

Research for the study leading to this book was conducted with funding from The Pew Charitable Trusts' grant for the Improving Campaign Conduct project from 1997 to 2003. A major objective of the grant was to study and to improve political discourse and campaign conduct of candidates and the political consulting industry in support of democratic renewal. The research on campaign industry attitudes, norms, and accepted campaign strategies and tactics was done to assess the state of the professional campaign industry and to evaluate the quality of campaigning generally. This book encapsulates knowledge gained from seven years of study using multiple surveys of the general public, campaign consultants, and political party leaders. Although the primary data collection method used was the opinion survey, focus groups and ongoing discussions with dozens of campaign professionals over seven years also contributed to this assessment of the health of American campaigning. Additional surveys and studies by others of candidates, journalists, organized interests, and the public supplement the study's surveys and systematic participant observation.

This book is the culmination of a larger body of research supported by the Improving Campaign Conduct project in the context of an ongoing research agenda about campaign conduct generated by the grant. Paul C. Light, Sean Treglia, and Michael Delli Carpini, formerly of The Pew Charitable Trusts, and Rebecca Rimel, president of The Pew Trusts, all provided remarkable support and confidence in the effort to study, assess, and improve American campaign conduct and ultimately our democratic processes. That support fostered varied and extensive publications about campaigns. That research built the foundation of this assessment of campaigning in America.

Like all outstanding scholarly works, this book owes a debt to many people, but the several studies funded by The Pew Charitable Trusts' Improving Campaign Conduct grant were particularly important to the building blocks of this assessment of American campaigning. The array of conferences, workshops, survey reports, articles, and books resulting from the project also contributed to this study, as did the dozens of scholars and practitioners who have published their research about campaigning with the project.

With this careful evaluation of the health of our campaigns, David Dulio and Candice Nelson, principal scholars on the Improving Campaign Conduct team, make a major contribution to our understanding about how American campaigning has changed at the beginning of the twenty-first century.

JAMES A. THURBER
Director, Center for Congressional
and Presidential Studies
American University

June 2005

Acknowledgments

As is the case with most scholarly work, this book would not have been possible without the help of countless individuals. First and foremost is James A. Thurber, the principal investigator on the Improving Campaign Conduct project at American University, which was the inspiration for this book. Without Jim's leadership and guidance, American University would never have gotten the funding from The Pew Charitable Trusts to conduct the grant project. Truly, without him all of the studies that our own project produced would not have seen the light of day. We are indebted to him for his leadership, guidance, generosity, and friendship. As Jim also mentions in the foreword, we also owe a great deal of thanks to The Pew Charitable Trusts for their financial support of our project and their desire to see us work toward better election campaigns.

We would also like to thank our colleagues who provided wonderful feedback on the manuscript as it went through its several drafts and as we worked through various issues in the book. Four anonymous reviewers provided very helpful feedback on earlier versions that improved the manuscript a great deal. We are grateful for the time they gave to our project. Colleagues at our own institutions also helped us through the process in a number of ways. At Oakland University, David Downing, former dean of the College of Arts and Sciences, and the former and current Chairs of the Department of Political Science, Michelle Piskulich and John Klemanski, provided great support. Pete Trumbore provided support through his wit and sarcasm and was a relief during stressful times.

Karen Meyer provided great administrative support throughout the process. At American University, Provost Cornelius M. Kerwin and William M. LeoGrande, Dean of the School of Public Affairs, provided tremendous support of the larger project from the beginning. At the Center for Congressional and Presidential Studies, Melissa Castle and R. Sam Garrett provided invaluable logistical and administrative support and assistance as well.

We would also like to thank Christopher Kelaher, the Director of Marketing and former acquisitions editor at Brookings Institution Press, for his support of this project as well as of the four previous books that have been produced by the Improving Campaign Conduct project. Several other individuals at Brookings were important to the completion of this book. Mary Kwak, the acquisitions editor, pushed us to revise the book in ways that substantially improved our work. We would also like to thank Robert L. Faherty, the director of the press; Janet Walker, the managing editor; Katherine Kimball, who copyedited the text; Carlotta Ribar, who proofread the pages; and Mary Mortensen, who provided the index.

This has been a collaborative process from the beginning, between the authors and among our colleagues. We are grateful for all the support; any remaining errors are our own.

CHAPTER 1

A Tale of
Two Campaigns?

Not only are we going to New Hampshire, Tom Harkin, we're going to South Carolina and Oklahoma and Arizona and North Dakota and New Mexico. We're going to California and Texas and New York. And we're going to South Dakota and Oregon and Washington and Michigan and then we're going to Washington, D.C., to take back the White House! Yeeeeeah!

—HOWARD DEAN, *after the Iowa caucuses, January 19, 2004*

In what is certainly an indelible image from the 2004 presidential race, Howard Dean's now infamous "scream" can be seen as a microcosm of the larger campaign. It was simultaneously a sign of the good and the bad that appeared throughout the election season. One might be tempted to ask, How can the scene that played out on caucus night in West Des Moines, Iowa, possibly be indicative of anything good? Well, if one goes back and looks at the full video of the speech, it is clear that Dean was speaking to a crowd of dedicated supporters who were fully behind their candidate—the *New York Times* called them "fiery"— and who wanted him to keep fighting for the nomination.[1] In addition, it was Howard Dean who can be credited, at the outset, with getting certain portions of the electorate intensely interested in the presidential election of 2004 with his fierce criticism of President George W. Bush. Dean also advanced campaigning in one particular area by taking advantage of a relatively new source of funds for candidates and information for potential voters—the Internet—as no candidate had done before. He constructed a campaign from the ground up with grassroots support (as is clear from the more than thirty-five hundred volunteers who traveled to Iowa from other states to work for the Dean campaign) in an era of campaigning that has come to be known more for television ads than house-to-house campaigning. Dean showed that insurgent campaigns can have some success, and he created, in part, the atmosphere that led to excitement and enthusiasm among Democrats that continued through until election day on November 2, 2004.

Obviously, however, all was not positive for the former governor of Vermont after the Iowa caucuses. Although his support in states like Iowa and New Hampshire had begun to slide before the caucuses, what truly brought on his downfall as the front-runner in the race for the Democratic Party nomination was the media coverage of his speech after the caucus results came in. Continually replaying the "Dean scream" solidly during the time between the Iowa caucuses and the New Hampshire primary, network and cable news completed the cycle they had begun, taking Dean from the darling of the primaries to the down and out.

This event, and its aftermath, is the bad that came out of this particular evening in West Des Moines. It illustrates the overwhelming power of both the media and the expectations set on candidates in presidential primaries. If the media had not played his "concession" speech over and over again, or if they had instead played the entire video clip—including the beginning, which illustrated the excitement in the crowd to which he was reacting—Dean might have had a chance to recover from his third-place finish in Iowa with a strong showing in New Hampshire, where he also had held a lead in the polls for the months leading up to the primary voting. However, the media cannot be blamed completely; it was quite a story and an intriguing video.[2]

This book is about the health of campaigning in America. Many pundits, commentators, and scholars are quick to say that our system of electing candidates is ill. They point to alleged problems such as decreasing voter turnout, increases in "negative" attack ads, the exacerbation of the permanent campaign by candidates' handlers and political consultants, the lack of media attention to important issues during the campaign, the decline in interest and efficacy in the electorate, and the increasing costs of seeking office, which are associated with the growing presence of massive amounts of money in campaigns, to name only a few. We do not wish to be so quick to judge, however. In the chapters that follow, we undertake an exploration of several key factors related to the health of our system of campaigning. There are unquestionably issues that need attention in our system of campaigning. But we believe there are also signs of hope. The 2004 presidential campaign, aside from its inauspicious start in West Des Moines for Governor Dean, illustrates what we mean.

It Was the Best of Campaigns

Campaign 2004 was, in the language of the literary classic *A Tale of Two Cities,* the best of campaigns and the worst of campaigns. Some aspects of the 2004 election cycle are clearly good news for our system of campaigning, but other features should make us question the health of modern campaigns. Consider, for instance, as a sign of the positive aspects of the 2004 election cycle, the record turnout of voters on election day. On November 2, 2004, roughly 121 million voters went to the polls and cast a ballot for either President George W. Bush or Senator John F. Kerry.[3] George Bush won more votes than any presidential candidate in American history—more than 60 million—and John Kerry received the second-highest vote total of any candidate in history. Sixteen million more Americans cast ballots in 2004 than in 2000, an increase in voter turnout of almost ten points; turnout in the election was 60.7 percent. This is notable because since 1960 the trend has been a decline in turnout in presidential elections—except in 1992, when turnout increased slightly thanks to the breath of fresh air H. Ross Perot gave to the race.

Just as important as the increase in the number of voters, however, is what brought these voters to the polls. Certainly, a large number of voters were self-motivated because of their feelings for one of the candidates: Democrats were excited about going to the polls to unseat President Bush, and many Republicans were just as excited by the opportunity to defend and vote for their candidate. The increase in turnout, however, would not have happened had it not been for a resurgence in old-fashioned retail politics. The grassroots campaigning started by Governor Dean in the weeks and months before the Iowa caucuses and the New Hampshire primary carried over into the campaigns of both general election candidates. In short, grassroots politics made a comeback in 2004. "Each party deployed hundreds of thousands of volunteers in a precinct-by-precinct voter-turnout drive . . . that strategists said was the most ambitious national campaign offensive they had ever seen."[4]

Today's presidential campaigns (as well as most competitive congressional campaigns and even some lower-level, down-ballot races) are mass-media based in that the main vehicle of communication is paid electronic media.[5] The 2004 election, however, was somewhat of a flashback to the days when retail politics and voter mobilization by face-to-face contact were not only important but vital to a campaign strategy.[6] This is not to say that the 2004 presidential candidates did not heavily employ television and radio ads. However, both the Bush and Kerry campaigns reported that they had "the largest turnout organizations in the history of the modern political era" to mobilize voters for election day.[7] In other words, the way in which voters were mobilized—by the tried-and-true, but often forgotten, method of canvassing and voter contact—is another positive result of the 2004 campaign.

The return to this kind of campaigning was driven to a large extent by both sides' realization that the end result was going to be close and that the side that did a better job of getting its supporters to the polls would most likely win. In this respect, the return to grassroots campaigning was motivated by self-interest. This kind of mobilization has been used in other modern elections, as has been clear in the Democratic Party's use of organized labor and other outside groups to conduct get-out-the-vote drives. However, considering the 1.4 million volunteers employed by the GOP to conduct voter contact and to both register and turn out supporters,[8] it is hard to argue that 2004 was not a new high in candidate and party mobilization efforts in the modern era. One study conducted after election day finds that 64 percent of voters were contacted by either the Bush or Kerry campaign or other groups over the course of the campaign.[9] The efforts to add to the registration rolls during 2004 should also be seen as a benefit that came out of this election cycle. Again, both sides engaged in unprecedented efforts to add names to the list of registered voters, and both sides boasted huge successes, claiming to have registered millions of new voters.[10]

Another encouraging sign from the 2004 campaign is that the electorate was highly engaged in the race between the two candidates and followed the campaign throughout 2004. Consider, for example, that in June 2004—five months before election day—nearly 60 percent of Americans surveyed said that they had thought "quite a lot" about the presidential campaign (up from only 46 percent of Americans surveyed at the same time in 2000); by September this figure had risen to nearly three in four voters (71 percent).[11] Members of the public also reported that they were paying close attention to the 2004 campaign: in June, 28 percent reported following the election "very closely"; by September this figure jumped to four in ten, about double what it had been in the past two presidential campaigns at a similar point in time.[12]

The public also seemed to be learning about the issues that were being discussed by the candidates. After election day, more than 85 percent of voters said that they had learned enough throughout the campaign to make an informed vote choice.[13] The public saw that the 2004 presidential election was a high-stakes election and that it was one of the most important in history—almost two in three felt that it "really mattered" who won the election.[14] In short, a large portion of the public generally grasped what was at stake, and they took the steps necessary to become active participants.

The electorate also saw clear differences in the candidates. There has been a good deal of criticism in the popular press in recent years that the two major parties have grown so close that there are no longer any meaningful differences between them. Many of these critiques come from those outside the two-party system, like Ralph Nader or members of the Green Party. However, many citizens (one in five, according to a July 2004 CBS News–New York Times poll, down from roughly a third of the public in several previous surveys) have these kinds of thoughts about the candidates who represent the Democrats and Republicans in the race for the presidency every four years.[15]

The argument that there are no differences between the candidates or the parties is difficult to make, however, about the 2004 campaign for the presidency.[16] There were large and important differences between Senator Kerry and President Bush on many key issues. On the domestic side, there were glaring differences between the candidates in the policy alternatives they offered with respect to many of the major policy problems confronting the United States, such as taxes, health care, job creation, education, Social Security, and homeland security. In foreign policy, the candidates certainly had different views on how to handle the "war on terror" as well as the war in Iraq; this was, in many ways, the focus of the campaign. These differences were not lost on the American people: by September 2004, almost 72 percent of Americans surveyed reported that President Bush and Senator Kerry took different positions on issues; this is a 16-point increase from the same period during the 2000 campaign.[17]

Another positive effect of the 2004 presidential election, it can be argued, is the importance of the three presidential debates. Not only did they have an impact on the state of the race—Kerry adviser John Sasso said that his candidate's performance in the first debate put Kerry "back in the game"[18]—but public interest in them was greater than it had been in most recent presidential debates. More than 62 million people watched the first debate (an audience about 35 percent larger than the one that tuned into the first Bush-Gore debate in 2000); many pundits and journalists thought that if Bush had scored a victory in that debate the race would effectively have been over. The public's interest in the 2004 debates was up nearly 20 percentage points compared with 2000 and 1996; only the 1992 debates that included H. Ross Perot exceeded 2004 in viewer interest.[19]

In addition, the public seemed to use the information that was communicated to them in the debates. The Annenberg Public Policy Center finds that "the public's knowledge of the presidential candidates' positions on issues such as tax cuts and re-importation of drugs from Canada increased after the three [2004] presidential debates."[20] Before the debates, for example, only 53 percent of Americans knew that it was Senator Kerry who favored prescription drug re-importation, while after the debates this figure rose to 68 percent; and before the debates, only 33 percent of Americans knew that Kerry had proposed repealing the Bush tax cuts that went to those making more than $200,000 a year, while after the debates 56 percent correctly identified this issue position.[21]

It Was the Worst of Campaigns

Certainly, however, not every development that transpired over the course of the 2004 campaign can be viewed as encouraging for our system of campaigning. The 2004 campaign was filled with examples of business as usual. If the truth be told, there were probably more problematic elements that emerged from the 2004 election cycle than positive signs.

For instance, some point to the huge sums of money that made 2004 the most expensive race in history as a clearly negative aspect of the campaign: $2.2 billion was spent on the 2004 presidential race in total, and the total dollars spent in all of the 2004 campaigns by all the different sources was nearly $5 billion.[22] The presidential candidates alone spent

$863 million in 2004, up from $509 million in 2000.[23] For many, the simple presence of this level of spending in an election is more than just disturbing, it is unethical.[24] At worst, campaign contributors are getting something for their money—a quid pro quo; at best, it seems like a waste to spend that kind of money on campaigning.[25]

Because modern campaigns are generally more capital intensive than labor intensive,[26] the dollars raised tend to be spent on paid advertising rather than old-school ways of political campaigning. The 2004 campaign was no different in this respect, as much of the candidate spending, of course, went to television commercials. For an example of the amount of money dedicated to this kind of spending, one need look no further than the final week of the campaign, during which "both candidates spent nearly $40 million on TV ads"; moreover, they spent "more than $400 million on TV and radio commercials since the ad wars began in earnest in March."[27] The free spending in 2004 did not end with the contest between George W. Bush and John Kerry; in a single U.S. Senate race—the campaign to fill John Edwards's seat in North Carolina—the two candidates, former U.S. representative Richard Burr and former Clinton administration official Erskine Bowles, spent nearly $12 million over the course of three months (July through September) and more than $26 million in total.[28]

Much of the story on campaign fundraising and spending goes back to Howard Dean. It was the Vermont governor who set the early fundraising pace in the race for the Democratic nomination, and he was the first (besides President Bush) to opt out of the public funding system of presidential matching funds that go to candidates in the primaries who accept certain spending limits. Dean's move to do without federal matching funds, of course, meant that he could raise and spend as much as he liked during the primary season. However, this strategic decision by the Dean campaign forced fellow Democrat Kerry to do the same; Kerry did not want to unilaterally disarm and thereby be in a position where he could not match the spending of the Dean campaign in later primaries, should the quest for the nomination reach such a point.

In an unprecedented move, the Kerry campaign, having sewn up the nomination, even contemplated, for a brief period, forgoing the federal funds provided to presidential candidates for the general election campaign. This was a threat to the public funding system for presidential contests, which had already been dealt a serious blow by three candidates' refusal of primary matching funds. Not only were those who did not like to see money in politics distressed at the total spending in 2004, but those who support the public funding of campaigns saw that very system come under heavy fire.

Candidate spending in 2004 is only half the story, however. In the first election cycle governed by the Bipartisan Campaign Reform Act of 2002 (BCRA; also known as McCain-Feingold after its two chief sponsors in the U.S. Senate), the spending by outside interest groups also reached a record high. The BCRA provisions, intended to curb the presence of unlimited and unregulated contributions from individuals, corporations, and unions, failed to stop outside interest groups from raising more than half a billion dollars themselves.[29] The spending by outside groups was highlighted by the activity of so-called 527 organizations—those groups that, because of their status in the tax code, do not have to report to the Federal Election Commission and are free to raise and spend as much money as they like. Specifically, 527 groups such as the Joint Victory Campaign 2004 saw contributions from individuals exceeding $10 million, and other groups, including MoveOn.org, America Coming Together, Progress for America, and the Swift Boat Veterans for Truth, received many contributions from individuals well in excess of $1 million.[30] If the architects of the BCRA meant to keep big donations out of campaigns, their level of success has to be questioned.

For others, disappointment in the 2004 campaign will be found not in the money spent or the way it was raised but in the tone of the campaign. As early as May 2004, the *Washington Post* described the campaign as characterized by "unprecedented negativity."[31] Indeed, the avenue most commonly associated with negative campaigning—television advertising—got heated up early in the campaign. Early on, some observers warned that 2004 might be the "the most negative campaign in history."[32]

Certainly, the presidential candidates had something to do with this, as they constantly criticized one another for this vote or that statement, that proposal or some other questionable activity. Starting early in 2004, the campaign was "marked by angry anti-Bush energy that first surfaced during the Democratic primaries and by relentless criticism of Kerry by the Bush campaign."[33] However, the nastiness of the 2004 cycle extended beyond the clashes between President Bush and Senator Kerry, into congressional races as well. For instance, in September, Wisconsin senator Russell Feingold's campaign manager, George Aldrich, warned Wisconsinites to "brace themselves for one of the most negative campaigns waged in Wisconsin history."[34]

Much of the nastiness was focused on a particular issue, one that many Americans saw as outside the set of topics that should have been a focus for the 2004 campaign—the candidates' activity during the Vietnam War, fought more than thirty-five years earlier. Even more important than the subject of the negativity, however, may be the source of much of it. Some of the 527s that raised huge sums of money during 2004 were behind many of the worst attacks on both candidates' service records. The most egregious of these was arguably the attacks by the anti-Kerry group, Swift Boat Veterans for Truth. The Swift Boat Veterans went so far as to question what then-lieutenant Kerry had actually done to receive the medals he was awarded (three Purple Hearts, a Bronze Star, and a Silver Star) for his service in Vietnam. They also questioned the accuracy of the reports that led many to call Senator Kerry a war hero. Groups working to defeat President Bush, however, did not go unheard on this topic, either. MoveOn.org ran a television advertisement alleging that Bush had received preferential treatment to get into the Texas Air National Guard and that, once there, he had not fulfilled his obligations and had been able to get out of service by requesting an early release to go to graduate school at Harvard.[35] One comment in particular by Senator Kerry epitomizes the sparring on this issue between the two sides: at a campaign rally, the Massachusetts senator told the audience, "I will not have my commitment to defend this country questioned by those who refused to serve when they could have."[36]

The theme of the candidates' service in Vietnam was persistent in the 2004 campaign, as it was one of the first issues raised by the Kerry campaign in their efforts to present him as a candidate who was "capable of managing world affairs and the war on terrorism as well as, or better than, Bush."[37] Kerry's service during the Vietnam War was also on display during the Democratic National Convention, when the candidate again tried to convince the American public that he could be trusted to fight the current war on terror as valiantly as he had fought in Vietnam.[38]

The media played a large role in shaping the more memorable moments of Campaign 2004. Unfortunately, some of them might better be forgotten. Certainly, the media's fascination with the "Dean scream" in the time between the Iowa caucuses and the New Hampshire primary hurt Dean's candidacy. This, however, is only one example of how the media's focus on process, punditry, and the campaign as a horse race left an important mark on the campaign.

Besides their coverage of Dean's speech after Iowans had caucused, the biggest media story of the campaign was arguably the controversy involving CBS News and Dan Rather's report about President Bush's service in the Texas National Guard. Briefly, Rather ran with a story on the CBS program *60 Minutes* using, as evidence, documents that turned out to be fraudulent (though truthful) and refused, for a lengthy period of time, to admit any wrongdoing on the part of CBS. However, the importance of this story goes beyond one reporter at one network.

The importance of this story is that the media in general were focused on the process of how it was reported and not on the issues central to this important story. Certainly, the use of forged documents to question the service record of the sitting commander in chief is worthy of discussion. However, little attention was paid by anyone in the media to the crux of the story. Great attention was paid to Marian Carr Knox, the secretary to Bush's former squadron commander and the purported source of the documents, when she said that she had not typed the documents in question. However, her assertion that the information in the documents was nonetheless correct seemed to get swept under the rug.[39] Once again, the media looked to the process rather than the more meaningful aspects of the story.

Much of the media coverage of the 2004 campaign illustrated a fascination with the presidential contest as a horse race—who was ahead and who was behind in the polls. For weeks, if not months, before election day, it was difficult to pick up a newspaper or turn on a radio or television broadcast without hearing what the latest polls were showing. Bush would be up one day, Kerry would gain ground the next and then take the lead, then Bush would gain the lead back again. All of this, of course, was nearly useless because, as the 2000 election showed us, the part played by the Electoral College renders national polls irrelevant to the outcome on election day. Even though reporters, journalists, and editors are keenly aware of this fact, national polls were the subject of much media coverage.

The quadrennial national party conventions were also a big story during the campaign. However, from one perspective they were not the successes that the candidates thought they were. First, although the public was more engaged in the election than they had been in quite some time, the major broadcast networks covered only three hours of each convention's proceedings—only one hour a night for three of the four nights were shown live by NBC, ABC, and CBS.[40] These programming decisions meant that speeches by some of the most recognizable members of each party—for example, Senator Edward Kennedy on the Democratic side and Senator John McCain on the Republican—were not broadcast.

It is hard to argue with ABC's Ted Koppel, who has described the national conventions as "nothing more than 'publicity-making machines.'"[41] Like those of the recent past, the 2004 conventions of both parties amounted to little more than four-day infomercials for the preordained candidate's campaign, with each and every move scripted and well planned out. In addition, each convention had the specific goal of connecting with the elusive "swing voters" in the electorate rather than engaging in activities more traditionally associated with political conventions, such as discussion of the party platform or policy fights within the party. Many of the scenes that students of conventions are used to seeing are now avoided as if they were radioactive; instead, conventions seek to show a "united" party and send the "right" message.

The Kerry campaign's focus on the candidate's war record continued to be on display during the Democratic National Convention in Boston. Kerry mentioned it in his speech, and retired officers from all branches of the military were on display, advertising their support of the candidate. Kerry was joined on stage for his acceptance speech by retired military officers and some of his former Navy crewmates.

The Republicans, too, put on quite a show for "persuadable" voters at their convention in New York City; they were even accused of being disingenuous during their convention when they gave prime-time speaking slots to public and popular figures such as Arizona senator John McCain, California governor Arnold Schwarzenegger, and former New York City mayor Rudy Giuliani. Clearly, the GOP was trying to put its best foot forward in communicating with those in the electorate who might not agree with everything in the Republican platform, as Schwarzenegger and Giuliani are both "at odds with the president and [the] conservative base on social issues such as abortion and gay rights."[42] Many also questioned the timing of the convention—it concluded only nine days before the third anniversary of the September 11, 2001, terrorist attacks—accusing the Republicans of using the anniversary for political purposes and political gain.

Many commentators, journalists, and pundits saw the three presidential debates as potentially decisive, especially because the first debate focused on foreign policy, which was commonly thought to be President Bush's strength. Although the three debates seemed to reach a number of potential voters, much of the media coverage addressed factors other than the issues. After the first debate, commentary focused less on the substantive points made by either of the candidates and more on the style and appearance of the candidates. In 2004 the focus was on the facial expressions of President Bush, calling to mind the 2000 debates, when much of the postdebate commentary centered on Al Gore's sighs and his impatience with his opponent. Indeed, the public may have been as influenced by Bush's petulant tone and appearance as they were by what the candidates said about Iraq, North Korea, or the global war on terror, since "perceptions can shift as commentators, analysts and spinners chew things over and selected sound bites are endlessly replayed on television, creating 'moments' that may have seemed particularly dramatic at the time."[43] This, of course, is nothing new to campaign debates in the United States: in 1992 George H. W. Bush was roundly criticized for looking at his watch rather than paying attention to his rivals or the audience.

Additionally, there was a great deal of discussion after the first presidential debate about a certain "bulge" in President Bush's jacket. Rumors started to circulate, mainly in a new medium for political discussion—the weblog—that Bush had a communications device in his jacket through which he was able to talk to his advisers during the debate. The Bush team had to respond to these stories and rumors rather than engage voters with their message, even resorting to a report from the president's tailor reassuring the public that nothing dastardly had occurred.[44]

Negative features of Campaign 2004 were present right up to and including election day. In a preemptive strike intended to avert a scenario similar to that in Florida during 2000, both Democrats and Republicans dispatched thousands of attorneys around the country (though particularly in battleground states), to get set for recounts where necessary and to file lawsuits claiming election fraud or voter intimidation. Democrats had their teams of lawyers (there were reports of two thousand in Florida alone) in heavily Democratic areas to deal with charges that Republican voter intimidation would keep many minorities from voting, and Republicans claimed to have attorneys in thirty thousand precincts across the country to challenge voters whose registration credentials were suspect. Both sides claimed their efforts were altruistic and done in the name of fairness—the Democrats said they simply wanted to make sure every vote was counted, and the Republicans said that they wanted to make sure that every vote was counted only once— but campaigns rarely engage in seemingly selfless behavior unless it produces some benefit as well.

Underlying Issues in 2004

Many of the issues discussed above—both positive and negative—are directly related to the art of campaigning.[45] At the root of many of these stories are decisions, actions, or personalities that contributed to how each main story line played out in the public arena. These additional, underlying features are as important to how the 2004 campaign was waged, and to its outcome, as the more visible aspects of the campaign. However, they received relatively little coverage compared with the stories noted earlier. Some may consider these underlying issues to be "inside baseball," important only to those who closely follow campaigns; in fact, they probably are. However, simply because they slip under the radar for most Americans does not mean they have no bearing on the campaign. In one sense, the stories about how decisions were made, what went into those decisions, and how those decisions were carried out are more important than those that get the most coverage. Without them, little else would happen during the campaign.

For instance, any explanation of the record turnout and heightened mobilization efforts by the candidates and their party organizations would be incomplete without an examination of the role that campaigning and campaigners played. Notwithstanding the success of these efforts and the most sophisticated and ambitious turnout plans in the era of modern campaigning, the behind-the-scenes contributions of political professionals cannot be underestimated.

On the GOP side, based on scientific research (the science, as opposed to the art, of campaigning) conducted by the campaign's chief strategist and pollster, Matthew Dowd, "the Bush operation sniffed out potential voters with precision-guided accuracy, particularly in fast-growing counties beyond the first ring of suburbs of major cities. The campaign used computer models and demographic files to locate probable GOP voters."[46] Not to be outdone, the Kerry campaign had a similar operation headed by Michael Whouley, who for much of the campaign, beginning in Iowa, was "shuttered away in 'war rooms,' constantly monitoring the ebb and flow of possible votes, precinct by precinct."[47]

Of course, in examining the success of these turnout operations, one cannot overlook the simple exercise of getting volunteers in the right place at the right time. Again, campaigners were at the heart of this work in 2004. In the end, voters came out in impressive numbers on election day because each campaign galvanized its supporters with the help of

tried-and-true tools of shoe leather and phone banks. Still, the importance of strategists and electioneering here cannot be glossed over. One of
the reasons the Bush campaign had the success it did in Ohio—both in
turning out its voters and, ultimately, in the election results (Ohio was the
state that put President Bush over the top in the Electoral College)—was
the practice get-out-the-vote drive ordered by campaign manager Ken
Mehlman during the summer months. In both Florida (another state key
to Bush's victory) and Ohio, the Bush campaign undertook a dry run of
their turnout effort, telling all their volunteers that "Saturday was 'election day'"; "people walked the precincts county by county, counted voters, monitored the numbers of doors knocked on and offered rides to
simulate our operation," and "turnout workers ran their phone banks
and contacted lists of voters 'just as if the election were being held.'"[48]
The importance of these kinds of efforts was captured by the political scientist Thomas Schaller when he noted, "We call them political campaigns
for a reason. Like a military campaign, the idea is to outflank your opponent, to move your resources around as quickly and in the most strategically advantageous way."[49] It was this kind of strategic thinking that
allowed both campaigns to turn out their voters in unprecedented numbers in 2004.

Voters were not only energized in 2004, they were also engaged. Campaigning and campaigners had a part to play here, as well. Why were so
many individuals engaged in the election? Mobilization efforts were
undoubtedly part of the answer, but the campaigns contributed in other
important ways. Both campaigns drew contrasts between their candidate
and the opponent, giving voters a clear choice.[50] For instance, the issues
that were at the top of many voters' minds—Iraq and the war on terror—
showed the decided differences between the candidates, as well as how
their campaigns positioned them to make their individual cases to the
public. President Bush tied the two issues together, saying that Iraq was
the central front in the war on terror, and apparently convinced the public that one went hand-in-hand with the other. Senator Kerry tried to separate the two issues, arguing that the war in Iraq had taken away vital
resources and efforts from the broader war on terror and calling Iraq a
"diversion" and "the wrong war in the wrong place at the wrong time."[51]
Although the campaigners on each team of advisers did not invent the
positions the candidates held on the issues, they helped create language
that their candidates used to convey those positions to the voters and
highlight the contrasts between the two men.[52]

Campaigners and campaigns are at the root of many of the positive and encouraging aspects of the 2004 campaign, but they are also the source of the disappointing elements, as well. All the money that was spent during 2004 by all those involved (save the matching funds taken by some Democrats in their primary campaigns and the roughly $75 million spent by each of the presidential candidates during the general election as part of the public funding system) was money that was raised from individuals and from political action committees. Countless numbers of individuals and groups gave money to candidates, parties, and outside organizations. Much of this money was raised with the help of professional fundraisers. Without these key players on the inside, candidates, parties, and outside groups would have a much more difficult time raising the money needed to wage a viable campaign. Furthermore, the decisions made by the Dean, Kerry, and Bush campaigns not to take matching funds during the primary season were made by strategists on the inside of the campaign organization. The Kerry team of advisers also had to struggle with whether to accept public money for the general election. In the end, their decision to participate in the public funding system was also a strategic and political move; they did not want Kerry, a Democrat, to be the first to opt out of this part of the public funding system.

Additionally, 2004 was viewed as one of the most negative campaigns in American history.[53] Both campaigns "came out swinging" early in the election year and engaged their opponent earlier than many anticipated. Those who made the decisions not only on when to engage the opposing candidate through paid advertisements on television, radio, and through the mail but also on what issues and language to use in engaging the opposition were those inside the campaigns. The political consultants and campaign advisers created the television and radio commercials and the direct mail flyers that communicated these "negative" messages to potential voters. Early in the campaign, the Bush team wasted little time going after their opponent as having been on both sides of many major issues (that is, flip-flopped) and as having continually supported higher taxes (a position that never plays well in a presidential election); Kerry, for his part, continually attacked Bush for his handling of the war in Iraq as well as the U.S. economy (for example, sending jobs overseas and tax cuts for the rich). These kinds of messages were not limited to the early months of 2004, of course, but continued throughout the campaign.

The focus on the candidates' roles in the Vietnam War was a conscious decision made by the Kerry campaign to remind the American public that he was a war hero and therefore had the requisite credentials of a commander in chief. The campaign also wanted to convince voters that Kerry could hold his own on the world stage and be as effective in the war on terror as President Bush. Whether this was the right or wrong decision, the issue was designed by the campaign itself.

War records were on display at the Democratic National Convention in July, where the Kerry campaign's goal was to reintroduce their candidate to the public and to convey their message that Senator Kerry would "make America stronger at home and respected in the world." This message, created by Kerry's team of advisers, was "designed to underscore the centrist and forward-looking image Kerry wanted to present to voters."[54] The consultants and handlers of the candidates crafted more than the words, however, at the national conventions. The "publicity-making machines" were designed to send a certain signal to those who were watching. All of this—from the messages spoken to the messages transmitted by visual images—was the making of the campaigns. In today's politics, every aspect of the four-day events—the look of the hall, the placement of the chairs on the floor, the list of speakers who address the crowd, even the speed with which the balloons fall after the nominee finishes his or her speech—is controlled by the campaigns to make sure that only the "right" message is heard and seen by the voters. So tight was the control on imagery from inside the Bush campaign that on the day of the president's speech, the hall was transformed. Workers tore down the stage used for the three previous nights' speeches and constructed a new circular stage—complete with the presidential seal—in the middle of the hall. This change was designed to bring Bush closer to the audience; and after three nights of hitting Senator Kerry rather hard, Bush "sought to soften the sharp-edged tone of the convention's first three nights with some personal reflections tinged with humor."[55] The Bush campaign staff tried to end the convention with a different message, one that helped them achieve the desired success (after the convention, the polls gave Bush a 52-43 lead over Kerry).

Although the three presidential debates provided an opportunity for the candidates to tell the public about their plans for the next four years and for the electorate to gather a good deal of information, they may have been tarnished by the tightly controlled rules hammered out by the two campaigns before they began. Everything from approved camera angles to the heights of and distance between the podiums, from what the candidates could have at their podiums to the choice of moderator, was negotiated beforehand in a thirty-two-page written contract. The agreement between the two campaigns "had been negotiated to make the encounter as antiseptic as possible":[56] neither candidate could approach his opponent during the debate or ask direct questions of his opponent; and the response time to questions was to be limited to two minutes. The agreement was entered into by both campaigns (negotiated by former secretary of state James Baker, for the Bush team, and Vernon Jordan, for the Kerry team), and was pushed by the campaigners, to try to remove the possibility of any "gotcha" moments from the debates, such as Al Gore's leaving his stool and approaching George W. Bush during a debate in 2000, making Gore appear overbearing and inconsiderate of his opponent. The Bush campaign made no secret that it wanted to limit the responses to questions to two minutes so that Senator Kerry might go over his allotted time and be alerted by the buzzer that was negotiated as a signal that a candidate's time was up. Again, the jockeying by the campaigns affected the campaigning itself. In this instance, it appeared to have little impact, since there was still plenty of "spin" after the debates—especially after the first debate, when the media focused on the president's facial expressions.

The importance of campaigning and campaigners extends beyond the candidates' campaigns. There was considerable activity on the part of outside interests—both parties and interest groups (many in the form of 527s)—during the 2004 campaign. Those behind the efforts of parties, political action committees, and 527 organizations are the same campaigners that were at the helm of the Bush and the Kerry campaigns. For instance, one of the top staffers of the active and influential 527 America Coming Together, Jim Jordan, had been John Kerry's campaign manager before being fired in late 2003. Other political consultants and former party operatives headed many other prominent 527 organizations that played a major part in the 2004 election.

Rationale for the Book

This book is about the health of American campaigning. "Campaigning," however, at least in our view, is different from "elections"; by *campaigning* we mean those concepts, decisions, actors, and processes that are associated with the everyday execution of a campaign for elective office. In other words, we view campaigning as a smaller piece of the general topic of elections. Thus we leave many questions aside in this exercise. We do not address topics that would be included in a broader discussion of the health of our electoral system, such as voter registration regulations and reforms, the administration of elections on election day (that is, ballots and voting mechanisms), electoral competitiveness (or the lack thereof), and the electoral rules we employ in most election contests (for example, single-member districts, winner-take-all rules, or the Electoral College).

Each of these topics is surely fair game in an examination of our electoral system. However, we consider these to be issues that are at a macro level of the process. We are interested, instead, in issues that may be considered to be at a micro level of our electoral process—the decisions that are made in campaigns, the actors inside those campaigns, and the exercises undertaken by campaigns. Many of the examples noted in our recap of the good and the bad of the 2004 campaign illustrate this point. Moreover, many of the ills that seem to plague our system are associated with this micro level. Decisions about what issues to focus on in a campaign, how to communicate candidates' stances on those issues, the money needed to wage a campaign in the twenty-first century, strategies that will result in victory on election day, and messages created by campaigns for their candidates are all questions that fit into our conception of campaigning. We agree with Mark Petracca, who notes that "our attention has moved away from the analysis of electoral institutions [as a discipline]. . . . In general we pay less attention to the dynamics of electoral institutions and the processes of campaigning than we do to those variables that seem to directly influence the voters' choice."[57]

There are certainly many specific questions that would be good candidates for such an inquiry, and questions about the health of our system of campaigning abound—as seen from the 2004 presidential election alone. However, for this exercise we restrict ourselves to four central topics that are focused on the way campaigns are actually conducted and waged in the United States. Specifically, we examine questions related to the control of modern campaigns, the quality of the most important players in the campaigning process, the role of money in our campaigns, and the ethics of the way our campaigns are conducted.[58] We examine these questions through the lens of political consultants, party elites, and the general public, based heavily on survey research conducted over a seven-year period beginning in 1997 and continuing through 2003. We augment our empirical data with examples and accounts from recent elections, with a specific focus on the 2004 presidential election because it provides several points of interesting comparison and evaluation.

We believe that each of these topics is important in any effort to judge the health and quality of our campaigns. The question of control in modern campaigns is central to the question of quality because it explores who controls the decisionmaking in campaigns on a daily basis. In other words, we believe determining who is in charge of the day-to-day decisionmaking in campaigns is important to the health of those campaigns because these decisions are often linked to other aspects of campaigning that can be criticized or questioned. If those involved are not of high quality, one might also question the results of the system in which they operate. The importance of the role of money in elections is self-evident. To some extent, however, this question also addresses control in elections, but from a different perspective. Who is paying for our elections matters a great deal when one considers the quality of the system of campaigning. The final question we consider—Are our campaigns conducted in an ethical and appropriate manner?—may be the most important. If campaigns are not being conducted with high standards, can we have confidence in the results of those elections? Although we expect campaigns to be waged with vigor, we also expect them to be conducted in a manner befitting the offices they pursue. One can question whether this is happening in today's campaigns.

The research we rely on in examining these questions comes from surveys of those who are involved in the processes of campaigning; the data are from their perspective. We offer an insiders look at the questions outlined above. Our work focuses on three critical campaign actors—professional political consultants, political party elites, and members of the general public—because of their important and special roles in our system of campaigning.[59] We do not, however, limit our exploration to our surveys of campaign actors. We supplement our own data with surveys of candidates, journalists, and other surveys of the public, among other data sources.

This book is the culmination of several years of work on a larger project, which was funded by The Pew Charitable Trusts. When we began this larger project, our first interest was to better understand political consultants. Throughout the latter part of the twentieth century, consultants came to play an integral part in American elections, and we wanted to know more about who these new campaign actors were, what they brought to the electioneering table, and what motivated them to enter politics. After three years of studying consultants through surveys, interviews, and participant observation, we decided to expand our study to other actors in the process of campaigning. We were still focused on consultants, but we wanted a different perspective on the work they do every day in campaigns and the effects of their work on the electorate. Therefore, we turned to examinations of political party elites, because they often work alongside consultants in the execution of campaigns (on behalf of either candidates or the parties), and the general public, because they are the targets of the efforts of consultants and campaigners.

The result of this entire grant project is a data set that we believe is unlike any other that has been used to study campaigns and campaigning. In the chapters that follow we report on seven surveys of campaign actors, as well as other data we have collected through other methods during the seven-year project, including focus groups with consultants, interviews with consultants and party elites, and participant observations made in several campaigns.[60]

Our data set is unique not because we ask questions of those who are at the heart of the campaigning process—there are a number of works that use surveys of participants in campaigns[61]—but because we bring together survey research focusing on multiple actors in the same outlet. More important, we designed our survey research for the comparisons reported in this book by posing the same set of questions to these multiple actors. We believe that what sets our data set and our work apart from others is that we can confidently make comparisons across different groups of campaign actors. In addition, in two cases—political consultants and the general public—we can make these comparisons over time because we have longitudinal data over three waves of surveys.

In the chapters that follow, we report on these data and address the four central questions about the health of our system of campaigning. We make frequent use of the 2004 presidential election to drive home these points, many of which are clearly illustrated in the contest between Senator Kerry and President Bush. We also believe that the presence of these factors over several election cycles (the surveys of consultants were done in three separate election cycles, the surveys of the general public were conducted over two) demonstrates the consistency of our survey findings.

Plan of the Book

In chapter 2 we tackle the question of who is in charge of our campaigns today. We begin by providing a brief historical overview of control of

American campaigns, beginning with those around the turn of the nineteenth century and continuing through the turn of the twenty-first century. Again, we are focused on who makes the day-to-day decisions in candidates' campaigns, so we look at political parties, candidates for office, and political consultants after their appearance in the 1930s.[62] This historical examination of the question sets the context for a discussion of modern campaigns.

We then turn to an exploration of the survey data gathered from those campaign actors who are at the center of political campaigns—political consultants, party elites, and, to some extent, candidates—and detail how each group of actors sees the status of control in campaigns. We begin with a description of how consultants and party elites view the importance of their peers as well as other actors central to this question. We add to this a discussion of consultants' and party operatives' views of who does what in modern campaigns and outline a division of labor that exists between the two in the provision of services to candidates' campaigns.

In chapter 3 we consider the state of our system of campaigning in terms of the quality of the actors in the process. This is the most data-heavy chapter in the book and includes comparisons of all the actors we surveyed (and, thanks to some additional sources of data, some that we ourselves did not) on questions about nearly every actor group in our system of campaigning. We begin by assessing the quality of candidates: In electing public officials, are we selecting from a set of solid choices? We also examine the role of the public in our system of elections in terms of their responsibilities in creating a sound system: Are voters doing their part and becoming well informed on issues and candidates? We then investigate the different groups' attitudes about actors who operate mainly behind the scenes of the process, specifically political consultants and party operatives. Finally, we consider the performance of journalists in the system through the eyes of the actors we interviewed. The evaluations of each of these groups of actors is made both over time and from the perspective of the other groups of actors, using the same survey questions. We believe this provides a unique picture of the state of the actors in our system of campaigning.

In chapter 4 we address the role of money in campaigns. We examine the attitudes and beliefs of consultants, party elites, and the general public on questions of money in politics and explore in detail their attitudes about reforms to the campaign funding system. Specifically, we consider consultants' views on the potential impact of the Bipartisan Campaign

Reform Act. We evaluate the early impact of the BCRA and speculate as to the consequences—both intended and unintended—of the law. We examine the role of money in campaigns with a specific focus on the 2004 cycle and how it compares with past election cycles.

In the last empirical chapter, chapter 5, we consider the ethics of American political campaigns in these times. In some respects, this is the most important question we could consider. Are our campaigns being conducted in an ethical and appropriate manner? If not, what does that say about the results of our elections? If a candidate wins through tactics that are unethical, can we have trust in our government—and can that candidate be considered a legitimate elected official? We examine the attitudes of several groups of electoral actors, focusing on different aspects of campaigning. We detail what each considers to be appropriate behavior in campaigns, as well as what each sees as unethical practices in campaigning. We also offer several examples of many of these practices from recent campaigns.

In chapter 6 we reflect on the main findings in our empirical examination of electoral actors' attitudes and beliefs and explore their meaning in the context of the lessons learned from the 2004 campaign. More important, we ask, What have we learned about the state of campaigning in the United States? Our answer may surprise the reader.

Before getting into our exploration of these questions, we want to provide some important notes to the reader about what follows. We began our larger project knowing relatively little about political consultants and the consulting industry. Historically, there has been, and there continues to be, a lack of data about much of what consultants do and the impact they have on campaigns. Stanley Kelley Jr. noted this deficit nearly fifty years ago: "There are few data for evaluating, with anything like scientific accuracy, particular propaganda techniques, and certainly not for the assessment of the effectiveness of 'public relations' in general."[63] Not much changed in the next forty years; in 1989, Mark Petracca noted this same lack of information.[64]

Tracking the behavior of consultants and their participation in political campaigns, even at the highest levels, still remains difficult. Some studies have tried to survey individuals in the field, but many of these have been small, targeted surveys that did not reach across the entire industry. Because of the limited data, we started our inquiry as an exploratory one, with the central objective of creating a baseline of knowledge about political consultants and their industry. We entered this endeavor with relatively few expectations because there had been little work devoted to the subject, compared with other topics in political science.

In addition, because we replicated so many of the questions we asked political consultants when we surveyed political party elites and the general public, we also were not sure how these two groups of actors would stack up compared with consultants. Having said that, we did have a few hypotheses we wanted to test, and those are presented in the following chapters. However, what follows is mainly a report on the data we have collected in our multiple surveys and additional methods of data collection. In many cases, we did not have an expectation of what we would see in the data. Where interesting and important patterns emerge—either over time or across electoral actors—we engage in a bit of speculation and present possible explanations for these patterns.

This leads us to a more important point. We view this book as a hypothesis-generating exercise, rather than a hypothesis-testing one. We hope this book encourages readers and other scholars to ask similar questions and generate new hypotheses that expand on our work. We believe that in many areas of study related to political consultants, political parties, candidates, the public, the media, and outside interest groups, as well as how each interacts with the others, we have only found the tip of the iceberg when it comes to scholarly investigation. We hope others pick up where we have left off and collect more data and test some of the hypotheses that the material presented here is sure to provide.

Finally, one methodological note should be made at the start. Although we include many different types of data, the reader should know that we rely mostly on the responses from the seven surveys we conducted of electoral actors. We believe this to be a rich method of studying the phenomena we are interested in. As Henry Brady notes, "Surveys . . . it can be argued, have revolutionized the social sciences. . . . No other social science method has proven so valuable."[65] However, a few caveats are in order, as is true of any work that relies on respondents' reports of their attitudes, beliefs, and, more important, behaviors. We have to put some faith in the survey respondents to accurately report their feelings and behavior.

This is especially true in the case of political consultants and party operatives. When we began this study, we were pleasantly surprised with the candor of the vast majority of consultants in discussions outside of the surveys, both on and off the record. We believe that the consultants were aware of the lack of scholarly attention their profession had received and were willing to talk about almost every aspect of their work. We are confident in the accuracy of their survey responses because their responses were not always complimentary, either to their peers or to their industry. The same can be said about party elites, as they were equally forthcoming in their responses to the questions we posed. We are also confident in the data collected from the American public. To some extent, we have to take a leap of faith with the public, as well; but then, so does every other study that utilizes public opinion data.

These points are not brought up to cast doubt on any of the findings reported in the following chapters. Rather, we want our readers to be aware of these limitations so they can make their own judgments about what to do and what data need to be collected when they begin to think about how future questions can be asked about similar issues.

CHAPTER 2

Who's in Charge?
Candidates, Consultants,
and Political Parties

After the spectacle that was the 2003 California gubernatorial recall election and the fiasco that was the 2000 presidential election recount in Florida, the question in the title of political scientist
Stephen J. Wayne's book, *Is This Any Way to Run a Democratic Election?* is certainly appropriate. It is also appropriate, however, in another
context—a context that is the subject of this book, and specifically this
chapter.

In an electoral environment that is dominated by twenty-four-hour
news coverage, thirty-second ads, special interest groups, and big-dollar
contributors and in which a number of competing interests vie for control
of election campaigns to further their own interests, the question arises,
Who is in charge of our election campaigns?[1] Rightfully so, the current
electoral landscape and this question have created a stir among myriad
commentators, pundits, and experts who all seem to have the same
answer: that because of the presence of these different factors our system
of campaigning is broken and is in dire need of fixing.[2] As noted in chapter 1, one important yet relatively uncovered story of the 2004 presidential campaign that had a significant impact on the outcome was the role
of campaigners. In this chapter we consider the question of authority and
control in modern campaigns by investigating the role of those who are
at the everyday helm of campaigns in the United States—the candidates

themselves but also those who work on their behalf as political consultants and political party operatives.[3]

Our analysis of how campaigns are conducted may surprise some
readers in that we conclude that modern elections are rather efficiently
carried out by different groups of actors engaged in different activities.
Candidates, campaign consultants, and political parties all share in the
responsibility of executing today's campaigns, and each contributes something that is necessary and valuable. A brief historical examination provides a better-informed context from which to explore the current state of
electioneering.[4]

A Swinging Pendulum of Control

The locus of control in American election campaigns has evolved over
time much as a pendulum swings on a clock. In the first electoral contests
in the United States, electoral power was firmly held by political parties.
Parties controlled every facet of campaigning; their power was so strong
that some have likened it to a monopoly of electoral power.[5] For myriad
reasons, the pendulum has since swung away from parties to what some
have called a candidate-centered electoral system. Many observers have
criticized professional political consultants for their role in this shift. One
of the most important critiques of the current state of campaigning in
terms of who is in control of campaigns comes from those who argue that
consultants have shoved parties to the side of electioneering and those
who argue that consultants have snatched control of campaigns away
from candidates.[6] David Broder, the longtime columnist for the *Washington Post*, summarizes this sentiment nicely in terms of presidential
campaigns: "Something strange and important has happened to the system of picking presidential candidates. Influence that was supposed to
move from political insiders to the broad public has been captured by
activists, pollsters, pundits, and fundraisers—not exactly the people re-
formers had in mind."[7] These claims, however, have little merit. Rather
than seizing control of campaigns, the entry and ascendance of political
consultants was one of many adaptations that parties and candidates
made to the changing electoral landscape; the swing of the electioneering
pendulum away from the parties was inevitable.

The first hotly contested presidential campaign in the United States
occurred in 1796 between John Adams and Thomas Jefferson. Parties
controlled much of this campaign: both sides distributed handbills and

pamphlets, and each vigorously debated the issues of the day.[8] The creation of statewide party organizations made interstate party activity possible.[9] Party organizations at the local level began to appear in the years following this contest, and their influence in campaigns only increased. From the earliest presidential campaigns and for many years after, campaigns were conducted as party-centered matters. However, parties were in control of much more than how the campaigns were fought; parties controlled everything from who would run in the election to what issues the candidate would run on. By the early years of the nineteenth century, party control of campaigns had become entrenched, and parties had become important actors in raising campaign funds, strategic and tactical decisionmaking, and voter mobilization.[10] This set the stage for the "machine" era, during which political parties were the dominant force in elections and in much of American politics generally.

"During the golden age of political parties . . . party organizations . . . bore the primary responsibility for contesting elections."[11] Parties were so much in command that by the end of the century candidates in some campaigns were almost completely uninvolved in spreading their message to voters.[12] Instead, it was the party that organized the events, created the handbills and circulars, and distributed campaign paraphernalia to potential voters. Equally important, the "management" of campaigns also fell to the party apparatus. The earliest campaign managers were party loyalists more interested in the slate of party candidates than in any one individual running for office.[13] The first efforts to manage candidates' campaigns were made by a committee of party leaders; management responsibilities would later be turned over to one individual in a campaign, but these campaign managers were never far removed from the party elite.

Parties enjoyed a great deal of power in election contests for roughly a century. However, toward the end of the nineteenth century and the beginning of the twentieth, the pendulum began to swing away from political parties. Beginning with the Pendleton Act of 1883, which created a federal merit-based system for civil servants that took away one of the parties' main power centers in the form of patronage and the spoils system, parties began to lose some of the electoral power to which they had grown accustomed.[14] This declining trend in party influence in electioneering continued in the early twentieth century with the reforms instituted by the Robert LaFollette–led Progressive movement, which instituted voter registration and ballot reforms, recall elections, and referendums and citizen initiatives. However, the Progressives dealt the biggest blow to party power in the form of the direct primary. "During the prereform part of the golden age of political parties local party organizations had absolute control over the nominating process."[15] After a move to the direct primary, however, the decision as to who would run for office was in the hands of the party rank and file, not the party bosses.

These reforms and changes to the electioneering landscape were the impetus for the movement away from parties. It took roughly fifty years for the pendulum to fully swing away from the parties and for them to reach their weakest point of electioneering power. As Paul S. Herrnson has argued, after their golden age, parties were little more than "peripheral organizations" that were, "at best, on the margins of the electoral process."[16] By the 1970s, election contests in the United States were said to be candidate centered, in that "candidates, not parties, were the central actors in election campaigns."[17] Because of the reforms of the Progressives and others, candidates were now "encouraged to develop their own campaign organizations."[18]

Professional political consultants began to play a central role in candidates' personal campaign organizations around the time of the early challenges to party power. Many argue that the California tandem of Clem Whitaker and Leone Baxter, and their firm Campaigns, Inc., which was formed in 1933, were the first political consultants, but they were really precursors to the modern consultant.[19] Those professional political consultants who came after Whitaker and Baxter did not create the context that confronted candidates and parties in the middle years of the twentieth century, however. Rather, their appearance in campaigns and later ascendance in the system was an effect of the changing electoral context, as was the decline of the parties. In addition to the parties' lessened electoral power, other changes to the electoral landscape paved the way for consultants to come onto the electoral scene. Dan Nimmo nicely summarizes this swing of the pendulum of electoral power:

A century ago candidates relied on their wits, their friends, and a few trusted allies to mount a campaign for office. Few men specialized in selling political advice. The campaign specialists of that day were primarily party politicians. . . . Today . . . [candidates] turn less to party leaders than to professional campaign managers for political expertise. Once a campaign craft pursued by relatively few public relations experts, campaign management has become a highly diversified industry serving a wide variety of clients."[20]

The weakening of the parties did not occur overnight. Neither did the ascendance of political consultants; rather, consultants gradually became the source of campaign services that candidates demanded. "From its start in 1934, the campaign management industry grew rather slowly. A few companies went in and out of business shortly after World War II, and some public relations and advertising firms started accepting political campaign clients in the late 1940s. [It was not until] the 1950s [that] there was a slow but steady expansion."[21] This, combined with the fact that political consultants were not fixtures in federal elections until the 1980s, further illustrates that consultants were not a cause of party decline but rather were a reaction to it.[22]

As the pendulum of electoral power was in full swing away from political parties and toward candidates' own organizations, the services that were once supplied by the party became the responsibility of candidates themselves. It was the candidate and his or her campaign manager who were responsible for building a campaign organization, developing the campaign's strategy, theme, and message, and devising tactics to implement that strategy and deliver that message. At this time, "party organizations were called upon for assistance in only a very limited set of campaign functions."[23]

The reasons for the power shift away from parties are many and varied. The increasing number of eligible voters at the time meant that parties could not help every one of their candidates as they once had in the ways to which they were accustomed (that is, on an individual basis).[24] Additionally, the great advancements in campaign technology that came about midcentury meant that candidates could take their case directly to the people rather than be tied to a party strategy and party message.[25] Arguably the most important aspect of this shift was the way candidates disseminated their campaign messages to potential voters. Because candidates could no longer depend on party activity to convey their messages, as they once had, candidates began to take advantage of the new technologies that were available to them. Television, the innovation in electioneering that has had by far the biggest impact on campaigns, allowed candidates to take their cases directly to the people.[26] However, the new technology brought with it the need for new skills to apply that technology. The use of television required know-how in areas of production, scriptwriting, editing, and other sophisticated and technical techniques. Candidates and their campaign managers rarely had the skills necessary to create television advertisements, so campaigns turned to those who did—political consultants.

Professional consultants provided not only media expertise but also services such as survey research and direct mail. Candidates used messages derived from scientific surveys and, through continual repetition, reached out to the voting public over the airwaves and through the mail. As Robert Agranoff observed more than thirty years ago, "Highly trained specialists are [now] needed to prepare and analyze public opinion polls, to run sophisticated advertising campaigns and to translate the results of data processing into useful political knowledge."[27]

Critics of professional political consultants argue that their presence in campaigns pushed parties into decline. However, "Cultural changes and other transformations, such as the progressive reforms that were designed to weaken the influence of local party bosses, the technological innovations of the 1950s and 1960s, and the party reforms and campaign finance legislation of the late 1960s and 1970s, all worked to bring about the decline of American political parties."[28] Consultants were a reaction to, rather than a cause of, party decline.

During the late 1970s and early 1980s parties experienced what some have called a resurgence or a revitalization.[29] Parties began to retool and adapt to the new electoral context created by both the new technology available to campaigns and the financial limits put in place by the campaign finance reforms of the mid-1970s. A major portion of this revitalization was a result of organizational modernizations and innovations in fundraising. Both the Democrats and Republicans built new headquarters near Capitol Hill in Washington, D.C., acquired more professional staff, and rededicated themselves to raising money. This allowed them to offer their candidates some of the sophisticated and technical services that were in demand.[30]

One development in particular put the parties on the modern electioneering map—their use of so-called soft money. Beginning in the mid-1990s, thanks to loopholes in the campaign finance regulations, parties began to raise and spend monies in amounts not limited by the law. This gave parties the means they needed to convey their own messages and be players in selected races across the nation through television and radio ads as well as direct mail campaigns. By now, the pendulum of influence in campaigns had begun to swing back in the direction of the parties.

The revitalization of the parties in their adaptation and the services they provided to candidates is well documented.[31] However, the parties would not have been able to reclaim electioneering power at this time without the help of consultants who were outside of the formal party organization. Both Republicans and Democrats, for example, hired consultants to help with their direct mail fundraising efforts in the early 1980s.[32] In addition, parties actually cultivated relationships with professional consultants so they could better provide services to their candidates.[33] Both parties hired consultants to collect and interpret public opinion data, and consultants were heavily relied on to help candidates create television ads in the parties' media studios. Moreover, parties hired media consultants to create the ads they were airing, paid for with the soft money they had been putting into their coffers.[34]

The decline in the power of political parties was not caused by political consultants' coming onto the scene and pushing parties into irrelevance. It is also difficult to make the case that political consultants have grabbed the reins of power away from candidates. Candidates have always had relatively little control over the management of their own campaigns. In the golden era of parties, when the machines were at their strongest, candidates had virtually no control over whether they would even run for office, let alone what issues they would campaign on, what their message to potential voters would be, or how their campaign would be conducted. Each of these issues was controlled by the party elite. As parties lost some of their power, candidates were left to fend for themselves. Candidates did not have the expertise to create radio or television commercials, to conduct or analyze scientific public opinion polls, or to craft sophisticated and targeted direct mail campaigns. In other words, at the same time that parties were losing their power thanks to the spread of earlier reforms, the mode of electioneering in the United States was shifting to one in which mass communications were a primary force. Candidates needed and demanded the services of political consultants from the beginning and never had control over many of the most important aspects of their campaigns.

David Menefee-Libey argues that campaigns are not candidate centered but are campaign centered.[35] His assessment of the role parties have played in American elections is not unlike those of most other scholars who have traced the ebb and flow of party power: parties are clearly weaker today than they were one hundred years ago. Menefee-Libey observes that "electoral politics has been radically transformed through the past half century in ways we are now coming to understand, and the parties have struggled desperately to adapt to that transformation." He argues that "for the weeks and months of campaigning that lead up to election day . . . contemporary American politics is *campaign centered.*"[36] "In most contemporary contests for national and statewide office, professionalized campaign organizations—not the parties, and not the candidates themselves—coordinate and mediate the most important aspects of our electoral politics."[37] Consider the case of Dennis Moore, a former district attorney in Johnson County, Kansas, who decided to run for Congress in 1998 and who, like the vast majority of candidates at this level who hope to be successful, looked to hire some professionals. Moore recalls his decision to hire Chris Esposito as his campaign manager: "When my kitchen cabinet was interviewing different applicants for the position of campaign manager, at one point Chris told me I would have three vetoes during the campaign at different times and after that all the decisions would be his. I told him, veto, veto, veto, to get it out of the way. And then I said to get on with it."[38]

Candidates are certainly the focus of our campaigns in that their names appear on the ballot, as well as on the organization that is created to run their campaigns. Candidates also are the ones on the front lines of the battle for campaign money: it is they who must "dial for dollars," asking potential supporters for contributions, and who give speeches and talk with voters. However, it is the professional campaign organizations that actually run the campaigns. It is the organization—most likely staffed with a campaign manager and professional consultants—that develops the campaign strategy, theme, and message, executes that strategy, and delivers the campaign communications. This is seen by many as a power grab by consultants. However, as noted earlier, candidates were never really in charge of their campaigns. In fact, "many candidates are far more directly involved in their campaigns today" than were candidates of the past century, who operated under the supervision of party bosses.[39]

We have gone from an electoral landscape dominated by parties to one dominated by political professionals. Parties are no longer the glue that holds individual candidates' campaigns together; this task now falls to professional political consultants and campaign managers. One has to look no further than the campaign teams of the 2004 presidential candidates to see this campaign centeredness. In Senator Kerry's inner circle of advisers, it was political consultants, rather than party operatives, who were at the helm. The *Washington Post* has noted that during the campaign it was "Bob Shrum [the longtime Democratic consultant and veteran of many presidential campaigns] . . . who [emerged] as the most influential shaper of Kerry's image and words"; Shrum's power, the *Post* continues, was "rivaled only by a select few including his business partner Michael Donilon . . . and Boston-based pollster Tom Kiley. . . . But [it was] Mary Beth Cahill, campaign manager and longtime adviser to [Senator Edward] Kennedy calling the final shots and overseeing the . . . operation."[40] During the campaign, Cahill "said six people equally dominated campaign strategizing sessions: Shrum, Donilon, and their partner Tad Devine, as well as pollsters Kiley and Mark Mellman and herself."[41] Noticeably absent here are any individuals from the Democratic National Committee. Although it was George W. Bush who, during 2003, picked Ed Gillespie to chair the Republican National Committee, the organization traditionally charged with heading up a president's reelection campaign, the Bush-Cheney campaign had an equally consultant-loaded campaign team responsible for its everyday decisionmaking, including media guru Mark McKinnon, pollster Matthew Dowd, and Bush's most trusted political adviser, Karl Rove, a former direct mail consultant.

The importance of consultants and their central role in campaigns today should not necessarily be thought of as detrimental to our campaigns. The current electoral order is one in which parties and consultants are cooperating partners. These two groups of actors have developed a division of labor that is quite efficient, both for their own needs and for the needs of their candidates.

Campaign Control: An Efficient Division of Labor

Control of candidates' campaigns in modern U.S. elections is not a zero-sum game. Simply because political consultants have a strong presence in campaigns does not mean that political parties are doomed or that they are irrelevant. The current electoral landscape includes a relationship between political parties and professional consultants in which they work together to help elect candidates.[42] In the present context, consultants provide certain services that are in demand, and parties provide others.

Consultant and Party Influence in Campaigns

As might be expected, consultants and political party elites did not completely agree on the strength of each group of actors' role in campaigns. In general, consultants were seen as the stronger of the two actors in the electioneering process, but fewer party staffers than consultants took this view. Consultants' attitudes were consistent with scholarly work in this area illustrating the changing nature of elections, as described above. Parties were once the only place to turn for electioneering help, but as electioneering changed, so did the locus of power in campaigns.

In our 1999 survey of the industry, professional political consultants reported that in the time that they themselves had been involved in politics, the role of parties had decreased at all levels. They saw the most dramatic decline at the local level; however, they saw the parties' role at the national level as nearly stable (see table 2-1). Consultants' views of their own role at this time was one of significant influence, and one that had grown more important over the time they had been in the consulting business. These attitudes changed slightly from the 1999 survey to the measure taken in 2002. Many consultants surveyed in 2002 felt that the parties' role had remained stable in campaigns, and they continued to report that their own influence had increased, although the increase was not as substantial as that reported in 1999.

Not surprisingly, party elites took a somewhat different view of their role in elections. Party operatives agreed that consultants' role had increased over time, but they reported that the role of parties had at least remained stable, and some even saw an increase in the parties' electoral presence. Although the numbers are limited, the respondents who were from the national parties and party committees reported views similar to those of consultants about the increased role that consultants play; the mean evaluations of national party staffers and political consultants all indicate that both groups see consultants as having an increased role in campaigns at all levels. More state party elites reported that consultants' influence had increased at the national level than at the state level. Conversely, more national party elites reported that consultants' influence had increased at the state level than at the national level. In other words, party operatives at the state and national levels found consultants' influence to have increased in those races in which they were not as directly involved—the state level for national party staffers and the national level for the state party operatives. We believe this may be because party oper-

Table 2-1. *Consultants' and Party Elites' Assessments of Change in the Role of Parties and Consultants*[a]

	Consultants		Party elites, 2002	
Role	1999	2002	State	National
Parties at the local level	2.38 (496)	2.76 (196)	3.52 (93)	3.3 (15)
Parties at the state level	2.71 (495)	3.13 (200)	3.89 (93)	3.7 (15)
Parties at the national level	2.90 (488)	3.22 (193)	3.83 (93)	4.2 (15)
Consultants at the local level	4.40 (501)	4.17 (202)	3.70 (93)	3.9 (15)
Consultants at the state level	4.44 (501)	4.29 (203)	3.95 (93)	4.3 (15)
Consultants at the national level	4.37 (490)	4.07 (199)	4.04 (90)	4.1 (15)

a. The question asked was, "Thinking back to when you first began working in [party] politics in a professional capacity—and comparing that to now—do you think the role of [political parties/political consultants] in electing candidates at the local, state, and national levels has increased, stayed about the same, or decreased?" Mean rankings are based on a scale in which 1 = decreased very much, 2 = decreased somewhat; 3 = stayed the same, 4 = increased somewhat; and 5 = increased very much. Numbers in parentheses are numbers of responses.

atives see themselves as still playing an important role in campaigns, and to admit an increase in consultant influence in the races they had a large part in may signal that they were not as relevant.

One possible explanation for these results is the differential reference point of consultants and party staffers when making their judgments. The consultants in the 1999 study had, on average, eighteen years of experience in the electioneering business, and those in the 2002 study, nearly twenty-three years' experience. This is in dramatic contrast to state party operatives, more than 70 percent of whom had less than two years' experience in their jobs. What is more impressive, 100 percent of the staffers at the national parties and party committees had less than two years' experience.[43] Respondents who have vastly different years of experience will have very different reference points in making these comparisons and judgments about the roles of consultants and parties. Consultants with many years of experience will have seen their power relative to that of the parties ebb and flow. Party elites who have fewer years of experience will not have these same experiences to draw on and will not have seen their party's influence fluctuate. In short, experience may make a difference in how those in the electioneering business see campaigns. Consultants, who have generally been in the business longer than party staffers, have seen trends and changes through the years; party operatives, who are generally new to their environment, have fewer experiences from which to draw.

The figures reported in table 2-1 are also understandable given the different location of the party operatives. State party elites reported stronger consultants' influence at the national than at the state level (the races in which they work and have influence). Similarly, national party staffers noted a greater increase in consultants' influence at the state than at the national level (their area of influence).

To some extent, the views of consultants are reflected in the conduct of the 2004 presidential campaign (as well as many other races from 2004 and other recent cycles). The main players in the presidential campaigns were all individuals hired by the campaigns, not representatives of the party organizations. The chairs of the national parties had no real presence in the day-to-day workings of the candidates' campaigns, except as surrogate spokespersons on occasion and as fundraisers for the party that would help elect their candidate (see chapter 4). As we note in chapter 1, even the national party conventions were scripted mainly by the campaign organization to reflect the message of the individual campaign.

What these data do not speak to are the specific tasks carried out in campaigns. There are some things in campaigns today that consultants are best equipped to handle, whereas others are best carried out by parties. The data from party staffers (especially those at the national level) may already be reflecting this point: there is not a zero-sum increase or decrease between parties and consultants; rather, as consultants have increasingly controlled campaigns, parties have taken on other important roles. On average, party operatives (and, to a lesser extent, consultants) reported that though consultants' influence increased, the importance of parties either held steady or increased somewhat.

Electioneering Services: Who Does What?

The increased role of consultants reported by both consultants and party elites can also be seen in other attitudes of these two important groups of electoral actors. Consultants and parties were again in full agreement that some electioneering services and tasks are better provided to candidates

Table 2-2. *Consultants' and Party Elites' Assessments of the Services Provided by Consultants and Political Parties*[a]

Percent

	Consultants		Party elites, 2002	
Rating	1999	2002	State	National
Strongly agree	55.8	63.9	10.9	13.3
Somewhat agree	34.0	30.2	59.8	60.0
Somewhat disagree	7.2	5.0	19.6	20.0
Strongly disagree	3.0	1.0	9.8	6.7
N	500	202	92	15

a. The question asked was, "Some people in the campaign industry say that political consultants today provide services to campaigns that political parties are incapable of providing. Do you strongly agree, somewhat agree, somewhat disagree, or strongly disagree with that statement?"

by consultants than by the parties. Nearly 90 percent of consultants in 1999 and 94 percent in 2002 agreed that consultants provided some services that parties could not; more interesting, however, is that party elites at both the state and national levels felt the same, although with a bit less consensus (see table 2-2). Only about 30 percent of state party elites, and slightly more than 26 percent of national party elites, disagreed with that assessment.

These results fit well with what else we know about the parties' efforts in campaigns over the past ten to twenty years. As noted above, toward the end of the 1970s the parties began to regain some of the electoral power they had lost in preceding decades.[44] Herrnson describes this as the "party-as-intermediary" era, which saw parties start to provide services candidates were demanding.[45] As parties recaptured some influence in campaigns, they began to revamp the way they provided services. The clearest example of this change is the use of the media production facilities that both parties had built during their revitalization. On the Republican side, according to Ed Blakely, the former director of the National Republican Congressional Committee's studio, before 1986 "about 25 to 30 candidates [got] the full treatment," which included discussions with the campaign's pollster, the party's regional field director, and one of the party's writers.[46] However, after a few election cycles had passed, the committee started to reduce the number of candidates to whom they supplied "full blown media campaigns" and increased the number of ads purchased from outside media consultants.[47] Finally, in the late 1990s, Republicans stopped all use of their media studio for campaign purposes. According to one National Republican Congressional Committee staffer, "Technology is changing so fast that it's just not cost effective for us to continue to upgrade our equipment in a recording studio. The resources there could be better used somewhere else."[48] Democrats have also significantly scaled back the use of their facilities, opting to outsource the production of television ads for their candidates to private consultants.[49]

In other words, the parties have made a conscious decision to look to consultants to provide certain electioneering services rather than try to produce or provide them themselves. This point was clearly demonstrated in consultants' and party elites' assessments of who is better able to provide certain services. We asked consultants and parties if consultants had replaced parties in providing certain services that candidates demand today. Again, there was a great deal of agreement between both sets of actors, though the two groups did show differences in the specific services they thought had been taken over by consultants. Political consultants surveyed in 1999 and 2002 agreed on the extent to which they had taken over provision of specific services from the parties. Consultants felt they were now the main providers of services geared toward message creation and delivery—in particular, strategic advice, paid media advertising, polling, and direct mail—all services that are geared toward developing and spreading a candidate's message (see table 2-3).[50] They also agreed on the services that they had not fully taken over, including fundraising and get-out-the-vote (GOTV) efforts.

The assessments of party operatives were, for the most part, similar to those of consultants. Party elites reported, though with less unanimity, that consultants had taken over for parties in the provision of paid media advertising and polling and, to a lesser extent, direct mail services to candidates. Party elites at both the state and national levels, however, did not feel that consultants had replaced them in the provision of strategic advice. Among the services reported in table 2-3, strategic advice was the one that consultants showed the most agreement on, with the highest mean ranking of all the services mentioned; most consultants agreed that their industry now provided this service to candidates. Among party elites, however, this service was the fifth highest for state party operatives and fourth highest for the national party respondents in terms of what services consultants have assumed in campaigns. This indicates that many party staffers felt they still had something to offer in the way of strategic

Table 2-3. *Consultants' and Party Elites' Assessments of Whether Consultants Have Replaced Parties in Providing Electioneering Services to Candidates*[a]

| | Consultants | | Party elites, 2002 | |
Service	1999	2002	State	National
Strategic advice	3.51	3.50	2.46	2.47
	(496)	(197)	(91)	(15)
Advertising and media	3.49	3.50	3.04	3.00
	(494)	(199)	(93)	(14)
Polling	3.42	3.31	3.14	3.20
	(486)	(200)	(92)	(15)
Direct mailings	3.31	3.35	2.85	2.73
	(487)	(194)	(93)	(15)
Opposition research	3.07	3.05	2.48	2.20
	(487)	(196)	(93)	(15)
Fundraising assistance	2.91	2.94	2.41	2.13
	(491)	(199)	(92)	(15)
Field and GOTV operations	2.65	2.60	1.78	1.67
	(490)	(193)	(93)	(15)

a. The question asked was, "Thinking specifically now, please tell me whether you strongly agree, somewhat agree, somewhat disagree, or strongly disagree that political consultants have largely taken the place of political parties in providing each of these services." Mean rankings are based on a scale in which 4 = strongly agree, 3 = somewhat agree, 2 = somewhat disagree, and 1 = strongly disagree. Numbers in parentheses are numbers of responses.

advice to candidates. Party staffers undoubtedly see their role in campaigning as one that includes delivering strategic help in some form. However, whether candidates and campaigns (which are likely to include outside consultants) listen to that advice is another story. Anecdotally, a former staffer at the Democratic Congressional Campaign Committee (DCCC) and now a media consultant, Martin Hamburger, reports that for many campaigns, this is little more than an illusion:

Upon entering the campaign headquarters on [my] first trip [as a DCCC staffer] . . . I realized something about my new world. I had assumed, and had hoped, that the campaigns we were working on looked toward the DCCC, if not me, as a sort of bank of knowledge and support. I found out they perceived us only as a bank. The impending arrival of a DCCC staffer was like the impending arrival of a wealthy great aunt. You cleaned up [the headquarters], tried to make a great impression, and hoped you were still in her thoughts when it came time to hand out the money. You listened patiently to any advice offered, to make the offerer feel valued. But you almost never thought about it long enough to follow it.[51]

Party elites also reported that they believed consultants had not replaced them in providing services such as opposition research, fundraising, and GOTV efforts. The party staffers we interviewed were adamant about this as well, especially with respect to fundraising and getting voters to the polls. They are clearly not convinced that consultants offered a better service in these areas. The thoughts on these services are best summed up by a former DCCC field director, Chris Esposito: "The party is more helpful than the consultant [in] raising money. That will never change. . . . People like myself can get on the phone and call labor leaders and say, 'Where the hell is the check?' . . . Consultants can't do that." "Consultants are blowing smoke if they think they are replacing the party with turnout plans."[52]

We can again turn to the 2004 presidential election for supporting evidence. In both campaigns, professionals handled the day-to-day strategy planning—Mary Beth Cahill, Bob Shrum, and Tad Devine at the helm of the Kerry campaign, and Ken Mehlman, Karl Rove, and Matthew Dowd calling the shots for the Bush team. In addition, each campaign hired one or more private firms to conduct polling (Dowd for Bush, Mark Mellman and Tom Kiley for Kerry) and create and place paid media ads (television and radio spots and direct mailings; on the television side it was the firm of Shrum, Devine and Donilon for Kerry and Maverick Media for Bush). However, the party did a great deal in the other areas. For all the money that each candidate raised during the primary season (through August 31, 2004, Bush had raised more than $250 million and Kerry more than $210 million),[53] the parties raised more. In total, GOP fundraising at the federal level totaled more than $870 million, and the Democrats raised more than $800 million; the Republican National Committee alone raised more than $390 million, and the Democratic National Committee more than $400 million.[54]

When it came to opposition research in 2004, the parties were again center stage. Leading up to the presidential debates, for example, at Republican National Committee headquarters in Washington, "the 'oppo' (opposition) research team had spent months poring over tapes of

Kerry's past debates. . . . [They] produced a thick binder titled '2004 John Kerry Debate Analysis.'"[55] The same scene played out leading up to the campaign: party staffers combed through Kerry's Senate voting record to find each and every instance in which he had cast a questionable vote. At the Republican National Committee, the research team "catalogued every vote, every statement, every offhand remark" made by every Democratic candidate who might have won the nomination.[56] There was a similar research team in place at the Democratic National Committee.[57]

Although campaign consultants Matthew Dowd and Michael Whouley were part of the strategic thinking behind the mobilization efforts of the two campaigns (see chapter 1), it was the party organizations that carried out many of these activities (in conjunction with the candidates' campaigns, of course).[58] In the end, "Each party developed hundreds of thousands of volunteers in a precinct-by-precinct voter turnout drive and poll-watching operation."[59] Political consulting firms simply do not have the staff required to handle these kinds of research or volunteer recruitment and mobilization efforts.[60] Therefore, the campaigns rely on the party organizations to provide the lion's share of these types of services.

The clear division in the mean rankings of both consultants and parties between services that are dependent on sophisticated technical knowledge, such as polling, media production, and direct mail, and those that are more dependent on a large staff and time, such as opposition research, fundraising, and GOTV operations, helps to illustrate the division of labor that exists between consultants and parties.[61] Consultants are the main providers of services centered on creating a message and delivering that message to voters; parties are still part of the electoral game when it comes to services that require more staff resources and time.

Complementary evidence is found in what candidates reported about where they turn for certain electioneering services. In a survey of candidates conducted in 2002, congressional candidates reported that, for the most part, they turned to consultants for the services that both consultants and party staffers identified as best provided by consultants, and they looked to parties for the same services that both groups said were best provided by parties. For instance, of all candidates surveyed, 49 percent said that they paid outside consultants to conduct their polling, compared with only 6 percent who reported that their polling services were provided by the party (or interest groups); these figures become more divergent when the field was limited to those candidates who ended up in competitive races—incumbents who were in jeopardy of losing their seats and hopeful challengers. Fully 86 percent of endangered incumbents said they used consultants, and only 7 percent got their polling from the party; 81 percent of hopeful challengers got their polling from consultants, compared with only 3 percent who got it from the party.[62] Similar trends were found for services such as media production and direct mail. However, the numbers were reversed when candidates' responses about services such as GOTV operations were tallied: 33 percent of all candidates reported that help with getting out the vote came from the party (or interest groups), compared with only 4 percent who said they used consultants. Of endangered incumbents and hopeful challengers only, 28 percent said GOTV help came from the party, compared with 0 and 6 percent of incumbents and challengers, respectively, who said consultants provided that service. Not one endangered incumbent, hopeful challenger, or open-seat candidate reported having relied on the party for campaign management advice.

The evidence presented above, however, is really only half the story. Consultants also reported that they welcomed party assistance with some electioneering services and that they considered that support valuable in competitive campaigns (see table 2-4). Interestingly, many of these were the services that consultants said they had not taken over from parties.[63] Specifically, consultants most welcomed help with campaign funds, followed by opposition research and polling. On the other hand, consultants consistently reported that the national party was less effective in its assistance with strategic advice and paid media advertising (issue ads or coordinated advertisements)—the electioneering services most consultants felt their industry had taken over from the parties. The findings from the 1999 and 2002 surveys of consultants were almost identical in this respect.

There are some curious results in these data. First, consultants reported that they welcomed the party organizations' assistance with polling—one of the areas that they felt they had taken over from the parties. That consultants welcomed this help from the parties does not mean, however, that the party organizations actually produced the service, in the same way they would provide funds or an opposition research report. Rather, in the case of polling, the party may have helped interpret polling data, but it was other outside consultants who produced the poll. Neither the Democrats nor the Republicans have in-house polling shops at their national headquarters. Instead, they hire consultants to gather and analyze survey data. This has been the case ever since the rejuvenation of the

Table 2-4. *Consultants' and State Party Elites' Assessments of Services Provided by the National Parties in Competitive Races*[a]

Service	Consultants		State party elites, 2002
	1999	2002	
Campaign funds	1.63	1.65	1.53
	(396)	(164)	(86)
Opposition research	1.86	1.86	1.84
	(390)	(159)	(88)
Polling	1.99	2.08	1.71
	(384)	(159)	(89)
Direct mailings	2.18	2.07	1.89
	(373)	(159)	(86)
GOTV operations	2.19	2.20	1.89
	(391)	(161)	(87)
Issue ads and coordinated advertising	2.33	2.25	1.90
	(386)	(159)	(87)
Strategy advice	2.79	2.71	1.84
	(392)	(160)	(89)

a. The question asked was, "I am going to read you a list of services that are sometimes provided to state parties and candidates by the national party organizations or Congressional Campaign Committees. Thinking about competitive races in your state, please tell me whether, in your experience, you think each service has been very helpful, somewhat helpful, not very helpful, or not helpful at all to the success of those campaigns." Mean rankings are based on a scale in which 1 = very helpful, 2 = somewhat helpful, 3 = not very helpful, and 4 = not helpful at all. Numbers in parentheses are numbers of responses.

party organizations in the early 1980s: Republicans originally hired consultants, including Richard Wirthlin, Robert Teeter, and Stanley Finkelstein, to conduct survey research, and the Democrats looked to consultants such as Peter Hart and Matt Reese.[64] The same holds true today. During the last eight weeks of the 2002 campaign, the National Republican Congressional Committee spent $5 million on polling, all conducted by consultants outside of the formal party structure; in 2004, the committee spent $1.2 million on polling, and the Democratic Congressional Campaign Committee spent $1.1 million.[65] Therefore, though consultants working in competitive races welcomed polling data from the national party, the data were not produced by the party as much as they were paid for by the party. Consultants are the main providers of this service today, and they welcome the data supplied by the party organizations.

Consultants reported that assistance with direct mailings was less helpful than assistance with campaign funds or opposition research; however, it was found to be helpful to more consultants than either strategic advice or other paid media advertising (issue ads or coordinated advertising). We believe that this is less a reflection of the helpfulness of direct mail assistance than of the dislike of many consultants for party efforts to commandeer the message during a campaign with the use of issue ads or some other kind of party-based message. This also is consistent with consultants' belief that the party should stay out of developing the campaign's message and the strategic plan for delivering that message. Although we have only anecdotal evidence of this, it is quite convincing.

Party-sponsored issue ads and coordinated advertisements can be a service to candidates. For one thing, they can provide cover for the candidate: if the ads attack the opponent, the candidate can respond, with a wink and a nod, "I am not the one running these ads. I have asked my party to stop running the ads, but I have no control over what they do." In other instances, however, they can be a hindrance. During the 1998 congressional campaign, the GOP launched an air war, called Operation Breakout, consisting of a series of television ads run in targeted districts across the country. One theme of the ads was the scandal involving President Bill Clinton and Monica Lewinsky. Consultants and candidates who were trying to campaign in districts where these ads were run sometimes found it hard to get out their own messages.[66] As one Republican party staffer recalls, "I had a candidate who . . . openly disavowed what we were doing and called me . . . two and three times a day telling me to take the issue ads off [the air]. I told him I wasn't going to do that. I believed in what we were doing. He didn't win, but I think it was the right thing to do. He certainly didn't lose because of what we were doing."[67] The consultants in this race very likely had a different interpretation—that the message they were trying to get out for their candidate was muddied by the work of the parties.[68]

During the 2002 congressional elections, this scene played out again in Iowa. Facing a tough reelection race, Republican Jim Leach, "who has long prided himself on running local campaigns with no out-of-state money," found that the national party was going to begin running ads in his district. Leach told his party brethren "that he did not want the national campaign committee to get involved." However, "Representative Thomas M. Davis III of Virginia, chairman of the National Republican Congressional Committee . . . told Mr. Leach that the national party was probably going into the district on his behalf, like it or not."[69]

This anecdotal evidence helps clarify the empirical data presented earlier. Political consultants appreciate help from the national party when it comes in the form of services that help them carry out the strategy that they have helped the campaign design, but they do not appreciate help when it comes in the form of advice from the party on how best to wage their campaign. Consultants see the party as a resource that can help them get their candidate elected. However, when it comes to strategy execution, they want to be left alone. Party intrusion into their campaigns may be less troublesome to consultants since the 2002 passage of the Bipartisan Campaign Finance Reform Act, which forbids the national parties to spend "soft money" on issue ads—a favorite practice of the national parties, before the BCRA, that allowed them to communicate a party message that may or may not have been consistent with the candidate's message.[70]

Candidates are not the only recipients of help from the national party organizations. State party committees also receive assistance from the national committees and the campaign committees. Because of this, we asked state party elites about the services they received from the national party and what they found to be helpful (see table 2-4). Aside from a slight difference in the pecking order of the services they welcomed compared with those consultants found helpful, one other general trend is important to point out. As compared with the consultant rankings, which ranged from roughly 1.6 (firmly between "very helpful" and "somewhat helpful") to 2.8 (closer to "not very helpful"), the state party respondents' mean rankings were under 2.0 for all listed services. What this indicates is that state party operatives were more welcoming of all services from the national party than were consultants.

One likely reason for this result is that state party operatives simply hold the services that come from their national party counterparts in higher regard than do consultants. It is not a stretch to think that state party elites would look favorably on something contributed to their organization by the national committee or campaign committees; they are, after all, part of the same party structure. Another potential explanation is that the state party operatives simply have fewer resources and less expertise than those at the national level. When assistance with any kind of electioneering service is offered to the state party, many welcome it with open arms because they have neither the staff required to produce it themselves (for example, an opposition research report) nor the funds required to pay for it (for example, a television commercial carrying the party message or a poll of voters in their state). Of course, some state parties are stronger than others, and some are more professionalized (and therefore have larger staff) than others. The state parties that are less professionalized and have smaller staff are quite likely those that look to the national party for any assistance they can provide. Along the same lines, some state party elites have not been in their jobs full-time because their state party organizations are less professionalized than some others. Because of this, some state party operatives simply may not have the expertise or experience needed to carry out some of the electioneering services.

The biggest difference between the mean rankings of consultants and state party operatives was found in the area of strategic advice. State party elites reported that, relative to other services from the national party, assistance with strategy was rather helpful. Again, this may be because state party operatives do not have the same kind of experience that those at the national level do. To some extent this notion is supported by data describing these campaign actors' career paths. Only two-thirds of state party elites reported having worked for a federal, state, or local elected official, compared with more than 86 percent of those national party elites we interviewed; only slightly more than half of the state party operatives had worked for a party organization other than the one they were working for in 2002, compared with 80 percent of the national party elites; and only slightly more than one-third of the state party staffers had worked as a political consultant, compared with two-thirds of the national party operatives.[71] Clearly, state party elites, as a group, are not as experienced politically as their national party counterparts (recall also the difference in years of experience noted above). This may help explain why state party operatives felt that the national party still had much to offer in the way of strategic advice.

Consultants' Clients: Beyond Candidates

Our data regarding parties' hiring practices provide further support for the hypothesis that a network of consultants has taken over in providing certain services to candidates and campaigns and that a division of labor exists between consultants and parties.[72] The practice of hiring consultants has deep roots at party headquarters and continues today. We asked party officials whether, during the 2002 congressional election cycle, their

Table 2-5. *Expected Hiring Practices of State and National Party Organizations*[a]

Percent

Consultant	Definitely will	Probably will	Probably will not	Definitely will not	N
	State party elites, 2002				
Pollster	63.7	24.2	11.0	1.1	91
Direct mail specialist	64.4	18.9	10.0	6.7	90
Fundraiser	33.7	19.6	23.9	22.8	92
Media consultant	40.9	27.3	22.7	9.1	88
	National party elites, 2002				
Pollster	73.3	26.7	0.0	0.0	15
Direct mail specialist	71.4	21.4	0.0	7.1	14
Fundraiser	69.2	23.1	0.0	7.7	13
Media consultant	80.0	13.3	6.7	0.0	15

a. The question asked was, "During the 2002 campaign cycle, does your [party organization/committee] plan to hire any of the following professional consultants? Please tell me whether you definitely will, probably will, probably will not, or definitely not hire [each type of consultant] during the 2002 campaign cycle."

organization would hire professional political consultants to provide certain services and products.[73] As the data in table 2-5 illustrate, party organizations turn to certain types of consultants more than others. The party operatives we interviewed said they hired consultants in the service areas that consultants reported they had taken over—those centered on message creation and delivery. Only slightly more than 12 percent of state party officials reported that they "probably" or "definitely" would not hire a pollster. A slightly higher percentage, roughly 17 percent, said the same about hiring a direct mail consultant. However, nearly half, 46.7 percent, said that they would not hire a fundraiser. Again, because parties have the staff and time resources necessary for fundraising, they do not need consultants to help them with this service. However, because polling and direct mail operations require more technical skills and facilities, parties more often look to consultants in these areas. Interestingly, only about 68 percent of state party elites reported that they would definitely or probably hire a media consultant (compared with 87.9 percent and 83.3 percent who said they would hire a pollster or direct mail specialist, respectively). This result most likely stems from two factors. First, state parties may not have the requisite funds to pay for the air time to run the ads a media consultant would make. In some areas, a week's worth of television ads can cost upward of $1 million.[74] Second, state parties may not engage in broadcast advertising because the national party can step in and do it for them. The state party is not likely to have a message it wants potential voters to hear that is different from that of the national party. Therefore, it is more efficient for the parties in Washington, D.C., to perform this service.

Of the national party operatives we surveyed, more than 93 percent said that their organization would hire a media consultant (see table 2-5). Clearly, this reflects the fact that the national parties and their party committees are major players in the air wars that occur during each election cycle.[75] Ads, whether they are from the Democratic National Committee, the Republican National Committee, or one of the Capitol Hill committees, have a large presence in congressional and presidential campaigns, as can be observed in the heavy dose of ads aired by the Democratic National Committee on behalf of their candidates in 2004.[76] Furthermore, every one of the national party elites we interviewed said their organization had hired or planned to hire a pollster; nearly 93 percent reported that they planned to hire a direct mail specialist. We are not arguing that parties are unable to perform these tasks; rather, parties turn to consultants because they choose not to invest in the technical facilities required for their production. Parties do not have calling houses in their headquarters where phone calls for survey research can be made, nor do they have the requisite facilities to produce direct mail pieces. Although parties have greater time resources than consulting firms to devote to providing some services, they do not have enough time to conduct a poll or create a direct mail piece for each of their candidates who would like them to do so. Instead, parties have found that it is much more efficient to hire consultants to do this for their candidates than to do it in-house.[77]

What is more, parties look to consultants for their own purposes, not just to help out candidates who demand these services. Although parties do hire consultants to provide services to their candidates, they also use them to conduct polling solely for the party or to create party-based television ads or direct mail pieces. Among state party operatives who said their organization was going to hire a pollster ("definitely would hire" and "probably would hire" responses combined), nearly one-third said the pollster would work exclusively for the party (see table 2-6). Similarly, almost 40 percent said the direct mail consultant they hired would work only for their organization; and more than 30 percent said the media con-

Table 2-6. *Expected Workload of Consultants Hired by State and National Organizations*[a]

Percent

Consultant	Party	Candidates	Party and candidates	N
	State party elites, 2002			
Pollster	33.3	7.7	58.9	78
Direct mail specialist	39.7	1.3	58.9	73
Fundraiser	56.5	0.0	34.5	46
Media consultant	31.1	10.3	58.6	58
	National party elites, 2002			
Pollster	28.6	0.0	71.4	14
Direct mail specialist	23.1	0.0	76.9	13
Fundraiser	25.0	8.33	66.7	12
Media consultant	28.6	0.0	71.4	14

a. The question asked was, "Will this [consultant] work exclusively for the party, exclusively for the candidates the party is supporting, or for both?"

sultant would work only for the party. The lion's share of the state party elites who said they would hire consultants reported that those consultants would work for both the party and specific candidates; only a small fraction said that the consultants the party hired would work exclusively for candidates. Similar patterns appear in the data from national party elites. In other words, parties look to consultants to help their candidates, but they also use the services consultants provide for their own purposes. For instance, all of the television ads aired by the parties in the 2004 presidential race were made by consultants hired by the parties.

Although others have addressed the idea that parties and consultants are allies rather than adversaries,[78] we believe the evidence presented here helps to further illustrate their partnership in the electoral game. If parties and consultants were truly enemies, it is reasonable to think that parties would not want to have anything to do with consultants. However, this is clearly not the case. Large majorities of party elites, at both state and national levels, reported that they would recommend political consultants to their candidates (see table 2-7). Between 80 and 100 percent of state and national party operatives reported plans to recommend pollsters, direct mail specialists, and media consultants to their candidates; this supports our notion of a division of labor in campaigns between parties and

Table 2-7. *Party Elites' Plans to Recommend Political Consultants to Their Candidates*[a]

Percent

Consultant	State party elites, 2002	National party elites, 2002
Pollster	91.9	86.7
Direct mail specialist	95.0	80.0
Fundraiser	60.8	86.7
Media consultant	82.4	100.0
N	74	15

a. The question asked was, "Would you recommend [this political consultant]?" Numbers in cells represent the percentage of sample respondents who answered yes.

outside consultants. State party operatives were less likely to report they would recommend a fundraiser to their candidates; this most likely derives from the parties' role as a major source of fundraising help for candidates. More than 86 percent of the national party elites, however, reported that they would recommend a fundraiser to their candidates; this may simply reflect that fundraising over the past four decades has been driven by the rules governing campaign finance, in particular, the Federal Election Campaign Act and its amendments. As Herrnson has noted of the 1971 law, "These reforms set the stage for [political action committees] to become the major organized financiers of election campaigns and drove candidates to rely upon professional campaign consultants to design direct mail fundraising operations."[79] Nonetheless, as our data indicate, consultants and parties both agreed that the party can be a big help with money matters in a campaign.

It is clear from the data presented in this chapter that consultants and parties are both in control of campaigns today. Although today's election contests are campaign-centered affairs, parties still play a role. Much of the Bush-Cheney campaign's work to get out the vote, for example, was done through the GOP's 72-Hour Project. Moreover, both the Democratic and Republican National Committees helped their candidates with their massive fundraising efforts.

Rather than grabbing control of campaigns from candidates or pushing parties to the side of the electioneering process, consultants stepped in to fill an electioneering void and to help candidates with the services that they demanded. Consultants and parties are currently engaged in an electoral partnership in which there is a clear division of labor between the two actors. Services are divided between those centered on message creation and delivery and those that require a great deal of staff resources and time, with consultants being the main service provider of the former and parties of the latter. Both state and national parties look to consultants for help with their own needs, as well; parties both recommend consultants to their candidates and hire consultants to perform services and deliver products to party headquarters. In effect, the pendulum of electioneering power has, for the moment, found equilibrium.

CHAPTER 3

Where Do We Stand?
A Comparative View
among the Actors

A thorough examination of the health of American campaigning must include an investigation of the players central to the process. How are different electoral actors performing within our system of campaigning? There are many different levels on which the main actors in campaigns could be judged. (In this book, we focus on candidates, the public, political consultants, political parties, and journalists as electoral actors.) Because of actors' different roles, however, these measures do not always overlap. Therefore, for each of these groups of actors we offer a general performance assessment, again based on our survey research and examples from recent campaigns. We have data from both inside and outside the campaign organizations that try to affect the makeup of our governmental institutions (consultants and political parties), as well as from those whose support the campaigns target (the general public).

Because the function of the different campaign actors can be conceived in many different ways, we avoid making normative judgments about what they should be doing in campaigns. We do not single out any particular ill or remedy; we do not, for example, advocate for a system with strong parties or one in which voters are well informed, because these are not the only ways in which elections can function. Rather, we try to describe the current state of affairs in modern campaigning. We believe that this chapter presents the question of the health of campaigning in a broad manner and allows readers to draw some conclusions about where our campaigns are headed in relation to their own expectations for the system.

Where Do We Stand? Candidate Quality, Inside and Out

There are a number of ways to conceive of candidate quality. In the scholarly literature on elections, and specifically election outcomes, important studies have illustrated that a candidate's political experience and name recognition in the community in which he or she is seeking office, as well as characteristics such as being a political activist and having a fundraising base, among others, have an important impact on candidate success, especially in terms of challenger quality.[1] For current officeholders, incumbency itself (and the advantages associated with it) makes a candidate tough to beat at the ballot box.

Interestingly, however, the traits or characteristics necessary for candidates to be competitive on election day are some of the same traits that lead many to criticize the pool of candidates from which voters must choose. For instance, to be successful today, candidates must have the ability to raise significant sums of money—Howard Dean jumped to the head of the pack of Democrats running for his party's presidential nomination early in the 2004 presidential primary season in part because he was able to raise more money than any of his rivals (also see chapter 4)— or have a great deal of personal wealth to contribute to their campaign— Senator Jon Corzine (D-N.J.) spent more than $60 million of his own money in his 2000 campaign. However, candidates who are able to raise large amounts of money are suspected of being either beholden to special interests or having big-dollar donors filling their campaign coffers. During the 2004 Democratic primary, John Edwards was considered to be in the running for the nomination partly because of his fundraising success. However, in a primary debate John Kerry, who went on to choose Edwards as his running mate for the general election, criticized Edwards for his fundraising success. Kerry noted that Edwards had "raised 50 percent of his money from one group of people"—trial lawyers, of whom Edwards had been one before running for the U.S. Senate in 1998.[2] Those who contribute their own money to their campaigns are sometimes accused of buying their way into office—a label some tried to attach to Jon Corzine after his 2000 Senate campaign.[3]

Candidates who have experience in the job are criticized for being "Washington insiders" or "career politicians" who are "out of touch" with the average American. Many challenger candidates in high-level races, in fact, cite as one of their qualifications that they are *not* from Washington, D.C. Countless candidates have run for Congress by running against Congress as an institution; and in 2000 George W. Bush was able to capitalize on his inexperience with national office by painting his opponent, Vice President Al Gore, as someone tied intimately to Washington and with no connection to life outside the Beltway. In 2004 John Kerry had to battle a similar image, even though his nineteen years in the U.S. Senate made him a well-qualified candidate for the highest office in the land. In the same debate noted earlier, John Edwards attacked Kerry on this very charge, rhetorically asking the audience of viewers, "Do you believe change is more likely to be brought about by someone who has spent 20 years in Washington, or by someone who's more of an outsider to this process—somebody who comes from the same place that most Americans come from?"[4]

Candidate quality, however, it can be argued, must be measured by more than the variables that make one likely to win on election day. It also includes the ability to do a good job once in office. What it takes to do a good job often depends on the office the candidate is seeking and the context in which the candidate is running.[5] As E. J. Dionne notes,

> Americans are opportunistic, fickle and capricious on the subject of experience in politics—which also means that we are practical and sensible. There are times when the voters are looking for a plumber, mechanic or doctor. The idea is to hire someone with a long track record who can fix problems and keep an eye on things. There are other moments when voters yearn for a preacher, an actor, a general—even a wrestler—who might lift their spirits by offering vision, or just by being different. . . . Occasionally, voters get so mad at the reliable mechanic (especially when one can't fix things) that they will turn to absolutely anybody.[6]

In other words, quality is in the eyes of the beholder—the American voter—and can mean different things at different times. Sometimes voters demand experience, at other times they want a breath of fresh air and change. This was at play in the 2003 gubernatorial recall election in California, Dionne continues, where at the time, "it's said, correctly, that Arnold [Schwarzenegger] has no government experience beyond his time on a couple of physical fitness commissions—i.e., no government experience. . . . Arnold has the kind of inexperience that [Governor Gray] Davis wishes he could now buy." Davis went on to be recalled by the citizens of California, mainly because he was blamed for the dire condition of the state budget at the time. One cannot know what is going through the mind of the public, and for this reason what the public considers to be a quality candidate can be difficult to define.

One constant running through our survey research has been electoral actors' different assessments of the quality of other specific actors in the electoral process. Judging from our survey research, it appears that candidates today are not held in high regard by some of those most qualified to judge them: political consultants. Consultants are in a unique position to judge the quality of candidates because they work alongside them during campaigns and see them in positions critical to an assessment of quality. Because, for the most part, consultants operate behind the scenes in a campaign, they see the candidate in a different setting from that available to the public and the news media. Consultants see how their candidate-clients react when their opponents launch attacks or when their campaigns take a turn for the worse; they see candidates respond to crisis situations.[7]

The stable and clear message from political consultants is that in terms of quality, today's candidates running for some of the highest national offices are lacking. In the 1998 survey, nearly 48 percent of all consultants rated the quality of candidates as only "fair" or "poor."[8] In the 1999 survey, only slightly more than 3 percent of all consultants found candidates at the time to be of "excellent" quality, and more than 13 percent said they were of poor quality (see table 3-1). The modal response from consultants in 1999 was that candidates were only of "average" quality. Consultants in 2002 gave candidates a slightly better evaluation, nearly 5 percent rating candidates as excellent, but most still reported that they believed candidates were just average. What is more, many consultants have consistently reported that they believe that over time the quality of candidates has decreased. In 1998 only slightly more than 17 percent of all consultants interviewed said that the quality of candidates for the House and Senate had "gotten better," but 42 percent said it had "gotten worse" in the time they had been in politics. In both 1999 and 2002, roughly 21 percent of all consultants we surveyed said that candidates for the House and Senate had shown an improvement in quality ("gotten a lot better" and "gotten somewhat better" taken together).

There were significant and important differences between Republican and Democratic consultants in how they viewed candidates.[9] More Republicans than Democrats gave U.S. House and Senate candidates a

Table 3-1. *Consultants' and the Public's Assessments of the Quality of Candidates Running for Office*[a]

Percent

Rating	Consultants		General public		
	1999	2002	March 2000	October 2000[b]	2002
Excellent	3.3	4.5	3.5	9.1, 13.4	3.4
Good	35.9	34.2	29.6	31.5, 35.4	31.4
Average	46.4	48.0	49.8	43.7, 37.6	46.7
Poor	13.3	12.4	12.0	10.2, 8.9	14.9
Very poor	1.0	1.0	5.1	5.4, 4.7	3.6
N	487	202	968	958, 950	1,059

a. The question asked was, "In general, how would you rate the quality of the candidates running for the House and Senate today?"

b. In this column, the first number represents respondents' views on presidential candidates, the second number, vice presidential candidates. In October 2000 the general public was asked, "In general, how would you rate the quality of [vice presidential candidates running for public office today/presidential candidates running for public office today]"?

high rating. For instance, when asked in 1999 to rate the quality of today's candidates, Republicans' mean rating was 3.39 compared with the Democrats' rating of 3.26.[10] This difference may be a function of the electoral fortunes of Republican candidates—from the middle to the late 1990s, Republicans were able to regain control of the U.S. House of Representatives for the first time since 1954 and took control of the U.S. Senate again, losing it only because Senator Jim Jeffords (I-Vt.) decided to leave the GOP and caucus with the Democrats, not because of any electoral shift. We believe that part of the Democratic consultants' negative views of their candidates was a result of their recent lack of electoral success.

In 2002 the difference between Republicans and Democrats grew even stronger, as Republicans' mean rating was 3.63 to Democrats' 3.14. Looking at the data another way shows these differences even more clearly. In our last measure of consultants' attitudes, more than 58 percent of Republicans said that they thought candidates were of either excellent or good quality, compared with only about 30 percent of Democrats. The noteworthy difference here is not between Democrats and Republicans, although that difference does exist, but between the 1999 results and the 2002 results. In 2002 more Republicans (by 14 percent) said that their candidates were of high quality than in 1999, and fewer Republicans (by 10 percent) rated candidates as average. The opposite pattern appeared for Democrats, as more Democrats (8 percent more) in 2002 said their candidates were average and fewer (10 percent fewer) said they were of high quality, compared with 1999. In other words, Republican consultants' attitudes got better over this short time, and Democrats' got worse. These data suggest that our original hypothesis has some value. From 1999 to 2002, Republicans were able to add seats to their House majority and were able to take back control of the U.S. Senate, continuing to frustrate Democrats. For this hypothesis to be fully tested we would need data over a longer period of time, preferably with Democrats showing some gains in House and Senate elections to see whether Democratic consultants' ratings of their candidates improved with better luck at the ballot box.

After the 2000 presidential election, less than a quarter of the voters surveyed reported being very satisfied with the choice between the candidates, up from 18 percent in 1996.[11] Our measures of the general public's satisfaction with today's candidates for public office are consistent with these findings. In the first survey we did during the 2000 campaign (immediately after the Super Tuesday primary), only 3.5 percent of all respondents reported that today's candidates were of excellent quality. Similar to consultants' attitudes, most Americans found candidates to be of only average quality (see table 3-1). However, the public was harsher on candidates: more of the general public (5.1 percent) said that the candidates were of very poor quality than did consultants (1.0 percent). The public's views of specific candidates, however, showed some improvement over their rating of candidates generally. During the survey conducted in late October 2000, more than 9 percent of all Americans reported that the presidential candidates were of excellent quality, and more than 13 percent said the same about the vice presidential candidates. The electorate showed similar pessimism compared with the earlier measure: roughly 5 percent of all Americans reported that the presidential and vice presidential candidates were of very poor quality. Our final measure of the public's attitudes about today's candidates, in November of 2002, continued to show similar patterns. Only slightly more than 3 percent of all respondents said that the candidates running for Congress were of excellent quality, while the modal answer continued to be "average."

During the height of the 2004 Democratic presidential primary race (February 2004), only 4 percent of Americans rated the candidates as excellent, 27 percent rated them as good, and 40 percent as fair; a full 17 percent said they were of poor quality.[12] This would appear to indicate a continuing and consistent pattern. The number of Americans who were satisfied with their choice of candidates was stable, compared with a similar point in 2000: only 15 percent were very satisfied, and 47 percent fairly satisfied, with their choice of candidates (this 62 percent who were at least moderately satisfied with their choices is the same that expressed a similar sentiment in 2000).[13] However, by the end of 2004 more voters reported being very satisfied with their choice of candidates (33 percent) compared with earlier in the campaign and compared with the same time frame of previous election cycles (24 percent in 2000; 18 percent in 1996; and 24 percent in 1992).[14] One caveat to these findings is that they are results from individuals who reported having voted in 2004. It may be that these respondents had higher opinions of candidates than the public in general; there is some evidence of this in our 2000 data as well.

Those individuals identified as likely voters generally gave higher ratings to candidates during the 2000 campaign.[15] In March 42 percent of likely voters said that the candidates were of either excellent or good quality, compared with just under 30 percent of those not likely to go to the polls. About 12 percent of likely voters gave candidates a negative rating (poor or very poor), compared with almost one in five of those not likely to vote. Similarly, in October of 2000, more than 12 percent of those identified as likely voters, compared with 6 percent of those identified as not likely to vote, said that the presidential candidates were of excellent quality (the difference grows to 10 points when we consider the responses "excellent" and "good" together—45.9 percent versus 35.9 percent). Moreover, less than 10 percent of likely voters said that the presidential candidates were of poor or very poor quality late in the 2000 campaign versus nearly 21 percent of those not likely to vote.

The same differences were found in ratings of the vice presidential candidates, 17 percent of likely voters reporting that they believed these candidates to be of the highest quality compared with only 10 percent of those deemed unlikely to vote. Interestingly, the vice presidential candidates in 2000—Dick Cheney and Joe Lieberman—got higher ratings (from both groups) than did the presidential candidates. This could be a function of myriad factors, but these candidates' lower profile in their respective campaigns is likely to be one of them. After all, it is the presidential candidates who are on the stump day after day, continually in front of the media, and the focus of their campaign's communications, such as television and radio ads and direct mail pieces.

This raises an interesting question about vice presidential candidates, however. Traditionally, vice presidential candidates have been relegated to playing the role of attack dog in the presidential campaign—going after their opponents in ways that presidential candidates cannot afford to because they want to stay above the fray or would pay too high a political price for the direct attacks. To this end, the attacks coming from vice presidential candidates are often harsher and more pointed than the rhetoric from the top of the ticket. However, if these candidates are engaging in the "negative" campaigning that most Americans say they dislike, the vice presidential candidates in 2000 did not see this reflected in their approval ratings in October of that election year. Maybe they were playing attack dog, but the public did not seem to notice. One account late in the 2000 campaign notes that while neither Cheney nor Lieberman played this role throughout the campaign, each did play the role at times:

> In the beginning, Joe Lieberman was a phenomenon, campaigning exuberantly as the first Jew on a major party ticket. Now, with polls showing a tight race just weeks before the election, his appearances are a bit less cheerful, his tone sharper. By contrast, Dick Cheney, criticized at the start as a humorless, lackluster campaigner, has lightened up a bit, sprinkling a few jokes and wry comments into stump speeches still laden with criticism of the Democrats. The "attack dog" moniker, once readily assigned to Cheney, now fits Lieberman as well.[16]

However, what may help explain our finding is each man's performance in the one event in which they were center stage—the vice presidential debate. In 2000 an estimated 25 million Americans watched this debate, and the general impression was of a dialogue between two men rather than a confrontation between two pit bulls. The two candidates "were reviewed like entertainers in every major daily newspaper, on broadcast and cable TV, and on the Internet." In many cases, they were like "a couple of gentlemen having a chat." Cheney and Lieberman were called, among other things, old friends, grown-ups, and seasoned politicians. Their dialogue was described as spirited, warm, charming, humane, and respectful. "Give it a rave," said CBS anchor Dan Rather. "This will go down as the best vice-presidential joint appearance on television since the television era in presidential and vice-presidential campaigns began." "Highly civilized, in many ways they articulated the positions of their campaigns more effectively" than their respective running mates, observed NBC anchor Tom Brokaw.[17] It may be that Americans watched the debate, heard and read what the opinion makers were saying afterward, internalized the others' experience of the performance, and reflected that in their assessment of the candidates.

President Bush and Senator Kerry, by the end of 2004, certainly got more favorable ratings from the public than had past slates of candidates. However, after the campaign, the positive feelings were mostly one-sided. Among Republicans, 63 percent expressed a high degree of satisfaction with the candidates. Democrats, though, began wondering if they had run a bad candidate, much like they wondered after the 2000 election when Vice President Al Gore was beaten by Bush.[18] In 2004 Democrats could look to an economy that was less than robust for much of the campaign and a war in Iraq that had not been as easy as promised and wonder how their candidate had lost; the stage had certainly been set for a victory, but the candidate did not deliver. Moreover, those in the middle—the swing voters—were very dissatisfied with the candidates in 2004. By the end of the campaign, only 35 percent of those who had not firmly made up their minds said that they were satisfied with the candidates.[19]

The good news in 2004 was that the candidates communicated their different views and policy positions to the voters: 68 percent of potential voters (Republicans, Democrats, and independents alike) said that Bush and Kerry took different positions on issues (only 21 percent said their positions were similar).[20] Furthermore, nearly two-thirds of all Americans, compared with less than half of the public in 2000, said that it "really mattered" who was elected to the presidency.[21]

The preponderance of evidence, however, still points to a public dissatisfied with their candidates for office—even in 2004, only a third described themselves as very satisfied. There may be a mitigating factor here, however, in that we asked mainly about candidates generally. It is possible that, had they been asked about the candidates running in their own states or districts, the general public would have given higher ratings to candidate quality. We may be picking up on a similar pattern in public opinion data that has been illustrated elsewhere—that Americans are rather fond of their own congressional representatives but hold elected officials in general in contempt.[22] We believe signs of this are present in the more positive ratings of candidates when we asked specifically about the presidential and vice presidential candidates in October of 2000.

Interestingly, the general public we surveyed illustrated some of the same partisan differences shown by professional political consultants. In the March 2000 and November 2002 surveys, Republicans were more likely than Democrats to give a higher rating to candidates. Republicans' mean ranking was 3.29 compared with Democrats' 3.16 in March of 2000, and 3.28 compared with 3.15 in November 2002. It may be that the electorate, like consultants, tends to give higher ratings to the quality of their candidates when those candidates are winning. Alternatively, it might simply be that fewer good Democratic candidates have been choosing to run. Candidates must decide well in advance whether they are going to seek office (they need to raise money and establish campaign teams), and the 2004 presidential race on the Democratic side was no exception. Those seeking the nomination to challenge George W. Bush had to begin preparations nearly two years in advance (Governor Dean filed papers with the Federal Election Commission on May 31, 2002). Two years before the campaign would be waged, President Bush's high approval ratings may have made him look unbeatable; when Dean announced his candidacy, 76 percent of the public surveyed in a Gallup poll approved of Bush's performance. This may have made some Democrats leery of a run in 2004. New York senator Hillary Clinton or New Mexico governor Bill Richardson could not have predicted Bush's slide in the polls or the vulnerability he showed later in 2004.

Quality Assessment: A Retrospective Analysis

Asking about candidates who have run for office is inherently a retrospective analysis. To be more specific in this examination, we asked different groups of electoral actors pointedly about these assessments. Have voters voted for a candidate they were later sorry to see serve in office? Have consultants and party operatives helped to elect a candidate they were later sorry to see serve? The evidence on these questions is split. Roughly half of all consultants in each of our three measurements (44.5 percent in 1998, 51.3 percent in 1999, and 56.6 percent in 2002) expressed regret over having helped elect at least one candidate throughout their careers. This is indeed troubling, since consultants are in one of the best positions to evaluate candidates. Potentially more important, however, are the reasons they report for their disappointment. Consultants report, for example, that these feelings were caused because the candidate did not keep campaign promises (29 percent reported this reason in 1999), the candidate engaged in unethical campaign behavior (26 percent), and that the candidate was not qualified for the position to which he or she was elected (18 percent).[23] Similar reasons were given by consultants in 2002, but the reason cited most often (given by 30 percent of the respondents) was that candidates had engaged in some kind of unethical behavior; this was followed by consultants' feeling that candidates had changed their political positions (about 17 percent), were not qualified for the positions they were seeking (about 14 percent), and had not kept campaign promises (about 13 percent).

A number of factors might cause professional political consultants to feel remorse for helping to elect a particular candidate. First, though many critics claim that campaign consultants are driven only by a desire to make money, research into their motivations shows that they are ideological individuals who care about the policy direction of government and are often spurred to become consultants by their own beliefs and a desire to see the political party they identify with be the majority party in government.[24] In addition, because of the cyclical nature of their work, consultants must take on a number of clients each election cycle in order to remain in business. Unfortunately, not all consultants can be picky in whom they take as clients, and some may feel they have to sign on to a campaign they might otherwise refuse because of the candidate. Many consultants are pragmatists who take on a wide range of candidates; a moderate consultant working for a conservative Republican candidate might end up being uncomfortable with that individual in office.[25]

One result readers may find particularly interesting is that so many consultants cited candidates' failure to keep campaign promises as one of the main reasons for remorse. This would be a surprise to consultants' critics and to those who take a cynical view of the modern campaign. One might ask, "Isn't this what we would expect? Consultants tell their candidates what they have to say during the campaign in order to get elected, and then the candidate-turned-officeholder reverts to the original position on the issue, the one he or she really believes in." This implies that consultants manipulate candidates into taking any position that will get them votes and that candidates are willing to do whatever it takes to get elected. However, we believe that for the vast majority of candidates and consultants, this is not the case. We believe that, rather than telling candidates what issue positions to take, consultants act in accord with Stephen Medvic's theory of deliberate priming.[26] Medvic argues that consultants help identify issues that are beneficial to the candidate's chances of winning and that those are the issues they highlight during the campaign. In addition, consultants help candidates find language that best communicates the candidate's position on these issues. This is far from the notion purported by consultants' critics, which suggests that candidates are driven by the polls. Unfortunately, the reputations (deserved or not) of two recent candidates—President Bill Clinton and Senator John Kerry—have done more to advance the critics' case. However, these are only two of the hundreds of candidates who run for federal office every election cycle, and we should not judge all candidates based on the reputation of a few.

Further evidence of partisan differences between consultants is found in this retrospective analysis. Republicans continue to show a less pessimistic view of candidates running for office today; in 1999 nearly 52 percent of Democrats said they had helped elect a candidate they were later sorry to see in office, compared with only about 45 percent of Republicans. Although Republicans show regret in smaller proportions, 45 percent is not an insignificant figure and is not one to be ignored. In addition, in 2002 roughly half of both Republicans and Democrats said the same. These data indicate that today's consultants continue to have a negative view of candidates.

More striking, however, is that large proportions of consultants who identified themselves as independents said they had helped a candidate get elected whom they were later sorry to see serve—almost 70 percent in 1999 and more than 77 percent in 2002.[27] The differences between partisans (Democrats and Republicans) and those who called themselves independents are clearly seen here. One of the reasons for these differences is that consultants who do not affiliate themselves with either of the major parties still work for candidates who are Democrats or Republicans. Independent consultants must also be pragmatic if they are going to stay in business, and therefore they must take on Republican and Democratic candidates. It is no surprise to see that consultants who consider themselves to be neither Democrat nor Republican but take Democrats and Republicans as clients show some regret in helping these candidates get elected. After all, they are independents for a reason.[28]

The view of political party operatives, the other source of electioneering aid for candidates, is more positive. Only about a quarter of state party operatives reported that they had helped to elect a candidate they were later sorry to see in office. Party staffers report reasons similar to those of consultants, citing unethical behavior, lack of qualification for the office sought, and failure to keep campaign promises as reasons for their remorse. Before taking the smaller number of regretful party operatives as a truly positive sign, two important factors should put these figures into some perspective. First, party staffers are much less pragmatic than consultants; they work only for Democrats or only for Republicans, and the party apparatus decides whom they will help in a campaign. For party officials, the outcome of the election is positive if one of their candidates wins and keeps the other party from gaining control of government.[29] For Republicans, any GOP candidate is better than a Democrat, and for Democrats, any Democratic candidate is better than a Republican. As long as party staffers help to elect a candidate of their own party, they are likely to be happy with the outcome—certainly happier than if the other party were to gain more power. Second, as noted in chapter 2, the consultants in our surveys had been in the business much longer than the party staffers we interviewed in 2002. Most of the senior-level state party staffers we interviewed had been in their positions for less than two years—some not for one full election cycle. What this means is that consultants have had a greater opportunity to be associated with a candidate they might later be sorry to see in office; simply put, they have worked with greater numbers of candidates and therefore have a higher likelihood of coming across a disappointing candidate. Many party operatives have been around relatively fewer candidates, because of their short tenure in their job, and are less likely to have worked with a candidate who might disappoint them.

Voters also showed some disappointment in candidates in this specific retrospective analysis. About one-third of the Americans we surveyed in March of 2000 said that they had once voted for a candidate they were eventually sorry to see serve in office. Again, the reasons for their regret are significant. Like consultants and party staffers, voters who were sorry to see a candidate serve most often reported the reason was that the candidate had not keep his or her campaign promises; about 40 percent of those who said they later regretted having voted for a particular candidate reported this as the reason. Other reasons were that they found the candidate lied or could not be trusted (26 percent), that the candidate changed his or her political philosophy (20 percent), or that the candidate was unethical in his or her behavior (12 percent).

Again, large differences were found between those who were more and less likely to participate on election day. In March 2000 likely voters were more inclined than those less likely to vote to say that they had voted for a candidate at one point that they were later sorry to see serve in office (39 percent versus 28 percent). This is an interesting and potentially important finding. One might expect the opposite result. One thing that may drive individuals from the electoral process is that they have seen what they believed to be good candidates turn into poor elected officials once in office. Likely voters in 2000 were more inclined to say that they had been disappointed by a candidate in the past, yet they remained engaged in the electoral process. In other words, likely voters are resilient to disappointment inflicted on them by candidates in the past and continue to be informed citizens and active in the process.

What does this body of evidence say about our candidates today? Professional consultants—whose access to candidates puts them in a strong position to evaluate candidates—and the general public do not believe that voters are picking leaders and representatives from the cream of the crop when they step into the voting booth on election day. Rather, they believe that they are choosing from an average bunch of Americans or between "the lesser of two evils." One citizen's sentiments, after voting in the 2002 election between GOP candidate Douglas Forrester and former Democratic senator Frank Lautenberg for New Jersey's U.S. Senate seat vacated by Robert Torricelli, sums this up nicely: "I usually vote for the lesser of two evils. But after this campaign, I'm not sure which one it is."[30] Clearly, these two important groups of campaign actors do not believe that the ideal type of candidate is running in today's campaigns. This evidence is softened slightly by the few results reported earlier indicating that likely voters report more favorable ratings of candidates than do those who are not likely to go to the polls. However, these data may be just as troubling, since it may the quality of the candidates that is keeping a significant portion of the electorate home on election day.

Where Do We Stand? Voters

Democratic idealists such as John Stuart Mill, John Locke, and Alexis de Tocqueville believed that a successful democratic system required an electorate that possessed a high level of political information. "The democratic citizen is expected to be well informed about political affairs. He is supposed to know what the issues are, what their history is, what the relevant facts are, what alternatives are proposed, what the party stands for, what the likely consequences are."[31] If the truth be told, the political science literature has consistently shown that voters do not meet this ideal. Rather, classic works such as Angus Campbell, Philip E. Converse, Warren E. Miller, and Donald E. Stokes's 1960 *The American Voter* and others that followed illustrate that the American public is not very sophisticated in terms of political knowledge. In fact, according to Larry Bartels, "The political ignorance of the American voter is one of the best-documented features of contemporary politics."[32] The conclusion in the literature is fairly consistent: "ordinary citizens tend to pay attention to politics only fitfully, and possess in consequence a thin, rather than thick, knowledge of it."[33] Some in the literature, including Norman Nie, Sidney Verba, and John Petrocik, have challenged this idea,[34] but recent research "has hammered away at the Nie argument, confirming the continuing validity of the image of citizens as 'low involvement' spectators of politics."[35] Even in the face of the modern scholarship that illustrates a more positive assessment of the electorate, "most voters . . . still fall short of the standards of classic democratic theory."[36]

Voter Information Levels and Decisionmaking

Among our survey respondents, both political consultants and the general public tended to agree with the findings of the political science literature. In other words, both groups also appear to be pessimistic about the information levels held by the American public.

The practical view from those inside today's campaigns whose responsibility it is to have a finger on the pulse of the electorate—consultants— is that the American public is not well informed on major policy issues. In the 1998 survey of consultants, only 1.5 percent of consultants rated the American people as "very well" informed, and more than 18 percent said that they were "very poorly" informed (see table 3-2). As in their evaluation of candidates, the modal response from consultants was not optimistic: nearly half thought that the electorate was "somewhat poorly" informed on major policy issues. Similar results were found in the 1999 survey of the industry, although the number of consultants who rated the electorate as very well informed increased mildly to 3.0 percent. Still, however, 18.9 percent said that, in general, Americans were very poorly informed.

Again, partisan differences are readily apparent. Republican consultants tended to be more pessimistic about the level of the public's knowledge than were their Democratic counterparts. Data from the 1999 sur-

Table 3-2. *Consultants' and the Public's Assessments of*
How Well Informed the Electorate Is[a]

Percent

Rating	Consultants		General public	
	1998	1999	March 2000	October 2000
Very well informed	1.5	3.0	22.5	26.7
Somewhat well informed	31.1	34.8	58.0	57.5
Somewhat poorly informed	48.9	43.8	13.0	10.5
Very poorly informed	18.3	18.9	6.6	5.3
N	196	500	987	998

a. Consultants were asked, "Overall, would you describe the American public as being very well informed on major policy issues, somewhat well informed, somewhat poorly informed, or very poorly informed?" The general public was asked, "Overall, would you describe yourself as being very well informed on major policy issues, somewhat well informed, somewhat poorly informed, or very poorly informed?"

vey of consultants shows that nearly 41 percent of the Democrats sur-veyed versus only roughly 31 percent of the Republicans (and 24 percent of the independents) reported that they believed the public was somewhat well informed on major policy issues. Moreover, 23 percent of Republicans (and 26 percent of independents) rated the electorate as very poorly informed, compared with only 12 percent of Democrats.

Candidates for office shared the pessimistic view of consultants; in fact, a higher share of candidates than consultants found the public poorly informed. Of candidates polled in a separate survey, "nearly three-fourths take the dim view that the American public is either very poorly (30 percent) or somewhat poorly (43 percent) informed on major policy issues. Twenty-five percent say the public is somewhat well informed and, dramatically, only 3 percent picked very well informed."[37] The view from inside today's campaigns is not a complimentary one with respect to the information levels voters bring to the voting booth.

These data are complemented by those from outside the campaign. In a recent survey of their profession, roughly two-thirds of political jour-nalists reported that the public is simply not interested in serious news.[38] A more direct measure illustrates similar findings. The general public's assessment of its own sophistication is slightly more favorable than that of consultants, candidates, and journalists, but not by much. When we asked Americans whether they felt they personally were well informed, only about one-quarter (in both the March 2000 and October 2000 surveys) reported that they thought of themselves as very well informed, though nearly 60 percent (again, across both waves) said they were somewhat well informed. Before concluding from these data that the American public is actually well informed on major policy issues, we must remember that, as when the public reports how frequently it votes, some respondents may be giving the socially desirable answer and overstating the extent to which they are informed about politics.

As in the evaluations of candidates, significant differences appeared between those members of the general public who were likely to go to the polls on election day in 2000 and those more likely to stay home. In March 2000 nearly four in ten likely voters considered themselves very well informed compared with only about 16 percent of unlikely voters. Moreover, there were large and potentially important differences between likely voters and unlikely voters in the numbers saying they were not politically informed, with less than 6 percent of likely voters saying that they were either somewhat poorly or very poorly informed, compared with one-quarter of those not likely to vote. These results carried over into the October 2000 survey, as the proportion of likely voters who said they saw themselves as very well informed was nearly double that of those identified as not likely to vote (34.9 percent versus 19.1 percent). Furthermore, more than 9 percent of those unlikely to vote on election day said they were very poorly informed, compared with only slightly more than 1 percent of likely voters. The difference between those who were likely and those who were unlikely to go to the polls is a double-edged sword. On the one hand, it can be taken as a somewhat brighter picture of the electorate: those who actually do participate are more informed than those who stay out of the process. On the other hand, it reinforces the suspicion that something about campaigns and the electoral system in general is turning some people off to the political process. This is similar to the differences, discussed earlier, between likely voters and unlikely voters in their attitudes toward candidates for office; likely voters had a better view of candidates than those less likely to vote. Again, the individuals who participated in the process had a more favorable view, but those who were not participating may have been turned off by the candidates themselves.

The partisan differences between consultants—Democrats were more likely than Republicans to see the American electorate as informed—

also appear in the public's rating of their own level of knowledge of major policy issues, but in the opposite direction. In March 2000 more Republicans and independents (both roughly 26 percent) than Democrats (less than 20 percent) reported that they considered themselves very well informed on major policy issues. This difference appeared again in our measure of the public's attitudes closer to the general election: in October 2000, 32.0 percent of Republicans rated themselves as very well informed on major policy issues, whereas only 22.6 percent of Democrats said the same.

During Campaign 2004 it appeared that voter information levels were increasing, however. Even before the height of the campaign, measures of the public's interest and attention to the campaign were up from previous presidential cycles.[39] As noted in chapter 1, survey research conducted during June 2004 showed that members of the electorate felt more interested in politics and the election in 2004 than they had at the same time in both 2000 and 1996; nearly 60 percent of all Americans reported that they had already given a lot of thought to the election, compared with only 46 and 50 percent who said the same thing in 2000 and 1996, respectively.[40] Moreover, by late in the campaign 71 percent of Americans said that they had given "quite a lot of thought" to the presidential campaign; this is compared with less than 60 percent who said the same in both 2000 and 1996.[41] The 2004 campaign also saw a large jump in the number of Americans who said that they were following the election very closely—40 percent said as much late in 2004, compared with only 22 percent and 24 percent in 2000 and 1996, respectively.[42]

Much of the increase in interest during the early portion of the campaign season was from Democrats and independents, a 16-point increase among liberal Democrats, an 11-point increase among moderate Democrats, and a 19-point increase among independents in the number who said they had given a lot of thought to the election (there were much smaller increases on the Republican side).[43] There is little doubt that on the Democratic side, the increased interest and attention was generated by the desire to boot President Bush from office and the high stakes attributed to this race for president.

The fact remains, though, that most of the general public is not well informed about politics.[44] However, that does not mean that our campaigns (and our elections in general) are damned. As more recent scholarly work argues, "One should not presume that there must be strong constraints across diverse issue domains or citizens must have textbook

knowledge about the political process in order to participate in a knowledgeable way"; rather, "individuals can make reasonable decisions . . .
without perfect information."[45] Many scholars have argued that low levels of political information may not be important either because voters
use cues to help them make decisions or because, given the sheer numbers
of uninformed voters, their individual decisions tend to cancel one
another out.[46] Some recent research has painted a more optimistic picture
of the American electorate, arguing that citizens have what it takes to
make sense of politics and campaigns even though they are not fully
informed.[47] The reason for this optimism in the literature is that scholars
have seen that voters can use information shortcuts or their own individual reasoning to make a decision on election day.[48]

For the most part, professional political consultants agree. In 1998
more than 85 percent of all consultants reported that they had some trust
and confidence in the wisdom of the American public to make a decision
on election day;[49] only 2 percent reported that they had no confidence in
the public's ability (see table 3-3). Similar results were found in the 1999
survey. Thus consultants, much like political scientists, seem to believe
that members of the electorate are able to sift through the informational
clutter that surrounds them and use the limited knowledge they have to
construct a choice on election day.

Again, some subtle partisan differences between consultants were
uncovered. Although Democrats were more skeptical of the public's level
of information sophistication, they were also more optimistic with regard
to the electorate's ability to make sound decisions in the voting booth.
Republican and Democratic consultants in 1999 were roughly consistent
in saying that they had a great deal of trust (slightly more than one-third
of each group said this); however, more Democrats said they had a fair
amount of trust and confidence than Republicans (47 percent versus
39.2 percent), whereas more Republicans (and independents) showed
pessimistic attitudes.

Political journalists were slightly less optimistic than political consultants: as of May 2004, only 31 percent of national journalists reported
having a great deal of confidence in the wisdom of the American people
on election day. This was down from 52 percent in 1999, at the end of the
Clinton presidency.[50]

Although much of the public sees itself as pretty well informed on
issues facing the nation, they have relatively little trust in their fellow citizens to make sound decisions at the polling place. Only about one in five

Table 3-3. *Consultants' and the Public's Trust in the Electorate to Make Good Decisions on Election Day*[a]

Percent

	Consultants		General public	
Rating	1998	1999	March 2000	October 2000
A great deal	42.6	36.5	18.3	21.0
A fair amount	42.6	43.3	49.3	48.3
Not very much	12.7	17.1	25.2	24.5
None at all	2.0	3.2	7.1	6.2
N	197	504	981	986

a. The question asked was, "Thinking now about the role of the public in politics, how much trust and confidence do you have in the wisdom of the American people when it comes to making choices on election day?"

Americans reported that they had a great deal of trust and confidence in the ability of their fellow Americans to make good decisions on election day (18.3 percent reported this in March 2000, 21.0 percent in October 2000). Compared with consultants' responses in 1999, the proportion of the American public who said they had no confidence at all in the electorate was more than double in March 2000 (7.1 percent of the general public versus 3.2 percent of consultants) and nearly double in October 2000 (6.2 percent versus 3.2 percent). Interestingly, with respect to their trust in their fellow citizens, there were no clear differences between members of the electorate who were and were not likely to vote in either of the surveys.

Although Republicans were more likely to believe they personally were well informed, they were less likely to report having confidence in their fellow Americans' ability to make sound decisions in the voting booth. These differences mirror those uncovered in the consultants' attitudes. In March 2000, nearly 30 percent of Republicans (and independents), compared with only 19 percent of Democrats, reported that they had little trust and confidence in their peers. As the presidential election of 2000 approached, a larger share of Republicans said that they had some confidence in the public at large, but it still did not match the three-quarters of Democrats who responded similarly. Moreover, more than 6 percent of Republicans said that they had no confidence at all in the American electorate.

In sum, some of the voluminous political science research is consistent with the beliefs of candidates, consultants, and journalists about the information level of the American public; majorities of each group found the public to be rather poorly informed. What is more, the public seems to agree. Pessimism is replaced by optimism in some of the literature, as it was in the attitudes of consultants, who saw some reason to be confident that the public can make a sound decision on election day. In other words, "people do not need large amounts of information to make rational voting choices."[51] Interestingly, the public did not share this same optimism about its fellow citizens.

Citizens' Views of the Polls: No Thanks

Although voters may be able to make choices on election day without having a full complement of information at their disposal, the fact remains that many Americans decide not to participate in the electoral process. The decline in voter turnout is well documented and has been well studied.[52] In fact, even in the face of changes to the electoral system (for example, eased registration requirements) and within the electorate (for example, the increased education level of Americans), the number of people taking an active role on election day continues to decline. Understanding this trend is important to our discussion here because it can give us a better picture of what the public thinks about the campaigns that are trying to persuade them to vote for their candidate and of the other actors operating in and around those campaigns.

In October 2000, we asked members of the electorate whether they would participate in the upcoming presidential election. Those who said that it was likely they would not vote in the election provided some enlightening answers as to why.[53] In open-ended responses, roughly 10 percent of respondents said they probably would not vote because none of the candidates represented them or "real Americans" (8 percent), that it was not worth their time (7 percent), or that they did not like the process of voting or did not believe in voting (8 percent). However, 17 percent said that they would not go to the polls in November 2000 because there were no good candidates to choose from—echoing the sentiments of voters, discussed earlier, that the overall quality of the pool of candidates they choose from on election day is poor.

One rationalization for the low voter turnout in the United States is that it is linked to a content electorate; according to this argument, people stay home from the polls because they are fairly satisfied with the way things are going. However, even in the face of a disgruntled electorate, participation has remained low. During the 2004 Democratic presidential primary, at a time when Democrats were as angry as they had been in a long time because of President Bush's positions on taxes, education, and foreign policy, even though there were record turnouts in the primaries and caucuses held during January and February, the percentage of the eligible electorate actually participating was very low.[54] In Iowa the preprimary context was set: "There are many reasons for the expected record turnout . . . but one supersedes all others: a searing desire to dethrone a president. . . . 'We didn't elect George Bush, and we won't let them take this election away from us this time,'" said one caucus goer; another added, "Right now, anybody who can beat Bush is fine with me."[55] "On a 15-degree winter evening, about 122,000 Iowa Democrats gathered in 1,993 meetings around the state to vote. While that turnout was close to a record, it was still less than 6% of Iowa's roughly 2.2 million voting-age citizens."[56] A study released by the Committee on the Study of the American Electorate reported that while New Hampshire voters turned out like never before on primary day, only 23.5 percent of eligible voters participated; in the primaries in Connecticut and New York, both Super Tuesday (March 2) states, voter turnout was at a record low.[57] The rage Democrats felt toward George W. Bush in early 2004 did not result in high levels of participation in the early primary states, as might have been expected.

What is interesting, however, is that general election turnout was different across the United States. Turnout increased in places where the presidential election outcome was unclear: because of the role played by the Electoral College and the states' winner-take-all systems of allocating electoral votes, the outcome in certain states—California, Texas, and New York, for example—was clear before election day, whereas the outcome in other states—Ohio, Florida, and Pennsylvania—was not, and there was a greater increase in turnout in these battleground states. In other states where the outcome was more predictable, the increase was only negligible. Therefore, 2004 illustrates that, contrary to the feelings of some that their vote does not matter, that "it's not worth their time" to vote because the outcome is assured, the American public can become engaged and turn out in large numbers.

Where Do We Stand? Electioneering Specialists

The days of campaigns fully staffed by amateur campaigners and volunteers are over. Today, electioneering is a professionalized business and an industry in its own right. In chapter 2, we address the specific question of who is in charge of our elections; here, we present some data on how actors inside and outside of political campaigns view modern political parties and political consultants—the two modern electioneering specialists.

In the past, parties were the backbone of campaigns, playing a major role in activities from candidate recruitment to getting supporters to the polls. Much has changed in campaigning since the golden age of political parties, however. Suffice it to say, political parties do not play as big a role today as they once did; as noted in chapter 2, this statement is generally agreed upon by both academicians and those in the trenches of campaigns. Here we are concerned with how other actors in campaigns view political parties today. We again turn to political consultants (inside the campaign) and the general public (outside the campaign) for their views on the quality of political party organizations today.

In today's electoral context, political consultants work alongside political parties in providing services and other electioneering help to candidates. Consultants' attitudes toward political parties are somewhat optimistic compared with their beliefs about candidates and voters. In 1999 more than one-quarter of the consultants surveyed reported that they believed the national political party organizations were of good quality, and another 4.4 percent described them as excellent (see table 3-4). In our 2002 measure, almost 31 percent of consultants rated parties as good, and more than 10 percent rated them as excellent. In both 1999 and 2002, however, roughly 20 percent rated them as poor, and about 5 percent as very poor.

As in consultants' evaluations of candidates, interesting, important, and telling differences appear between Democrats and Republicans. In 1999 only slightly more than 30 percent of Republicans said that the quality of the national parties was either excellent or good, compared with about 32 percent of Democrats. In 2002, however, many more Republicans gave a positive rating to their national party organizations— a total of 61 percent. On the Democratic side, the share offering these positive ratings decreased to only about 29 percent. On the Republican side, these figures amount to a 31-point increase from 1999 to 2002 in ratings of good quality, whereas among Democrats there was a 3-point decrease from 1999 to 2002. Moreover, the number of Republicans saying their party was just average or poor ("poor" and "very poor" taken together) decreased by 20 percent and 12 percent, respectively. On the Democratic side, the percentage rating their party organization as average

Table 3-4. *Consultants' and the Public's Assessments of the Quality of National Party Organizations*[a]

Percent

Rating	Consultants		General public		
	1999	2002	March 2000	October 2000	2002
Excellent	4.4	10.6	3.0	4.9	3.1
Good	25.6	30.7	25.9	27.3	22.8
Average	43.6	34.7	47.7	49.2	46.1
Poor	21.8	19.1	17.5	13.1	21.9
Very poor	4.7	5.0	5.9	5.6	6.1
N	473	199	954	950	1,057

a. The question asked was, "In general, how would you rate the quality of political parties?"

also decreased (by 8 percent), but the share rating the quality of their party as poor increased by 11 percent.

It may be that Republican consultants gave higher ratings to their national party organizations in 2002 because of the electoral successes the party enjoyed in 2000 and 2002, just as consultants may have given higher ratings to their winning candidates. The reader will recall that in 2000 the Republican National Committee was able to lead the GOP to a victory in the presidential election after eight years of Democratic control. The committee raised more than $379 million ($212.8 million in hard money and $166.2 million in soft money) and was able to become heavily involved in the "air war" of 2000 by airing television commercials (mainly with soft money) on behalf of the Bush campaign.[58] Almost immediately after the 2000 election, in which Bush lost the popular vote to Al Gore and the GOP felt it had underperformed at the polls, the party began to look ahead to 2002 and ways to drive up its turnout levels. Republicans developed their most expansive turnout effort early in 2001 and tested it in a few gubernatorial races that year. In 2002 they put their new effort—which they called the 72-Hour Project—into full effect. Some in the party attribute many of their close wins in 2002—U.S. Senate wins in Minnesota and Missouri, for instance—to this new turnout effort.[59] It is possible that Republican consultants looking at those efforts, either from afar or close up, saw just how effective their party was becoming. Democrats, on the other hand, may have seen the same activities and become frustrated with their own party's efforts and disappointments at the ballot box. Again, to fully test this hypothesis, data over a longer period of time would be required.

The beliefs of those outside political campaigns—the general public—are similar to those of individuals within the campaigns—political consultants. Although the electorate's evaluations were not as positive as consultants' in 2002, in the 2000 election cycle (March and October surveys), roughly 30 percent gave parties a favorable rating (either excellent or good); this figure fell to about 25 percent in 2002 (see table 3-4). Slightly more likely voters than unlikely voters rated political parties as either excellent or good. Unlikely voters were slightly more inclined to rate parties as average in March 2000. A similar pattern appeared in the October 2000 study; in this measurement, however, those more likely to vote were more likely to be critical of the parties, with more likely voters giving a negative rating (22 percent among likely voters versus 14 percent among unlikely voters). After the 2004 election, the Pew Research Center asked individuals who reported having voted in the presidential election to grade the political parties on their performance; 17 percent gave an A to the GOP but only 9 percent to the Democratic Party. The modal response for the Republican Party (33 percent) was a B, and the largest share (37 percent) gave the Democrats a C.[60]

Evaluations of political consultants—the other main supplier of electioneering services today—are different from those of political parties. First, political consultants are undoubtedly the least-known quantity in modern campaigns. Although the general public is bombarded with consultants' work every election cycle, in the form of polls, television and radio commercials, and direct mailings, it is the candidates and the parties, who pay for those services and products, that are much more visible and salient to voters. Certainly, some in the electorate know who James Carville, Paul Begala, Bob Shrum, and Karl Rove are, but it is safe to say that few everyday Americans have specific knowledge of even a few political consultants. The likelihood that anyone could pick a political consultant out of a lineup is even less when we consider that many Americans cannot name their own senator or member of Congress. Still, we believe that, for comparison purposes, asking for evaluations of consultants was important.

We expected that the general public would have little to say about political consultants or that most would simply deal with the question by rating consultants as average. However, though a fair proportion of Americans in both 2000 (March and October) and 2002 recorded their

Table 3-5. *Consultants' and the Public's Assessments of the Quality of Political Consultants*[a]

Percent

Rating	Consultants		General public		
	1999	2002	March 2000	October 2000	2002
Excellent	6.0	5.5	4.4	6.5	4.7
Good	43.7	46.5	26.9	27.3	26.6
Average	40.4	41.5	46.5	46.0	35.9
Poor	8.7	6.0	15.9	12.5	23.4
Very poor	1.2	0.5	6.3	7.7	9.3
N	483	200	892	873	824

a. The question asked was, "In general, how would you rate the quality of professional campaign consultants who advise the candidates?"

attitudes this way, most registered a more meaningful opinion (see table 3-5).[61] Interestingly, more Americans had a positive opinion of consultants (either excellent or good) than a negative one (poor or very poor). More than 30 percent of respondents had a positive view of consultants, compared with only about 20 percent who had a negative view. There was no difference between likely and unlikely voters in their ratings of political consultants in either wave of our study. These results may be driven by the relative anonymity of consultants. Those most likely to vote—whom one would expect were more informed and engaged—did not show any difference from those who were less likely to vote. The share of Americans who had a negative view of consultants did climb to about one in three, however, during 2002. This is consistent with the Pew Research Center's data on ratings after the 2004 campaign as well, since only 7 percent of the public gave consultants an A grade and 31 percent gave them a B.[62]

Not surprisingly, political consultants had a rather upbeat view of themselves and their industry. Less than 10 percent of all consultants in both 1999 and 2002 rated their peers as poor or very poor. Roughly half of all consultants reported that the members of their profession were either of excellent or good quality. Moreover, a majority of consultants reported that they believed the quality of their peers had improved over time.

These findings are important for the simple fact that political consultants are thought by many in the popular press and scholarly literature to be responsible for a number of problems associated with modern campaigning, from negative advertising to the increasing costs of campaigns and from wanting to fill their pockets with campaign cash to being electioneering mercenaries.[63] However, the public's attitude as expressed in our surveys did not reflect these criticisms. Again, this may be because few in the public knew much about who consultants were and what it is they did, though this situation is changing as consultants are becoming more visible in the process, mainly through the press. However, that consultants were not rated as low as candidates should not be ignored.

Where Do We Stand? Journalists

Today's journalists play a key role in campaigns, as they are one of the main mediums through which potential voters get political information; they inform the electorate on the important happenings in the campaign, and they can help set the campaign agenda by focusing on certain issues. In a media age defined by the twenty-four-hour news cycle, nonstop news on cable television stations devoted entirely to news coverage, and the increasing role of the Internet in news reporting, journalists are always looking for stories to cover. Because of this, during any campaign season reporters are an important avenue through which citizens hear about the campaign. Through both television and print reports, potential voters are given information about candidates' backgrounds, issue beliefs, visions for the future, and probably most noticeably, standings in the polls. Today's journalists often act as gatekeepers of political information in that events, decisions, and candidate activity are filtered through their journalistic prism.

Campaigns and journalists need each other during a campaign, however. Campaigns are a source of news stories for reporters, and news stories are a potent way for the campaign to get its message out to potential voters. However, reporters' desire to get a story does not always mesh with candidates' desire to spread their message. The kind of stories reporters write about in newspapers and talk about on television news broadcasts are rarely the kind of in-depth pieces journalists of the past produced. Those sorts of stories apparently do not sell papers and attract ratings.

In chapter 1, we discuss two examples of this phenomenon that were important to the 2004 campaign: the CBS News story about President Bush's National Guard service based on false documents and the Swift

Boat Veterans for Truth attacks on John Kerry. The CBS News story is fairly clear. After the veracity of the documents used in the CBS story was brought into question, the rest of the media paid great attention to the process of how the story had come about and what the consequences would be for Dan Rather, the long-time anchor for the CBS evening news. There was relatively little coverage of the main substantive part of the story—Bush's alleged preferential treatment. We believe that this illustrates the kind of story the media are after and how the preference for such stories can affect candidates' campaigns. As long as the Rather story was hot, the campaigns had difficulty getting the media to pay attention to their messages, undermining what is usually an important way for campaigns to disseminate their message to the public.

The case of the Swift Boat Veterans for Truth is a splendid example of how the media can affect the debate in a campaign through the stories it chooses to cover. When the anti-Kerry group launched its advertising campaign in earnest in August 2004 with an ad claiming that Senator Kerry had lied to get the medals he won in Vietnam, they spent very little money on airing the ad—"only a few hundred thousand dollars worth of ads, but each played over and over—free—on the cable channels, CNN and MSNBC as well as Fox."[64] The media made the Swift Boat Veterans' ads into one of the big stories of the campaign. By paying attention and devoting airtime and column inches to the story of the Swift Boat Veterans, and in the process repeatedly airing the original ad, the media helped keep the story in the news. The Swift Boat Veterans presented a good story for the media because the crux of the story ran counter to the Kerry campaign's message—that Senator Kerry would make a fine commander in chief. It made the Kerry campaign's job of spreading its message extremely difficult. It also made it difficult for the Bush campaign to convey its message; rather than talking about issues they wanted to discuss, they had to respond to questions about the Swift Boat Veterans and whether President Bush was going to condemn the attacks. However, given the damage the Swift Boat Veterans' ads did to Senator Kerry during the month of August and beyond, the Bush campaign was probably content to keep the focus on the story. After election day, Kerry campaign staff members admitted that they had not done enough to counter the charges.[65]

Ratings are also garnered through short, hard-hitting stories that are often less about issues in the campaign than about topics such as which candidate is ahead in the polls or which candidate was caught changing his or her issue position.[66] An example from the 2004 Democratic primary process illustrates this clearly. Soon after retired general Wesley Clark entered the race for the Democratic nomination on September 17, 2003, the story that led the nightly news coverage and was in the headlines of papers and on the covers of news magazines was not what the former NATO commander would do to solve the problems with the deficit, Social Security, or Medicare but how he had jumped to the top of the polls. There was much less discussion of his positions on any number of important issues.[67]

The kind of story that today's journalists tell is also nicely depicted by data suggesting that during the 2000 presidential campaign, the average sound bite from either Al Gore or George W. Bush was only 7.8 seconds long on network news programs.[68] Additionally, the amount of time in total that Gore and Bush were heard speaking in their own voices on network news programs between Labor Day and election day was eighteen minutes for Gore and fourteen minutes for Bush.[69] It was the reporters, analysts, and pundits, rather than the candidates, who told the stories and communicated to the public.

Reporting in today's newspapers and on today's television broadcasts is arguably more adversarial than ever before. One way journalists play their watchdog role is through ad watches—stories in which candidates' television commercials (or other communications) are critiqued and picked apart by journalists. Tim Russert, NBC's Washington bureau chief, may have been one of the first to call for this kind of investigation into campaigns' communications when, during the 1988 presidential campaign, he argued that NBC should start "to identify and highlight visually inaccurate statements, misleading claims or false implications" in a campaign's advertisements.[70]

During the 2004 presidential race between George W. Bush and John Kerry, NBC News ran several stories (on air or on its website) about the content of each candidate's ads. The network asked former CNN reporter Brooks Jackson, who had started a website (www. FactCheck.org) in conjunction with the Annenberg Public Policy Center at the University of Pennsylvania for similar purposes, to examine ads for both Kerry and Bush; Jackson found problems with some of the ads running on both sides.[71] For instance, Jackson noted that one ad contained the language, "George Bush? He supported tax breaks for exporting jobs and he raided Social Security to pay for a tax cut for millionaires." However, he continued, the "Social Security trust fund has just as many IOUs in it now as it would have had those tax cuts never been passed."[72] Similar problems were found in Bush's ads; one ad in particular included the following audio: "Some people have wacky ideas like taxing gasoline more so people drive less. That's John Kerry. He supported a 50-cent-a-gallon gas tax." Jackson observed that the basis of the ad was "one quote, [and] two newspaper clips [from] a decade ago" and that Kerry "never voted for it, never sponsored a bill, doesn't support it now and they [the Bush campaign] would have you believe he still favors that."[73] The *Washington Post*, along with several other major newspapers, ran a series of similar stories picking apart the campaign ads run by both candidates.

However, because of the profit-driven nature of news organizations, critiques of campaign ads can sometimes go overboard. The election news stories that get the most attention today are those in which candidates have been caught lying, have flip-flopped on an issue, have made some revelation about their past, or have embarrassed themselves. Reporters seem to seize on these kinds of stories because they are the ones that sell papers and garner ratings. When journalists investigate a campaign's communications looking for something newsworthy, they are looking for the one charge that is not substantiated with evidence or the visual that has been doctored to send a certain message.[74] In other words, reporters "jump on inconsistencies, untruths, or misrepresentations in political advertising."[75]

We are not arguing that these kinds of stories are not important or useful to the public. However, in the quest for more airtime or column inches, if a reporter fails to uncover something major in a campaign's communication, he or she "has almost no choice but to focus on minor problems or stretch the evidence."[76] In one of the pieces that appeared in the *Washington Post*, the media critic Howard Kurtz notes that an ad done by MoveOn.org comparing John Kerry's service in Vietnam with George Bush's service in the Air National Guard during the same time period "deals with Kerry's war exploits but not his controversial statements and returning of his award ribbons after Vietnam. Similarly, it deals with a gap in Bush's Guard record but not the risks of his decision to fly fighter jets. And the ad's accuracy is undercut by fake reenactments, such as the stamping of Bush files with 'priority' and 'failure to appear.'"[77] Analyzing ads to find misleading or even false information in an effort to protect the public is an important cause, but bringing attention to an ad comparing the candidates' service records because it fails to mention the risks of flying fighter jets or because it uses a re-creation of file folders rather than originals does not seem to meet the standard originally designed for these kinds of stories. It is almost as if journalists look at campaign ads assuming they are going to find something wrong or dastardly; when they fail to uncover anything truly sinister, they find something to criticize anyway. One would be hard pressed to find a story in which the media told potential voters about a good ad run by a campaign.

According to one account, today's journalists view themselves as "arbiters of the political system."[78] However, the financial pressures, such as the drive to sell papers and improve ratings, placed on news organizations today can influence the content and quality of reporters' work, according to journalists themselves.[79] In a recent survey of the industry, journalists identified some major flaws with their profession: 78 percent of national journalists and 77 percent of local reporters agreed that "too little attention is paid to complex issues," 64 percent and 59 percent of national and local journalists, respectively, said that "the distinction between reporting and commentary has seriously eroded," and roughly 40 percent of both national and local reporters expressed the opinion that "the emergence of the 24-hour news cycle is weakening journalism."[80] The media's focus on stories like those noted here, from Dan Rather's false documents to the Swift Boat Veterans for Truth advertisements to ad watches that search for missteps by campaigners, may be lowering the quality of coverage and the benefit to the public. About one-third of reporters and 45 percent of news executives in one survey said that the criticism that today's press is more adversarial than necessary is valid.[81]

Members of the electorate give reporters and journalists relatively good marks for quality, however. In our surveys of the general public in 2000, more than one-third of all Americans reported that political print journalists were of excellent or good quality; about 18 percent, however, rated the quality of these reporters as either poor or very poor (see table 3-6). These types of ratings increased through the 2002 measurement. Reporters and journalists on television received slightly higher ratings from the public: nearly 40 percent of the respondents in all three surveys reported that political broadcast journalists were of excellent or good quality (see table 3-7).[82] Still, in 2000 roughly one in five Americans said that these journalists were of poor quality; this kind of negativity toward political journalists held across likely voters and unlikely voters alike, and no significant differences were uncovered in March or October. The number of Americans giving negative ratings to broadcast journalists

Table 3-6. *Consultants' and the Public's Assessments of the Quality of Political Print Journalists*[a]

Percent

Rating	Consultants		General public		
	1999	2002	March 2000	October 2000	2002
Excellent	4.6	3.0	5.0	4.6	5.9
Good	25.5	26.1	31.6	31.2	29.2
Average	38.3	36.5	46.2	45.5	39.1
Poor	22.6	26.1	12.2	12.8	20.3
Very poor	9.0	8.4	5.0	5.9	5.4
N	499	203	961	948	1,048

a. The question asked was, "In general, how would you rate the quality of print journalists who write about politics in newspapers or magazines?"

increased, however, to about one in four in 2002. The Pew Research Center's data on the public's ratings of the media are similar: only 8 percent of voters graded the press as having done A work in 2004 (19 percent gave the media an F).[83]

As one might expect, members of the electorate who identified themselves as Republicans were much more negative than Democrats about both print and broadcast journalists. Republicans gave journalists a lower mean ranking across all three surveys of the general public. In the general public survey conducted in October 2000, Republicans gave print and

Table 3-7. *Consultants' and the Public's Assessments of the Quality of Political Broadcast Journalists*[a]

Percent

Rating	Consultants		General public		
	1999	2002	March 2000	October 2000	2002
Excellent	0.8	2.0	6.7	7.5	8.0
Good	16.4	15.3	31.0	30.8	31.4
Average	29.3	34.7	41.5	41.3	35.5
Poor	33.1	26.2	14.3	12.8	19.2
Very poor	20.4	21.8	6.5	7.5	5.9
N	495	202	969	958	1,064

a. The question asked was, "In general, how would you rate the quality of broadcast journalists who talk about politics on the radio or television?"

broadcast journalists mean rankings of 2.99 and 3.05, respectively; Democrats' mean rankings were 3.36 and 3.40, respectively.[84] It is no secret that many Republicans believe the press has a liberal bias, and these findings reflect that belief. In fact, in a survey during the 2004 campaign by the Pew Research Center, "forty-two percent of Republicans [saw] bias [in media coverage] toward the Democrats, up from 37 percent in the last presidential campaign."[85] Republicans feel that they, their candidates, and their policy alternatives do not get a fair shake from today's reporters. Whether or not this is the case is less important than the perception that it is.

Those in the public who hold less favorable views of the press have strong opinions. Those who are critical of the press corps report that the latter are "arrogant" and "cynical."[86] In another recent survey, 57 percent of Americans said that members of the media "often" let their personal preferences affect the way they report the news, and 28 percent said that reporters "sometimes" let their personal views affect their reporting.[87]

The view of today's political reporters and journalists from inside the campaign is much different from that of the general public. Political consultants have a more critical view of the modern press corps than do everyday Americans. This finding has been constant throughout our research dating back to 1998, when 68 percent of all consultants gave journalists a negative rating. In 1999 we split out these ratings into print and broadcast journalists, and the focus of consultants' negativity became clear. Roughly equal proportions of consultants reported that print journalists were of good, average, and poor quality: about 30 percent rated print journalists as either excellent or good, 38 percent said they were average, and almost 32 percent rated their quality as either poor or very poor (see table 3-6). Consultants' attitudes toward broadcast journalists were much more negative: a solid majority (more than 53 percent) gave them a negative rating (see table 3-7). Less than 1 percent of all consultants reported that today's broadcast political journalists were of excellent quality. Similar results were found in the 2002 survey of consultants. Political consultants also reported in large numbers, about print and broadcast journalists alike, that the quality of political journalists had declined over time. Roughly 50 percent of the respondents in the 1998 survey reported that political journalists had declined in quality, and this number increased to about 60 percent in 1999 and 2002 when we asked consultants about broadcast journalists. The negative ratings that political consultants gave to the modern press corps may be linked to the more adversarial nature of the relationship between the two groups of actors.[88] When journalists started to actively monitor and comment on, and sometimes criticize, the job that consultants were doing in the form of ad watches, the relationship became strained. Consultants most likely look at reporters as individuals to be wary of, even though these same journalists can help spread the message consultants have helped define and cover the events that their campaigns hold.

The partisan split that appears within the electorate does not surface among consultants, however. In both 1999 and 2002 nearly as many Democrats as Republicans gave a negative rating of broadcast journalists, and only slightly more Republicans than Democrats gave negative ratings to print journalists. Clearly, all consultants have complaints about journalists—print and broadcast alike. Complaints from inside candidates' campaigns were clear even before a single vote was cast in the Democratic primary season. Before the Iowa caucuses, Howard Dean was complaining that "the established press" had "attacked us for months." Dean's campaign manager at the time, Joe Trippi, remarked that negative media treatment "comes with the territory" in a campaign and said that the Dean campaign would not be stopped from "standing up and fighting back" against the bad press they were getting.[89] In May 2004 the Kerry campaign was complaining about the amount of coverage their candidate was getting compared with President Bush.[90] The sentiment coming from inside campaigns in modern times is probably best summarized by the Bush campaign's media guru, Mark McKinnon, who equates the media with "dangerous zoo animals."[91] These examples illustrate the antagonistic relationship that exists between reporters and campaigns. Because the press and the campaigns have different goals, which are often in conflict—the press wants to sell newspapers and increase television ratings, the campaigns want their messages clearly disseminated—these two actors often clash about the kind of stories that grab the headlines. The media continued to give attention to the CBS News story and the Swift Boat Veterans' story because the stories fed their thirst for ratings, not because they fit with either campaign's message. It is no wonder that the consultants we interviewed expressed great displeasure with how the media do their job in modern campaigns.

The ratings of different electoral actors presented in this chapter do not paint a terribly optimistic picture of modern campaigning. The view from both inside campaign organizations (from political consultants) and outside the campaign (from the general public) is that all the major political

Table 3-8. *Consultants' and the Public's Assessments of Different Campaign Actors*[a]

	Consultants		General public		
Actor	1999	2002	March 2000	October 2000[b]	2002
Candidates	3.27	3.29	3.15	3.29, 3.44	3.16
	(487)	(202)	(968)	(958, 950)	(1,059)
Political	3.45	3.51	3.07	3.12	2.94
consultants	(483)	(200)	(892)	(873)	(824)
Print	2.94	2.89	3.19	3.16	3.10
journalists	(499)	(203)	(961)	(948)	(1,048)
Broadcast	2.44	2.50	3.17	3.18	3.16
journalists	(495)	(202)	(969)	(958)	(1,064)
National party	3.03	3.23	3.03	3.13	2.95
organizations	(473)	(199)	(954)	(950)	(1,057)

a. Mean ratings are all based on a scale in which 1 = very poor, 2 = poor, 3= average, 4 = good, and 5 = excellent. Numbers in parentheses are numbers of responses.

b. Where two numbers are given in this column, the first represents respondents' views on presidential candidates, the second, vice presidential candidates.

actors in modern campaigns—candidates, voters, parties, reporters, and consultants—are mired in mediocrity. Table 3-8 presents a summary of these ratings. The clear finding is that both consultants and the electorate assess all the actors as solidly average. Few of the mean rankings reported in table 3-8 move significantly away from 3—representing "average" in the response set—in any of the attitudinal measures we took. Consultants received the highest mean rankings from their peers in both 1999 and 2002; their views of candidates were less positive, though far more so than their views of parties and especially of journalists. The public, on the other hand, gave their highest mean ranking to candidates and journalists and much less positive ratings to consultants and parties.

Although the preponderance of evidence presented here indicates that actors both inside and outside of a campaign organization do not hold the major players in modern campaigns in high regard, the health of our system of campaigning goes beyond the actors involved in the process. In fact, one could argue that what transpires before election day matters little relative to the final outcome. If our system manages to elect good people to office, and if those elected carry out the will of the people, then the means by which we arrive at this end are of lesser consequence. On one side of the electoral coin, our surveys of consultants and the general public show what political science has known for quite some time—that voters are not well-informed individuals. The other side of the coin holds somewhat better news: most consultants—those individuals inside modern campaigns with the responsibility of communicating with voters—have faith in the voting public to make sound choices on election day; however, fewer members of the electorate trust their fellow Americans when they enter the voting booth. Unfortunately, more bad news is found in further evidence presented in this chapter, which indicates that many political professionals (consultants and party staffers) and voters regret at least one choice they made with respect to candidates—for consultants and party operatives, regret about the success of a candidate they helped get elected, for voters, about whom they chose to vote for.

CHAPTER 4

Money, Elections,
and the Impact of Reform

Perhaps the most disturbing characteristic of campaigns in the United States is the inequality in the resources, particularly money, that candidates face in their campaigns for office. There is no better example than the 2004 presidential election campaign: in March of 2004, President Bush had $110 million in the bank, forty-six times the amount available to John Kerry.[1] And this was part of a presidential financing system where partial public funding in the prenomination phase and full public funding for the general election was supposed to provide a level playing field, at least for major-party candidates.

It was not just Bush's remarkable fundraising, however, that led to an inequality in financial resources during the 2000 and 2004 presidential contests. Presidential candidates are not required to participate in the public funding system. Candidates who feel they can raise more money than the system will provide are free to refuse public funding. This also allows them to avoid the spending caps that accompany the public funding. In 2000 George W. Bush was the first major-party candidate who went on to become his party's nominee to opt out of the public financing system. Four years later, thanks in part to his great fundraising success on the Internet, Howard Dean also opted out—as did John Kerry later in order to make up the huge gap in funding relative to Bush. Of course, Bush also abandoned the public money in 2004. These candidates' decisions to reject public funds in the prenomination phase of the campaigns

88

created a two-tiered funding playing field—those candidates with what seemed like unlimited monies and those who were subject to fundraising and spending limits because they had agreed to take public funding.

In the 2000 presidential primary season, John McCain held on while other contenders, citing an inability to compete with George W. Bush's prodigious fundraising apparatus, dropped out of the contest for the Republican nomination.[2] In the end, however, McCain, who accepted partial public funding, was unable to compete with Bush's private donations; Bush outspent McCain two to one in the nomination phase of the campaign.[3] As a result, McCain, who had shown some early success in the GOP primaries with victories in New Hampshire, Arizona, Michigan, Connecticut, Massachusetts, Rhode Island, and Vermont, simply could not keep up with the money Bush had at his disposal.

Howard Dean's fundraising success in the summer and fall of 2003 led him to believe that if he refused public funding, and the spending limits that came with it, he would have enough money to be competitive not only with his Democratic rivals during the primary period but also with President Bush, who faced no primary challenge, during the postprimary season. Once Dean took the lid off spending, John Kerry felt that to be competitive, he too needed to raise and spend as much as possible; in December, Kerry took out a $6.4 million mortgage on his Boston townhouse to finance his campaign.[4]

What was more striking, and potentially damaging, than the nominees' refusal of public funding during the prenomination phase of the election was that for a brief period during the summer months, the Kerry campaign considered forgoing full public funding in the general election as well.[5] Because the Democratic convention would be held a full month before the Republican convention, Kerry had three months to spend the $75 million in public funds given to the major-party nominees, whereas Bush could continue to raise private money during the month of August and had a shorter time frame in which to spend the general election money. In the end, however, Kerry decided to accept the general election grant.

The experiences of candidates in the 2000 and 2004 presidential elections suggest that, unless the financing system for the presidential nomination process is changed by 2008, no candidate who hopes to be a serious contender will accept partial public funding in the prenomination phase.[6] What is more, candidates may even forgo public funding in the general election. If that happens, the level playing field for presidential election funding envisioned by the Federal Election Campaign Act of 1971 will be erased.

The role of money in our campaigns is one area of concern to longtime election observers and the public alike. The cost of running for elective office is one factor thought to contribute to the cynicism about elections in the United States. Each election cycle brings new accounts of the rising costs of elections and the amount of money needed to compete in those elections. In response to these rising costs, candidates in federal races have been focused on raising the requisite funds to run competitive races. In the 2000 presidential election, George W. Bush stunned his Republican competitors for the nomination by reporting campaign receipts of $37 million through June 30, 1999, a full seven months before any Iowa caucus goer or New Hampshire primary voter would begin the process of choosing a nominee.[7] Four years later, presidential candidate Howard Dean similarly shook up the Democratic prenomination race by announcing 2003 third-quarter receipts of almost $15 million.[8]

Almost $4 billion was spent during the 2000 campaign (at all levels in all races) by candidates, parties, and special interests.[9] Spending in the 2004 elections exceeded that amount by nearly $1 billion, reaching $4.8 billion in total; spending in the presidential race alone surpassed $2 billion.[10] The massive amounts of spending did not stop at the top of the ticket. Four months before the November elections, and still months before the heavy fall media advertising began, candidates had spent $12 million in the U.S. Senate election in Pennsylvania, $9 million in the South Dakota Senate race, and more than $6 million in Senate races in Florida, California, and Wisconsin.[11] By the time the election was over, the two Senate candidates in South Dakota had spent just over $35 million, making it the most expensive Senate race in 2004; $26 million was spent in Pennsylvania, and $23 million in both California and Florida. Furthermore, on the House side, incumbents Martin Frost and Pete Sessions collectively spent $9 million in their battle in the Thirty-Second Congressional District in Texas.[12]

Although Howard Dean set the record for the largest amount of money raised by a Democratic presidential candidate in a single quarter (with his $15 million haul in the third quarter of 2003), the two general election candidates, President Bush and Senator John Kerry, continued to break fundraising records during the spring of 2004. By the end of May, the Bush campaign had raised more than $200 million, and the Kerry campaign close to $150 million.[13] The total raised by all presidential candidates was $537 million, 62 percent more than what presidential candidates had raised at this same point in the 2000 cycle.[14] As part of the $2.2 billion spent in total in the 2004 presidential race, the candidates' campaigns themselves spent $863 million, a 63 percent increase over the $509 million spent in 2000.[15]

Candidates for the U.S. House and U.S. Senate also were busy raising (and spending) large sums of money. Partially as a result of the higher individual contribution limits in the Bipartisan Campaign Reform Act (BCRA), in the first fifteen months of the 2004 election cycle congressional candidates raised $583 million, 35 percent more than during the same period in 2002.[16] In the end, House and Senate candidates surpassed the billion dollars raised during the 2000 election cycle, bringing in more than $1.1 billion in 2004.[17] What is more, both the Democratic and Republican National Party Committees reported great fundraising success, even without the opportunity to raise soft money. Hard-money receipts for the national party committees were significantly higher through March 2004 than they had been in previous election cycles, and in the end, as a result of more aggressive fundraising, both the Democratic and Republican campaign committees raised more in hard money, $1.2 billion, than they raised in hard and soft money combined in each of the 2000 and 2002 election cycles.[18] Given the amounts of money being raised and spent by candidates for public office in the United States, it is no wonder that the effect of money on the health of American campaigns is questioned.

Money and Elections: The Actors' Views

To start to understand the views of those both inside and outside the campaign, we asked political consultants and members of the public some general questions about the role of money in elections. The sheer amounts of money raised and spent for federal elections in the past decade raise legitimate questions about how much money is too much. For some Americans, the presence of large amounts of money in campaigns is viewed as unethical because it has the potential to create an appearance of corruption in the campaign whereby campaign money means the promise of something once a candidate becomes an elected public official. Others outside campaigns may not go as far as to say spending large sums of money is unethical, but they may wonder why such massive amounts are necessary and what they are spent on, and they may believe spending levels have consequences for our campaigns. Although those inside modern campaigns (the consultants) are more knowledgeable on topics such as the need for and uses of campaign money, they also quite likely have thoughts on the effects of campaign money that can give us important insights into the status of our campaigns.

The Public's View of Money and Elections

When asked what the general public thought about the amount of money spent on elections, three-quarters of the American public "strongly agreed" that "too much money is spent on elections." When we combined those who strongly agreed with those who "somewhat agreed," we found roughly 90 percent of Americans in all three surveys agreeing that there is too much money being spent in campaigns in the United States (see table 4-1). As illustrated elsewhere, there was disparity of opinion among Democrats, Republicans, and independents. However, in this case, the partisan differences uncovered were not about whether too much money was being spent but rather in the extent of agreement. In our 2002 study, 84 percent of Democrats strongly agreed that too much money was spent on campaigns, compared with 78 percent of independents and 70 percent of Republicans. These differences aside, it is clear that Democrats, Republicans, and independents alike overwhelmingly agree that too much money is spent on politics.

The American public also appears to think that money affects both the kind of candidates that run for office and what candidates have to do to attract campaign contributions. We asked our respondents in both 2000 and 2002 what they thought of the following statements: "It's possible that good candidates don't run for public office because of the amount of money needed for a campaign" and "To have a chance to win, candidates are forced to go against the public's interest to support special interests who donate money" (table 4-1). Between 82 and 92 percent of Americans in all three of our surveys thought that good candidates were forgoing elective office because of the amount of money needed to run a competitive campaign. These figures are predictable, given our finding in chapter 3 that the American public does not think that candidates running for elective office are of the highest quality. In 2002 only one-third of the general public rated candidates running for office as excellent or good; two-thirds of the general public deemed candidates just average or worse. However, unlike our findings on the quality of candidates, here we found

Table 4-1. *The Public's Assessment of the Role of Money In Elections*[a]

Percent

View	March 2000	October 2000	2002
There is too much money spent on today's campaigns	91.2 (987)	87.6 (981)	91.6 (1,093)
It's possible that good candidates don't run for public office because of the amount of money needed for a campaign	89.5 (980)	82.4 (983)	91.3 (1,102)
To have a chance to win, candidates are forced to go against the public's interest to support special interests who donate money	75.4 (973)	65.3 (979)	77.6 (1,085)

a. Numbers in cells represent the percentage of respondents who said they "strongly agree" or "somewhat agree" with each statement. Numbers in parentheses are numbers of responses.

no difference between likely voters and those not likely to vote on any of the questions we asked about the role of money in politics. Although we might expect that those less likely to vote would be distressed about the negative implications of money on campaigns, it seems that likely voters also think money adversely affects campaigns. Despite their concerns about the impact of money on elections, however, they still vote.

Slightly fewer Americans think money compromises candidates' representation of issues. Between two-thirds and three-quarters of the public surveyed thought that to be successful, candidates had to represent special interests who donated money to campaigns over the public interest.[19] The importance of any differences is dwarfed, once again, by the large majorities in each group of partisans.

The relationship between campaign contributions from special interests and the representation of those interests in Congress has long been studied by political scientists. Although there is little, if any, evidence that money buys votes, there is a widespread perception that campaign contributions at least buy access to lawmakers—access ordinary citizens rarely have.[20]

Consultants' View of Money and Elections

To get a perspective on the relationship between campaign contributions and policymaking from inside the campaign, we asked political consultants in our 1998 survey if they thought campaign contributions influenced public policy. Consultants were less concerned about this problem than the general public; 41 percent of consultants thought it was "not much of a problem," compared with 35 percent who thought it was "somewhat of a problem" and just 24 percent of consultants who thought contributions' influence on policymaking was a "major problem."[21] Unlike the general public's responses to questions of money in politics, serious differences between Democratic and Republican consultants appeared on this question. Thirty-eight percent of Democratic consultants thought the influence of contributions on policymaking was a major problem, whereas only one Republican identified it as such. In contrast, two-thirds of Republican consultants surveyed said it was not much of a problem, compared with just 25 percent of Democratic consultants.

It is possible that the disparity in views between Democrats and Republicans is reflective of the respective power bases of the two parties in Congress. Because Republicans control both houses of Congress, Republican consultants may not see much relationship between money and policy. Republicans' policy alternatives have a much easier time getting though the legislative process than do those of Democrats. Therefore, to Republicans the movement of GOP-backed initiatives would only look like the natural flow of legislation, rather than a push by a special interest group. Democratic consultants, on the other hand, may think that Democratic policy issues are not being adequately addressed because campaign contributors are influencing Republican policy decisions to kill their proposals. However, as with Republican and Democratic consultants' differing views of their candidates, testing this hypothesis would require a longer time frame and a change in control of Congress.

Our surveys of the general public seem to confirm our speculation that the costs of running for office may contribute to cynicism about elections in the United States. To get a perspective from inside the campaign, we asked consultants in our 1998, 1999, and 2002 surveys if they thought that the way money is raised contributed to voter cynicism.

Approximately two-thirds of consultants in all three surveys thought that the way money is raised contributed "a great deal" or "a fair amount" to voter cynicism (see table 4-2). What is more, there was a slight increase in this perception over time, from 61 percent in 1998 to 69 percent in 2002. Democratic consultants were consistently more likely to report that fundraising practices contribute to voter cynicism; three-quarters of the Democrats surveyed held this view in all three years,

Table 4-2. *Consultants' Assessment of the Effect of Fundraising Practices on Voter Cynicism*[a]

Percent

Extent of effect	1998	1999	2002
A great deal	24.6	33.8	31.9
A fair amount	36.7	32.2	36.8
Not very much	32.7	24.4	21.6
None at all	6.0	9.6	9.8
N	199	500	204

a. The question asked was, "Thinking now about voter cynicism and what causes it, please tell me whether you think the way money is raised in a campaign has a great deal of impact in causing voter cynicism, a fair amount, not very much, or not at all."

compared with about four in ten Republican consultants in 1998 and slightly more than half of Republicans in the two latter studies.

It may be that Democratic consultants are more likely than their Republican colleagues to think that fundraising methods contribute to voter cynicism because they see their party's identifiers as less wealthy and thus less able to make campaign contributions. They may see their party's voter base as less financially involved in the political system and consequently more skeptical about the role of money in politics, thinking that all the money is coming from "wealthy Republicans." Of course, the data reported earlier on the parity in donations between the candidates, parties, and outside groups in recent elections dispels this myth. However, opinions are often shaped by perceptions, and even though consultants are, as a group, well informed about aspects of the campaign like fundraising totals, this may still be their perception.

It was also over the period of our studies that George W. Bush demonstrated his prolific abilities at fundraising, first for his presidential campaign, then for Republican candidates in the 2002 elections, and finally his 2004 shattering of fundraising records he had established four years earlier. We suspect that some of the opinions of consultants on campaign money may be tied to their own party's fundraising success, just as some of their opinions about the quality of today's candidates may be colored by their electoral success.

The nexus of money and consultants in elections has been a major point of criticism about the consulting industry generally and of consultants' role in elections in particular. In a scathing article in the *Washington Post* in the spring of 2000, Susan Glasser suggested that no one benefited more from the rising costs of campaigns than political consultants.[22] Glasser's article includes numerous examples of the wealth consultants glean from their professional activities—vacation homes and expensive cars, to name only two—and implies that consultants have been driving up the costs of campaigns to line their own pockets.

In our 1999 survey we asked consultants about their motivation for entering the business, and just 11 percent said they got into political consulting for the money. The main reason for becoming a consultant, given by 52 percent, was their political beliefs or ideology. Even when asked what their main motivation was for continuing in the profession, only 24 percent said money. The picture political consultants paint of themselves is quite different from the one portrayed in the Glasser article and in the many other critiques of the industry.[23] According to our survey findings, as well as other evidence we have collected over the course of our larger project, political consultants both enter and stay in the profession for political or ideological, not financial, reasons.

The foregoing analysis presents an American public dissatisfied with the role of money in American campaigns: Too much money is spent on elections, the costs of elections deter some qualified candidates from running, and the fundraising process may give undue emphasis to the objectives of special interest groups. Consultants concur that the way campaigns are funded in the United States contributes to voter cynicism. Although the views of the American public are remarkably consistent over time and across party lines, the views of consultants are not. Democratic consultants are more likely than their Republican colleagues to see money as a cause of voter cynicism. These differing views may be a reflection of the two parties' relative power bases in the federal government and could change with a change in governmental control or party power.

Rules and Reform

The costs of campaigns, the way money is raised, and the influence of money on policymaking have long been the basis for discussions about campaign finance reform. The modern era of campaign finance reform began with the passage of the Federal Election Campaign Act of 1971 and its 1974, 1976, and 1979 amendments. The act established voluntary public funding of presidential elections and created contribution limits, but not spending limits, for candidates for federal office. As special interest money, first in the form of funding from political action committees and then so-called soft money, began to permeate American elections, campaign finance reform bills were actively considered in the House and the Senate from 1987 to 2002.[24]

In 2002, after years of stalemate, the Bipartisan Campaign Reform Act, also called McCain-Feingold, for its two chief sponsors, Senators John McCain and Russ Feingold, passed the House and Senate and was signed into law by President George W. Bush. The constitutionality of the new law was immediately challenged, and in December 2003 the Supreme Court found the major provisions of the law to be constitutional.[25]

The central components of the BCRA were the prohibition on national political parties' raising soft money after the 2002 elections and the prohibition on interest groups' spending soft money on issue ads thirty days before a primary election and sixty days before a general election. By 2002 soft money had become a major source of funds for both the Democratic and Republican Parties. In fact, in 2002 the Democratic Party raised more soft money ($246 million) than hard money ($217 million).[26] In the same year the Republicans, who were less dependent on soft money than the Democrats, still managed to raise $250 million in soft money, compared with $442 million in hard money.[27] Issue ads had become as common as candidate advertising itself. David B. Magleby and J. Quin Monson, in their study of issue advocacy in the 2002 elections, find that in a number of races, "interest groups spent an equal amount or greater amount of money to help elect a candidate than did the candidates themselves."[28] Because issue ads did not directly advocate the election or defeat of a candidate, they were not subject to the contribution limits imposed on parties or interest groups.[29]

Consultants' View of Reform

Because consultants must work within the campaign finance laws, we were curious about their general views of campaign finance reform and their more specific views of how the BCRA would change the electoral landscape. In our 1998 survey of consultants we asked their opinions on five campaign finance reform proposals: public financing of congressional elections, providing free television time, eliminating soft money, increasing individual contribution limits, and limiting issue advocacy spending.

Table 4-3. *Consultants' Assessment of Selected Campaign Finance Reform Proposals*[a]

Percent

Proposal	Excellent	Good	Only fair	Poor	N
Public financing of con- gressional elections[b]	25.5	16.5	11.5	46.5	200
Free television time	29.1	21.6	19.1	30.2	199
Ending soft money	15.6	17.1	34.2	33.2	199
Increase individual contri- bution limits	38.9	27.3	14.1	19.7	198
Limit spending by issue advocacy groups	13.8	14.3	23.5	48.5	196

a. The question asked was, "As I read you some changes that have been proposed to reform the way political campaigns are financed, please tell me how you would rate each in terms of benefit to the country."

b. Public financing for candidates who accept spending limits.

As table 4-3 shows, support for campaign finance reform was lukewarm, at best. Although two-thirds of the consultants surveyed supported increasing individual contribution limits and barely half supported free television time for candidates, less than half of all consultants supported public financing ("excellent" and "good" assessments combined), and more than two-thirds of consultants opposed ending soft money and limiting issue advocacy spending. In other words, before the BCRA had seen the light of day on Capitol Hill, professional campaign consultants reported to us that they were unenthusiastically in favor of one aspect of the campaign finance reform measure—increased contribution limits—and very much against the two changes that were at the heart of the BCRA reforms—eliminating soft money at the national level and limiting interest group issue advertising before election day.

There is also anecdotal evidence that political consultants generally oppose most campaign finance reform proposals. Democrats were particularly concerned about the effect of the ban on soft money, given the party's dependence on soft money. James Jordan, the former executive director of the Democratic Senatorial Campaign Committee and for a time the campaign manager for Senator John Kerry's early presidential campaign, said in an interview in 2001 that "members of both parties should give some serious thought to the law of unintended consequences. This bill will have a truly profound effect on the role and functions of the

Table 4-4. *Consultants' Prediction of the Impact of the BCRA on the Role of Political Parties*[a]

Percent

Party level	Increase	Stay the same	Decrease	N
Local	17.8	72.2	10.0	180
State	36.7	48.9	14.4	180
National	19.7	42.2	38.2	173

a. The question asked was, "Do you think the new Bipartisan Campaign Reform Act (or BCRA) will change the role of political parties at [the local, state, or national level]? Do you think the BCRA will result in an increase of the role of political parties at [each level], a decrease in their role, or don't you expect much change?"

political parties and will thereby profoundly change, perhaps in some negative ways, electoral politics."[30]

Three of the five reforms we asked consultants about in 1998—raising the limits on individual contributions, ending soft-money contributions to national party organizations, and limiting issue advocacy spending—were the three main provisions of the BCRA. Because consultants have to work within the rules laid out by campaign finance regulations, we wanted to know how they thought electioneering would change in a post-BCRA environment.

Specifically, we asked consultants in 2002 whether they thought the role of political parties would change at the local, state, or national level as a result of the BCRA. The results are presented in table 4-4. Almost three-quarters (72 percent) expected the role of local parties to stay the same, almost 18 percent thought the role of local political parties would increase, and 10 percent expected that local political parties' involvement in elections would decrease as a result of the BCRA. This is not particularly surprising, given that, as noted in chapter 2, consultants do not think state and local parties play much of a role in elections.

At the state and national level, however, the political consultants surveyed did expect some change in the respective roles of state and national party organizations. Although the most common response among consultants was that the parties' role would stay the same, roughly 37 percent of consultants thought the role of political parties at the state level would increase—the same percentage of consultants who expected the role of political parties at the national level would decrease. What we do not know from these data, however, is whether consultants surveyed expected state party organizations to become more involved in elections at the expense of the national party organizations. This would not be surprising, because under one provision of the BCRA, state parties are allowed to continue to raise and spend small amounts of soft money. As a result, we would expect consultants to think the state parties might pick up some of the fundraising authority the national parties had had with respect to soft money.

We found little differences between Democratic and Republican consultants in their expectations for the roles of local and national party organizations as a result of the BCRA. There were, however, differences between Democratic and Republican consultants as to how they thought the role of state parties might change under the BCRA. Democratic consultants were more likely than their Republican colleagues to expect an increase in the role of state party organizations. Forty-four percent of Democratic consultants, compared with just 31 percent of Republican consultants, thought the role of state political parties under the BCRA would increase. In contrast, half of Republican consultants thought the role of state party organizations would stay the same. This may be because in the pre-BCRA era, the Democratic Party was more dependent on soft money than the Republican Party (see the figures noted earlier on soft-money fundraising by the national parties). Given that state parties under the BCRA could still raise some soft money, Democratic consultants, more than their Republican colleagues, may have expected state parties to pick up the slack left at the national level.

We also asked consultants what impact they thought the BCRA would have on services traditionally provided by the national party organizations or congressional campaign committees. We hoped to further examine our hypothesis about a division of labor between consultants and parties in modern electioneering. Not surprisingly, given the BCRA's prohibition on soft money raised by the national parties, campaign funds and coordinated advertisements were the services consultants expected the parties to be least helpful in providing. Forty-four percent of consultants thought the parties would be less helpful in providing campaign funds, and 38 percent thought the parties would be less helpful in providing coordinated advertisements (see table 4-5). This is consistent with our finding, presented in chapter 2, that consultants believe they have already replaced parties as the main service providers for media advertising and that, when the parties provided this service, it was not very helpful to them anyway.

Table 4-5. *Consultants' Prediction of the Impact of the BCRA on Party-Provided Campaign Services*[a]

Percent

Service	More helpful	No change	Less helpful	N
GOTV operations	33.3	38.8	27.9	165
Direct mailings	29.4	37.4	33.2	163
Opposition research	30.1	52.1	17.8	163
Polling	28.8	44.8	26.4	163
Campaign funds	26.7	29.2	44.1	161
Coordinated advertisements	22.6	39.0	38.4	159
Management or strategy advice	13.9	60.0	26.1	165

a. The question asked was, "Now please think about the impact of the new Bipartisan Campaign Reform Act on the helpfulness of each of these services provided by the national party organization or Congressional Campaign Committees. Thinking again about competitive races, do you think providing each of the following services will be more helpful once this act goes into effect, less helpful, or don't you expect much difference?"

The finding with respect to campaign funds also fits into our earlier conclusions. Fundraising assistance was one area in which consultants felt they had not replaced the parties, and in which they welcomed party assistance. Given the continued importance consultants placed on the role of parties in campaign funding, it is not surprising that consultants felt the BCRA would have an adverse affect on the role of parties in this area.

Republicans were slightly more likely than Democrats to expect the parties to be less helpful in providing these services. Forty percent of Republicans, compared with 34 percent of Democrats, expected less help from the parties with campaign funds, and 36 percent of Republicans, compared with 28 percent of Democrats, expected less help from the parties with coordinated advertisements. As table 4-5 shows, the BCRA was expected to have less impact on get-out-the-vote (GOTV) operations, direct mailings, polling, opposition research, and management or strategy advice; Republicans and Democrats were in relative agreement on the impact of the BCRA on these services. Again, this is not surprising, as consultants felt these services, with the exception of GOTV and opposition research, were among those they had taken over from the parties. Furthermore, this supplements the data reported in chapter 2 confirming the division of electioneering responsibilities between consultants and parties today. Consultants failed to see the impact of the BCRA on this

Table 4-6. *Consultants' Prediction of the Impact of the Soft-Money Ban on 2004 Political Campaigns*[a]

Percent

Impact	Percent
No effect because ways to get around the law will be found (loopholes)	35.3
Increase third-party campaigns and independent expenditures	16.2
New methods of fundraising; more hard money	14.2
Negative impact (no specific mention)	13.7
Decrease importance of state and national parties	6.9
Positive impact (no specific mention)	3.9
Ban will not be upheld by Supreme Court	2.5

a. The question asked was, "On November 6th, the Bipartisan Campaign Reform Act of 2002 became law. This law bans national political parties from raising and spending soft money. How do you think the ban on soft money will affect campaigns in the 2004 elections?" Multiple responses were allowed on this question; those responding "Other" or "Don't know" have been omitted.

division of labor in those areas that are focused on message creation and delivery, in contrast to those in which parties concentrate on more time- and staff-intensive activities. The vast majority of consultants reported that strategic advice and coordinated advertising from the parties would be even less helpful than before enactment of the BCRA, whereas GOTV operations and opposition research would be more helpful than during pre-BCRA election cycles.

We asked consultants how they thought the BCRA might more generally affect political campaigns in 2004. As table 4-6 shows, although slightly more than one-third (35.3 percent) of consultants thought the new law would have no effect, because there would be ways to get around it, a majority of consultants expected the BCRA to have some impact on the 2004 elections. Sixteen percent of consultants expected an increase in third-party campaigns and independent expenditures, 14 percent expected it would lead to new methods of fundraising, and 14 percent expected some sort of negative impact but did not give specifics.

Democratic and Republican consultants both agreed that the BCRA would affect the 2004 elections. More Republicans than Democrats said that the law would have a negative impact generally (18 percent of Republican consultants compared with 11 percent of Democratic consultants) and to expect a decrease in the importance of state and national

Table 4-7. *Consultants' Prediction of the Impact of Restrictions on Issue Ads on 2004 Political Campaigns*[a]

Percent

Impact	Percent
No effect	20.1
Increase the quality of campaigns; lessen negative campaigns	16.2
Increase third-party campaigns and independent expenditures	10.8
Decrease media advertising; increase direct mail and phone work	7.8
More negative campaigns earlier	7.8
Negative impact (no specific mention)	7.4
Redirect funding and advertising away from parties	5.4
Ban will not be upheld by Supreme Court	15.2

a. The question asked was, "From 1996 through the 2002 elections, political parties and interest groups ran 'issue ads,' paid for with soft money, that did not expressly advocate the election or defeat of a candidate. The Bipartisan Campaign Reform Act prohibits these types of ads by political parties and interest groups 30 days prior to a primary election and 60 days prior to the general election. If this ban is upheld by the Supreme Court, how do you think it will affect political campaigns in the 2004 elections?" Multiple responses were allowed on this question; those responding "Other" or "Don't know" have been omitted.

parties (11 percent of Republicans compared with just 4 percent of Democrats). Democrats were slightly more likely than Republicans to predict new methods of fundraising and the presence of more hard money in the election (19 percent of Democrats compared with 10 percent of Republicans).

Finally, we asked consultants if they thought the restriction on issue ads run by interest groups and paid for with soft money would affect the 2004 elections. Table 4-7 presents the results. One-third of consultants thought the BCRA would be meaningless in the 2004 elections, either because it would have no effect (20 percent) or because it would not be upheld by the Supreme Court (15 percent). When asked to assume the new law would hold up in court, consultants cited impacts such as an increase in the quality of campaigns and a corresponding decrease in the amount of negative campaigning (16 percent), an increase in third-party campaigns and independent expenditures (11 percent), an increase in direct mail and phone contact (8 percent), more negative campaigns earlier in the election season (8 percent), and a general negative impact (7 percent). There was not much difference between Democratic and Republican consultants on these assessments, though slightly more Democratic consultants (11 percent) than Republican consultants (4 percent) expected a decrease in media advertising and an increase in direct mail and phone operations.

The Public's View of Reform

Although our surveys did not ask the public about specific campaign finance reform proposals, other survey data collected do address this issue.[31] When asked in 2000 whether they favored limiting individual campaign contributions or allowing unlimited contributions, seven in ten of the Americans surveyed favored limiting contributions.[32] Also in 2000, almost two-thirds of Americans (64 percent) favored limiting how much of their own money candidates for federal office could spend on their own campaigns;[33] the same poll found 76 percent of Americans favored limiting the overall amount of money federal candidates could spend on their campaigns, and in June 2001, 62 percent of Americans strongly agreed that there should be a limit to the amount of money political parties could spend on federal elections.[34] Clearly, Americans want less money to be spent in elections and think restrictions should be placed on individual, party, and candidate spending. This is in contrast to the majority of consultants who, in our 1998 survey, reported that they favored increasing individual contribution limits.

When asked specifically about the effect of campaign finance reform on the influence of money in politics, Americans were cautiously optimistic that reform would reduce the influence of money in politics. In March 2001, two-thirds of Americans thought stricter campaign finance laws would reduce the influence of money in politics; a year later, just over half (55 percent) thought new laws would be effective in reducing the influence of money in politics.[35] However, when asked specifically if the BCRA would reduce the influence of big business on government, six in ten Americans surveyed were skeptical of the law's effect and thought "things would go on much as they did before."[36] The public seems to be hopeful that campaign finance reform will change the role of money in politics yet at the same time skeptical of specific reform proposals.

Money in Campaigns in the Post-BCRA Era

Even before election day it was clear that the Bipartisan Campaign Reform Act was affecting the 2004 elections. The increase in individual contribution limits from $1,000 to $2,000 per candidate per election enabled candidates to raise record amounts of money. By the time of the conventions, the two major-party presidential candidates had raised $684 million, almost twice the $350 million raised at the same time in 2000. Of this total, $300 million came from contributions of $1,000 to $2,000, amounts that had not been permissible before the BCRA was enacted. Such donations constituted 44 percent of Senator Kerry's total donations from individuals and 57 percent of President Bush's overall individual donations.[37]

However, the increase in limits was not the only story of individual contributions in 2004. During his presidential bid, Howard Dean successfully used the Internet to raise funds in small donations—less than $200—for his campaign. Almost 60 percent of the contributions to the Dean campaign were in amounts of $200 or less.[38] Both the Bush and Kerry campaigns followed Dean's Internet fundraising success; Kerry and Bush raised about $78 million each in small donations. The total amount of small donations raised by all presidential candidates was $205 million—four times as much as was raised in small donations in 2000.[39]

Apart from the sheer amounts of money raised in donations of less than $200, the pattern of giving of small donations was also interesting. Although the Dean campaign was successful in raising small donations early in the nomination period, other campaigns were not. Only 18 percent of the Kerry campaign's $78.8 million in small donations were received before Super Tuesday; George W. Bush raised just 17 percent of his $78.4 million in small donations before March 1.[40] Once Kerry became the presumptive nominee of the Democratic Party, his small contributions increased; between March and August, 40 percent of the contributions to the campaign were in amounts of $200 or less.[41]

Candidates were not the only ones buoyed by the increased contribution limits. The political parties also enjoyed fundraising success. Some Democrats feared that the ban on soft money would put their party at a financial disadvantage vis-à-vis the Republican Party, but that did not prove to be the case. In total, the Democratic National Committee raised $402 million, compared with the $392 million raised by its Republican counterpart.[42] The Democratic Senatorial Campaign Committee raised $87 million, while the National Republican Senatorial Committee raised $75 million. Only on the House side, through the efforts of the National Republican Congressional Committee, did the Republicans outperform the Democrats, the Republican committee raising $175 million to the $92 million raised by the Democratic Congressional Campaign Committee.[43]

Although the parties were able to successfully compensate for the ban on soft money, soft money did not disappear in 2004. Recall that many of the consultants we surveyed in 2002 thought that money would raise its head in new ways after the BCRA was enacted; 35 percent thought ways would be found to circumvent the law, 16 percent thought there would be an increase in third-party campaigns or independent expenditures, and 14 percent thought there would be new methods of fundraising. They were all correct.

The 2004 election cycle was supposed to be the year that "big money lost its influence in American politics."[44] Soft money remained an important factor in electioneering in the 2004 elections, however, in so-called 527 organizations. In fact, these groups were the main avenue for wealthy Americans who wanted to have an impact on the campaign, now that the BCRA barred them from making six- and seven-figure contributions to political parties. "Six of the top 10 donors to 527 groups [are] billionaires, and all are on Forbes magazine's list of richest Americans. Eight dollars out of every $10 collected from individuals by Democratic-leaning 527 groups came from donors who gave at least $250,000 each," according to a study reported in the *Washington Post*.[45] Republican-leaning 527s were not to be outdone: of the monies collected by these groups, nine out of ten came from donors who gave more than $250,000.

An uncertain beginning, owing to a court battle over the constitutionality of the new law—decided by the Supreme Court in *McConnell v. Federal Election Commission*—and Republican challenges within the Federal Election Commission itself caused 527s to start slowly. "Many traditional sources of big money—corporate chieftains and companies such as Microsoft, Boeing, and General Electric—were reluctant to give to [527s] for fear of becoming entangled in lawsuits challenging the legality of the groups."[46] Democrats, however, had little choice but to take advantage of the loophole left by the new regulations. Because the conventional wisdom at the time was that Democrats would be disadvantaged by the new law, there was an early movement to try to find a way to erase the suspected GOP advantage. Harold Ickes and the Democratic National Committee's chair, Terry McAuliffe, reached the same conclusion and launched an effort to "continue the flow of soft money to nonparty groups."[47]

The need was even greater in early 2004, as the Kerry campaign was well behind the Bush team in fundraising; as noted earlier, at one point the Bush campaign had forty-six times the resources of the Kerry team. One Democratic operative active in starting a 527 noted the urgency Democrats faced: "There is no question that Bush has $100 million and Kerry is down to zero. It's very important that there are alternative voices out there talking about the Bush record."[48] Three groups, America Coming Together, the Media Fund, and MoveOn.org, began raising money early to assist the Democratic presidential nominee.

Two of the groups, in particular, made a splash early in 2004; the Media Fund and MoveOn.org ran radio and television ads during the spring and summer of 2004 in key battleground states to promote the candidacy of John Kerry. In March alone, the Media Fund and MoveOn.org spent almost $10 million on television ads in key states.[49] Meanwhile, America Coming Together was formed to handle the "ground war." The group's organizers pledged to raise $75 million for a massive voter contact program in seventeen key states.[50] By the end of the campaign America Coming Together had spent just over $76 million, while the Media Fund spent $54 million and MoveOn.org $21 million.[51] The operatives behind America Coming Together were very efficient in their fundraising. They repeatedly approached donors who would write them large checks; "91 percent of contributions to [America Coming Together's] 527 committee [came] from donors giving $100,000 or more."[52]

Because of President Bush's fundraising ability and because of the uncertain regulatory environment surrounding the issue, Republican-leaning 527 organizations were slower to form. The former chair of the National Republican Congressional Committee, Representative Tom Davis (R-Va.), has said of the lack of GOP donors to 527s, "Our people were too skittish."[53] Moreover, President Bush was expected to be able to raise and spend as much money as he needed to take on the eventual Democratic nominee. In fact, the Republican National Committee asked the Federal Election Commission to regulate 527 organizations under the BCRA by prohibiting soft money and restricting the airing of issue ads. In May 2004 the commission decided against regulating 527 organizations, at least until after the 2004 elections. After that it did not take long for conservative activists to start to match their liberal counterparts in contributions to 527s favoring Bush's campaign. By midsummer, two Republican-supported 527 organizations—Progress for America and the Leadership

Forum—began to raise money to support the Bush-Cheney ticket, but their fundraising efforts lagged far behind those of the Democratic 527s.[54] By a few weeks before the election, however, Republican groups were out-spending their Democratic rivals by a margin of six to one; between late August and mid-October, Republican-leaning 527s had raised more than $48 million compared with the Democratic groups' $8 million.[55] In the end, Progress for America spent about $36 million in 2004, and the Swift Boat Veterans (who later called themselves Swift Boat Veterans and POWs for Truth) spent about $22 million.[56]

By early July, 527 organizations had raised more than $190 million and spent about $164 million.[57] In the end, they raised almost $576 million, and spent $585 million,[58] in soft money—unlimited contributions from wealthy individuals who in previous election cycles had contributed to the Republican and Democratic Parties. Contributors to these groups were familiar names. Financier George Soros claimed the most attention when he pledged $10 million to America Coming Together in late 2003. The flow of big contributions did not stop with Soros, however. Other wealthy individuals contributed millions to various 527 organizations.[59] The largest contributors to Democratic-leaning 527 organizations were Soros, who gave a whopping total of $23 million to 527 organizations, and Peter Lewis, who contributed $22 million. Large contributors to Republican-leaning 527s included Bob Perry, who gave $8 million— $4.4 million of which went to the Swift Boat Veterans and POWs for Truth—and Alex Spanos, who contributed $5 million.[60]

The Bipartisan Campaign Reform Act may have removed the political parties' dependence on soft money and increased hard-money contribu-tions to the party committees, but it did not remove soft money from the political system. Soft-money contributors invested in 527 organizations, which were not regulated by the Federal Election Commission and were therefore not subject to the disclosure requirements of the 1971 Federal Election Campaign Act. In 2004, 527s were the new, and potentially extremely important, players in the electoral arena. Consultants' predic-tions that new sources of money would flow into campaigns outside of the BCRA regulations proved to be true.

Another provision of the BCRA that was in play early in the 2004 pres-idential election was the stand-by-your-ad requirement. One provision of the law required candidates for federal office to approve their radio and television ads. For television ads, either the candidate had to appear in the ad and say "I'm [name of candidate], and I approve this message," or a likeness of the candidate had to appear, with the candidate's voiceover stating his or her approval of the ad. Representative David Price (D-N.C.) sponsored the provision to try to reduce negativity in campaigns. Price thought that were they required to appear in the ad and endorse the ad's message, candidates would be less likely to air negative material about their opponents. There was general agreement that much of the advertising during the Democratic primaries was positive, and Price attributed this more positive tone to the stand-by-your-ad provision.[61]

Kenneth Goldstein, a scholar at the University of Wisconsin and an expert in political advertising, discounts the effects of the stand-by-your-ad provision in the Democratic primaries. Goldstein contends that primary advertising generally is more positive than advertising in the general election.[62] However, although much of the advertising during the Democratic primary was positive, the general election campaign became engaged early in 2004. Of the $684 million raised during the prenomination period in 2004, $468 million was raised and spent after John Kerry became the assumed nominee of his party.[63] Some observers warned that the 2004 election might be the "most negative campaign in history."[64] Although the money spent by both candidates between March 1 and the conventions was ostensibly prenomination spending, in practice it was spent to influence the outcome of the general election, and much of it was spent on negative ads.

The consultants we surveyed did not favor much of anything related to campaign finance reform. Although we do not have empirical data, it was clear early on in the 2004 election that the stand-by-your-ad provision was another reform loathed by political consultants. Karl Struble, a media consultant, describes the feelings of media consultants most graphically: "It's like throwing a turd in the middle of a punch bowl. . . . I hate it aesthetically."[65] Not only did media consultants dislike the way the provision changed the feel of political ads, they also resented sacrificing the precious seconds needed to deliver the disclaimer. In the words of Larry McCarthy, a Republican consultant, "Thirty seconds [the length of a typical television ad] is already a very small window to deliver a message. Now it's cut even further."[66]

This chapter has shown some disturbing evidence about the role of money in American campaigns. The American public is cynical about the role of money in elections—they think too much money is being spent on elections and that the costs of campaigns adversely influence both who runs for office and what candidates have to do to get elected. Political consultants agree that money contributes to problems in the electoral system—specifically, it feeds the cynicism of the American public toward modern campaigns. The Bipartisan Campaign Reform Act of 2002 was the first major campaign reform in thirty years, and yet it does not seem to have measurably improved the campaign process. Wealthy contributors are still players in American elections and arguably in less discernible ways than they were before enactment of the BCRA. Moreover, the 2004 elections were the most costly elections ever in the United States. Perhaps the only bright spot in this bleak picture is that the Internet seems to have encouraged small donors to get involved in the political process, and the number of small donors contributing to both political parties and candidates increased sharply in 2004.

CHAPTER 5

Ethics and the Health of American Campaigning

During the third and final presidential debate of 2004, the candidates were asked whether they believed homosexuality was a choice. In addressing this question, Senator Kerry invoked the name of Vice President Dick Cheney's daughter, Mary Cheney, an openly gay woman who occupied a high-level position in her father's campaign. Earlier, in the lone vice presidential debate, Senator John Edwards had also made reference to the Cheneys' daughter. The Cheneys—both the vice president and his wife, Lynne—took umbrage at the mention of their daughter's name by Senator Kerry. After the last presidential debate, Lynne Cheney called the use of her daughter's name "a cheap and tawdry political trick."[1] Was this Senator Kerry trying to honestly and earnestly answer the question in an appropriate manner, or had he crossed a seemingly undefined line of the standards of conduct?

American elections are supposed to be fought in a spirited and competitive manner. However, we also expect our elections to be conducted ethically, fairly, appropriately, and in a manner befitting the offices being pursued, so as to leave no doubt as to the outcome and how it came about. In fact, this may be the most important aspect of our system of campaigning considered thus far.

Defining what *ethical* means is difficult, and one can quibble over what exactly constitutes an ethical campaign. The perceived negativity of the 2004 presidential race created an early stir throughout the campaign.

After John Kerry became the presumptive Democratic nominee in early March, the Bush campaign started to air advertisements that were critical of Kerry and challenged his nineteen-year voting record in the United States Senate. These early "attacks" from the Bush campaign led some to say that Campaign 2004 was the earliest and most intensely negative campaign in recent history.[2] By May 2004, Kathleen Hall Jamieson observed that there was "more attack now on the Bush side against Kerry than you've historically had in the general-election period against either candidate," and Darrell West was predicting the "most negative campaign ever," noting that "if you compare the early stage of campaigns, virtually none of the early ads were negative, even in '88."[3] The general public agreed with these sentiments. As of June 2004, nearly half of all Americans (45 percent) surveyed by the Pew Research Center reported that the campaign was too negative.[4] Interestingly, more of the public reported that Kerry had been too critical of Bush (44 percent) than vice versa (only 33 percent said that Bush was too critical of Kerry). However, those individuals "who [had] seen a lot of ads [were] equally likely to criticize both Kerry . . . and Bush . . . for being personally too negative" (about 40 percent of those surveyed reported this sentiment about both candidates).[5]

Some would argue that the kind of negativity U.S. campaigns have come to be known for is unethical. This is especially true of ads that approach the ethical line in their use of "facts." For instance, the Bush campaign aired an ad that said the Kerry health care plan would be "government run," when, in fact, his plan would have used the current system of private health insurance. The Kerry campaign aired an ad saying that President Bush would reinstate the draft (Kerry himself said there was a "great potential" for this to happen), though Bush had repeatedly denied the claim.[6] For some, all negative advertising and campaigning is unethical and is destructive to our campaigns (as well as to the government that results from those campaigns); for others, it is only candidates and campaigners fighting to win an election the best way they know how.

There is an ongoing debate in American politics about the impact of this so-called negative campaigning. Whether negative television ads help or hinder the health of campaigns is a widely debated issue. Some scholars argue that negative ads turn voters off to the process and contribute to voter cynicism and low turnout.[7] Others have found that, on the contrary, negative campaigning and negative advertising can lead to higher levels of issue knowledge and even increased turnout.[8] Still others argue that some ads that are traditionally characterized as negative should actually be described as "contrast" ads and that these ads actually provide more information to voters than purely positive ads, increasing voter information about candidates and thereby enabling voters to make more informed decisions.[9] In other words, attack ads may be negative, but they may also be informative and truthful. If one considers the evidence pointing to the former, a clear case can be made that negative campaigning is unethical and bad for our system of campaigning. However, if one examines the evidence that points to the latter, the answer is murkier.

The arguments that negative advertising is not detrimental received some complementary evidence in 2004. As noted in chapter 2, more Americans were interested in the 2004 campaign and had been paying attention as of June than at the same point in either of the two previous election cycles, and they saw real differences between the candidates. Almost half of the electorate reported at that time that the campaign was too negative. The correlation here, and its implication, is too important to ignore. What tends to be termed *negative* may not necessarily be bad for our elections. In the debate about negative advertising, what is unethical in campaigning is not always clear.

Nonetheless, there have been certain instances in each of the last three election cycles (2000, 2002, and 2004) that clearly cross the ethical line or at the very least generated great debate about their appropriateness and ethical nature. During the 2000 Republican primary campaign, an organization working to support Governor George W. Bush ran advertisements before the New York State primary stating that Senator John McCain, Bush's main rival for the nomination, had voted against breast cancer research. The television ads in question cited a few items that the senator had voted against, which "were included in more than $13 billion in what [McCain] characterized as pork-barrel spending requested by lawmakers."[10] The McCain campaign, as well as others, challenged the truthfulness of the ads, citing numerous other votes, over the course of his lengthy career, in favor of other bills that provided money for breast cancer research. Whether the Bush ad was ethical is debatable. Its statement was technically true—McCain did vote against the bill in question—but did it go too far?

The now infamous "RATS ad" became well known to those following the 2000 campaign. The ad in question, a thirty-second spot paid for by the Republican National Committee, was designed to compare the proposals of the two candidates in the race—Governor George W. Bush and

Vice President Al Gore—that would provide prescription drug coverage as part of the Medicare system. Using some creative filmmaking techniques, the media consultant who created the ad—Alex Castellanos, of the firm National Media—flashed the phrase "BUREAUCRATS DECIDE" across the screen to describe Gore's plan from the perspective of the GOP. However, as those words scrolled across the screen, the portion of the word "BUREAUCRATS" that spells "RATS" was isolated for an instant (it was visible in only one of the nine hundred video frames in the ad).[11] Both the Republican National Committee and Castellanos claimed that the word "RATS" flashing across the screen was complete coincidence and that the filmmaking techniques employed were used to make the ad "more interesting" and give it a "visual drumbeat."[12] Democrats argued that it was an attempt at subliminal advertising, something that is considered unethical by experts in the advertising field. The ad is what many would call a contrast ad, in that it compared Bush's prescription drug plan to Gore's, telling potential voters about both candidates' ideas for a policy solution; this, one could argue, is the kind of informative campaign that benefits our electoral process. However, was this done in an unethical manner? Were the Republicans out to trick voters into casting ballots for Bush? If so, the desire to have an election contest in which the conduct is unquestionable was not realized.

Democrats and their supporters also engaged in questionable tactics during 2000. The NAACP (National Association for the Advancement of Colored People) National Voter Fund paid for and aired an ad in support of Al Gore's bid for the White House featuring the daughter of James Byrd, saying the following:

> I'm Rene Mullings, James Byrd's daughter. On June 7, 1998, in Texas my father was killed. He was beaten, chained, and then dragged three miles to his death, all because he was black. So when Governor George W. Bush refused to support hate crimes legislation, it was like my father was killed all over again. Call George W. Bush and tell him to support hate crimes legislation. We won't be dragged away from our future.[13]

The facts expressed are beyond dispute: James Byrd was brutally killed on June 7; Ms. Mullings's feelings cannot be questioned; and Bush had not supported the hate crimes legislation referred to in the ad. However, the ad also implies a connection that may or may not exist. As one observer has noted, "The real ethical question surrounding this ad arises from the implied message, which is clearly something along the lines of: George W. Bush doesn't care if black people get dragged to their death behind pickup trucks."[14] Implications are a difficult subject in campaigns. Is there any way for us to know what Bush's feelings were? His lack of support for the legislation mentioned in the ad may be one indicator, but he did support another piece of legislation on the same topic. Did this ad live up to the highest standards of ethical conduct?

In 2002, during the U.S. Senate race that pitted incumbent Max Cleland (D-Ga.) against challenger and sitting U.S. House member Saxby Chambliss (R-Ga.), the Chambliss campaign ran an ad attacking Cleland's record on homeland security. The ad included pictures of Osama bin Laden and Saddam Hussein. This ad was particularly distasteful in light of Cleland's heroic service in the Vietnam War. He not only served his country, he lost both legs and an arm in the process. Arguably, this is a case in which the ethical line was crossed. The Chambliss campaign steadfastly denied that this ad was in any way an attack on Max Cleland's patriotism; rather, they argued that it was a legitimate critique of Cleland's voting record on homeland security, specifically, his votes against President Bush's preferred version of the bill that created the Department of Homeland Security.[15] Following the uproar created by this ad, the Chambliss campaign created a second version of the ad in which the Bin Laden and Hussein images were taken out of the opening sequence and replaced by more neutral images.[16]

Ethically questionable campaigns and instances within campaigns are not a strictly recent or modern phenomenon. Ethical misconduct has been an abiding presence in the American electoral process from the earliest campaigns. In contested elections in the early years of the nineteenth century, campaigns tossed about accusations with racial, ethnic, religious, and treasonous undertones and implications without a second thought.[17]

During the 1964 campaign between President Lyndon Johnson and Senator Barry Goldwater, the Johnson campaign aired what has come to be known simply as "the daisy ad": Sitting in a field, a little girl picks at the pedals of a flower and counts along—one, two, three, four, five. . . . When she reaches the number nine, her voice is replaced by an ominous voice, counting down from ten to one, and the camera zooms in on the girl's eye. When the countdown is complete, a bomb explodes, and a mushroom cloud appears in the girl's pupil. Lyndon Johnson's voiceover then famously says, "These are the stakes, to make a world in which all of God's children can live, or to go into the darkness. We must either love each other or we must die." Without ever mentioning Goldwater's name, the ad seems to be saying that if Johnson's opponent were to be elected, the end result would be nothing short of nuclear war.

Finally, consider the infamous Willie Horton ad run by a third-party group on behalf of George H. W. Bush's 1988 bid for the White House against Massachusetts governor Michael Dukakis. The ad in question told the story of a prisoner, Willie Horton, who had been released on a furlough from prison while serving a sentence for killing a boy, only to commit a rape while out of jail. Horton had been released under Dukakis's governorship, and the ad was used to cast Dukakis as soft on crime. Most observers found the ad to have crossed the line.

In each of these cases, candidates, or their campaigns, stretched the truth about an opponent to get votes. There are many examples throughout U.S. campaign history of what former president Bill Clinton has called the "politics of personal destruction"—from the Federalists calling Thomas Jefferson a godless Francophile to the opponents of Grover Cleveland making a campaign issue of his illegitimate child to Clinton's own battles with personal scandal.

Questions about the ethics of campaigns in American politics are not likely to go away. The campaign of 2004 was rife with examples of this kind of behavior from the onset. The first campaign ads run by President Bush were designed to portray him as a strong leader during challenging times for the nation. Included in these challenging times, of course, were the terrorist attacks of September 11, 2001. The Bush ads tried to convey to the public that it was Bush who had guided the nation through this ordeal. The ads' visuals—a flag waving in front of a fallen World Trade Center building and the flag-draped coffin of a fallen firefighter being pulled from the rubble—elicited a great deal of criticism from Democrats and some 9/11 victims' families. Critics said that Bush was using 9/11 for political gain. The GOP and the Bush campaign defended the ads as depictions of Bush's record during that time.[18]

The Kerry campaign can also be challenged on its ethical standards during the early part of the 2004 race. In one of the few scholarly attempts to consider ethics from a campaign perspective, L. Sandy Maisel has written that candidates should take care not to overpromise in their campaign rhetoric. Maisel makes a distinction between statements like "If I am elected, I will introduce legislation to outlaw practice X, and I will work as hard as I can to achieve passage of that legislation" and "If I am elected, I will introduce legislation to outlaw practice X, and I will see that that legislation is passed."[19] In Maisel's view, the first is ethically acceptable and the second is not. What is the difference? Under the U.S. system of checks and balances instituted by the Founding Fathers, Maisel argues, no official in the U.S. government has the power to do what the candidate promises in that second statement. At numerous campaign stops, John Kerry belted out what could be construed as a promise: "My pledge—and my plan—is for 10 million new jobs in the next four years."[20] His website reported that "John Kerry is unveiling a comprehensive economic agenda that will unleash the productive potential of America's economy to help it create 10 million jobs in his first term as President."[21] One can argue that a pledge is not a promise, but this pledge was certainly considered a promise and was reported and interpreted as such. Is this appropriate? Whether promise or pledge, is it a violation of ethical standards to announce an ambitious plan that the candidate is unlikely to deliver?

These several stories raise the question, Are questionable or unethical campaigns the exception, or are they the rule? The manner in which elections are conducted in the United States is a theme of our research, the central question, in fact, of the larger grant project of which this book is a part.[22] The question of ethics and ethical behaviors is implicit in our research. In our surveys, we asked political consultants, party operatives, and the general public a series of questions designed to help us understand each actor's views on the ethics of modern campaigning, allowing us to present a view from both inside campaigns and out.

The views of political consultants are especially important in an investigation of the ethics of campaigns. In many campaigns across the nation, consultants are now at the center of decisionmaking; and they often receive most of the blame for the ills of modern campaigning such as the creation of negative television ads, the focus on personal characteristics of candidates, and the trivialization of issues, among others.[23] Their role in creating ethical (or unethical) campaigns, therefore, is essential to any discussion of electioneering ethics. We also examine the general public's views of campaigns in terms of ethics, in an attempt to measure the perception of campaign ethics from the perspective of those whom consultants seek to influence and also to understand the effects of any potentially unethical activity.

The Ethics of Today's Campaigns

Before turning to the specifics of potentially problematic activities in modern campaigns, it is useful and worthwhile to examine how different campaign actors view today's campaigns in a general sense. Do they see them as fairly clean and appropriately conducted or as havens for unethical activity?[24] We asked political actors about ethics in two ways. First, we asked consultants and party elites about the ethics of professional consulting; given the several criticisms that have been levied against consultants and their ethics, we thought it important to examine their own views of the industry. We asked the public about the ethics of campaigns in a more general way. Central to each of these questions is the perception of how often unethical practices occur. There is good news and bad news in our survey data. First, for the good news: those inside campaigns—professional consultants and party operatives—generally see consultants' activity in the everyday functioning of today's campaigns as not characterized by unethical practices. The general public, on the other hand, was cynical about ethical practices in campaigns.

A View from Inside the Campaign

Professional consultants and party operatives were fairly optimistic about the conduct in today's campaigns. Only 23 percent of the respondents in the 1999 consultants' survey reported that they thought unethical practices occurred in campaigns either "very often" (9.6 percent) or "fairly often" (13.7 percent); what is more, these views were consistent over time—just under 25 percent said the same thing in 2002 (7.6 percent said very often, 17.2 percent fairly often).[25] That political consultants do not see campaigns as havens for unethical activity should not come as much of a surprise. After all, they are deeply involved in campaigns, in the trenches trying to win races for their clients; they would be unlikely to question what they do on an everyday basis as anything more than business as usual. However, these same practices may appear unethical to others who are less familiar with the rigors of modern campaigning or who simply are not as close to the industry.[26]

We found stark differences among consultants in terms of party affiliation—or, in this case, lack thereof. As illustrated in table 5-1, partisan consultants—those who call themselves Democrats or Republicans—were much less likely to report that unethical practices occur with any frequency than those who did not associate themselves with one of the two major parties. In the 1999 survey, more than half of all consultants who identified themselves as independents reported that unethical practices happen in the business on a fairly regular basis—either very often or fairly often. This is in contrast to Democrats and Republicans, nearly a third of whom reported

Table 5-1. *Consultants' and Party Elites' Assessments of the Prevalence of Unethical Practices by Consultants, by Party Affiliation*
Percent

Respondent	Very often	Fairly often	Sometimes	Rarely	Not at all	N
Consultants, 1999[a]						
Republican	9.2	9.7	49.2	29.7	2.2	185
Democrat	6.5	13.0	52.4	27.6	0.4	246
Independent	24.6	26.3	38.6	10.5	0.0	57
Consultants, 2002[b]						
Republican	4.4	13.2	42.6	36.8	2.9	68
Democrat	9.5	16.2	45.7	28.6	0.0	23
Independent	4.3	34.8	47.8	13.0	0.0	23
Party elites, 2002[a]						
Republican	2.5	7.5	32.5	50.0	7.5	40
Democrat	0.0	8.7	43.5	43.5	4.3	46

a. The question asked was, "In your view, how common are unethical practices in the political consulting business? Do unethical practices happen very often, fairly often, sometimes, rarely, or not at all?"

b. The question asked was, "In your view, how common were unethical practices in the political consulting business for this election cycle? Do you think unethical practices happened very often, fairly often, sometimes, rarely, or not at all?"

that ethical problems occurred either rarely or not at all. The partisan differences lessened in the 2002 survey. Here, fewer independents (39.1 percent) felt that unethical practices frequently occurred. However, they still significantly outpaced both Democrats and Republicans.

The views of consultants who did not ally themselves with either the Democratic or Republican Party are curious, indeed. In a world that defines a person by the party with which he or she is affiliated, the sheer number of independents (12 percent of the sample in the 1999 study) is striking.[27] However, the 30-point difference between how independents see the campaign business and how partisan consultants see it is difficult to explain. It may be that those consultants who described themselves as independents were simply more fed up with the system in general, and they may have viewed the work of their colleagues who call themselves Democrats and Republicans through a more critical lens.

One other change from 1999 to 2002 was the increase in the number of Democrats who said that unethical practices occurred regularly—from

19.5 percent in 1999 to nearly 27 percent in 2002 (Republicans remained steady at about 18 percent in both waves). One explanation for this shift is the electioneering behavior in the two election cycles that occurred between the two measurements—from the RATS ad to the Chambliss campaign's spot featuring Osama bin Laden and Saddam Hussein. Although we cannot know for sure, it is possible that Democrats took note of these ads, both of which were GOP projects, and their concerns were reflected in their responses.

The sizable difference across the partisanship of consultants aside, that one-quarter of all consultants said that unethical practices do occur is not insignificant. More than 40 percent of all consultants in each wave said that unethical practices sometimes occurred in the consulting industry; in addition, only 1 percent in both 1999 and 2002 said that unethical practices never occur. Although the "sometimes" response is subjective, this finding does point to a more critical view of the consulting industry and campaigns in general on the part of consultants.

Although a sizable number of consultants said that unethical practices occurred at least fairly often, few party operatives—only about one in ten—said that unethical practices occurred very often or fairly often in today's campaigns. Moreover, party officials were the least suspicious of unethical conduct; fully 46 percent said unethical practices happened rarely. In fact, more than half of the party officials surveyed said that unethical practices happened rarely or not at all. A comparison of the partisan breakdowns of results from party operative and consultant surveys shows both similarities and differences. Unlike consultants, party operatives (combining both state and national party elites) showed no significant partisan differences in their assessments of how often unethical practices occur in consulting and campaigns; in the consultant data, it was independents who voiced opinions different from those of the partisans. Because we are dealing with party staffers we are, by definition, only considering partisans.

The reasons for these differences may be linked to how closely each of these two groups sees what happens not only in the political consulting industry but in campaigns generally. Professional consultants, by virtue of their role in the day-to-day operations of modern federal campaigns, are closer than party operatives to campaigns generally and to their industry in particular; thus it makes sense that they would perceive some unethical conduct in their industry but not much. Party officials, in contrast, are

Table 5-2. *The Public's Assessment of the Prevalence of Unethical Practices in Campaigns*[a]

Percent

Rating	March 2000	October 2000	2002
Very often	39.7	32.2	39.3
Fairly often	32.8	28.5	32.9
Sometimes	21.4	32.7	20.8
Rarely	3.2	4.3	4.9
Not at all	3.0	2.3	2.0
N	973	959	1,099

a. The question asked was, "In your view, how common are unethical practices in campaigns? Do unethical practices happen very often, fairly often, sometimes, rarely, or not at all?"

more removed from the process and are not as often in a position to see the occurrences that might qualify as unethical.

The Public's View of Campaign Ethics

On a much more pessimistic note, roughly two-thirds of the general public we surveyed said that unethical practices occur in campaigns very often or fairly often (see table 5-2). Although the modal response to the question of unethical consultant behavior (table 5-1) was either "rarely," in the case of party operatives, or "sometimes," in the case of consultants, the modal response from the general public was that unethical practices happen very often in today's campaigns. Across our surveys, roughly one in three Americans responded that something unethical very often happens in campaigns, and another 30 percent that these practices happened fairly often. These are troubling figures, and they do not bode well for either our campaigns or the results they produce. The differences between Republicans, Democrats, and independents were insignificant (though slightly more independents than partisans said unethical practices happened frequently). More likely voters said they believed unethical practices occurred very often or fairly often than those categorized as not likely to vote (77 percent to 70 percent in March, 63 percent to 59 percent in October). Given the large numbers in each category, however, the important point here is not the difference between the groups but that this belief was so widespread. More interesting is that though likely voters were more apt to report unethical practices in campaigns, they still remained engaged in campaigns and were not deterred from voting. This is similar to findings, presented in chapters 3 and 4, that likely voters are more inclined to express some regret about having voted for a candidate in the past and to perceive money as having an adverse effect on campaigns than were those less likely to vote. In addition, likely voters more often reported that ethical transgressions of the candidate were the cause of this disappointment and regret than their nonvoting counterparts.

One interesting aspect of these data is the shift over time in the public's assessment of the frequency of unethical practices. From March 2000 until October of that year, the proportion of the electorate who thought unethical practices occurred very often or fairly often decreased by 5.5 percent, and by November 2002 it had returned to the earlier (March 2000) level. In the first and last measurements (March 2000 and November 2002), 72 percent reported they felt unethical practices happened frequently, but only about 60 percent did in October of 2000. A possible explanation for this, and one that deserves future study, is that fewer instances of unethical practices are brought to the public's attention during the height of a presidential election cycle than at other times. In presidential years, because the presidential race attracts so much attention from the media, the congressional races are not on the public's radar screen; during midterm years, however, the congressional races are the only game in town, and there are 435 congressional races and 33 or 34 U.S. Senate races, though the vast majority are not competitive. When one considers the kinds of stories that the media like to cover—those that are sensational, scandalous, and negative—the coverage may include more stories about nasty things that happen during these campaigns. Because there are more of them, there is more fuel for the fire.

The Ethics of Campaign Tactics

We also asked consultants, party elites, and the general public to evaluate specific campaign practices that could be considered ethically questionable: focusing on an opponent's negative personal characteristics rather than issues, making statements that are factually untrue (that is, lying), and making statements that are factually true but taken out of their original context. We also asked the different actors about other practices that might be more relevant to each. For instance, we asked consultants about the use of push polls and the use of so-called contrast ads noted earlier;

we asked the general public about candidates' making promises that the candidates know are impossible to keep.

The Public's View of Campaign Tactics

During the period in the 2004 presidential campaign that is usually a quiet time in presidential campaigns—the summer months before the nominating conventions—there was quite a bit of activity on the part of both the Bush and Kerry campaigns. In keeping with the trend noted by scholars and journalists, the tone of the dialogue was decidedly negative. Debates about the war in Iraq and the economy dominated as they had through much of the campaign to that point. Right after John Kerry selected John Edwards to be his running mate on the Democratic ticket, however, another issue popped up—the candidates' values. In his own race for the White House during the primaries, Edwards had become known for his standard stump speech, which included references to the values instilled in him in his childhood home in small-town North Carolina and through his father's job in a mill.[28] After his selection as the vice presidential nominee, Edwards joined his running mate on the campaign trail where they both touted their values, hoping to connect with voters. Values became an issue for the Bush campaign during this period, as well. The candidates did not limit their remarks to their own values, however, instead taking aim at each other's. The *Washington Post* ran a headline that read, "Rhetoric on Values Turns Personal; Attacks Sharpen in Presidential Race." The story quoted candidate Edwards as saying at one rally, "I understand that President Bush is going to be out today, as he does every day, talking about values. Values is not a word on a piece of paper. Values is not part of a political slogan. Values are what's inside you"; Bush responded at a campaign rally: "And now just last weekend, [Kerry] even tried to claim he was the candidate with conservative values. I know, I know, but I'm quoting his own words. Believe it or not, that's what he said"; Bush was also quoted as saying that Kerry was "out of step with the mainstream values so important to our country and our families."[29]

Taking shots at the opposing candidate rather than confronting issues important to the electorate is one of the things many believe has turned voters off to campaigns. Campaign statements of this kind can get quite ugly at times. In past campaigns, candidates have taken issue with an opponent's marriage, divorce, sexuality, and family. During a 2004 congressional campaign, incumbent U.S. representative Jerry Weller (R-Ill.)

found his fiancée under attack from his Democratic opponent. In the early summer of 2004, Weller announced his engagement to Zury Rios Sosa, who happened to be the vice president of Guatemala's Congress. Weller's opponent, Tari Renner, released a statement after the wedding announcement calling Sosa "'a leader in the Guatemalan Republican Front' run by her father, former president Jose Efrain Rios Montt, 'whose dictatorship was charged with genocide by the United Nations.'" Weller responded by saying, in part, "My engagement to Zury is not an issue in this election. . . . To tarnish one [of] life's joys, marrying the woman you love, is simply beyond the bounds of decency."[30]

Statements alluding to a candidate's personal life, personality, or personal characteristics in a political campaign are usually viewed as inappropriate. As table 5-3 illustrates, in both March and October 2000, fewer than one in ten Americans thought focusing on the negative personal characteristics of an opponent rather than on issues was an acceptable way to campaign; two-thirds said that it was unacceptable (the rest identified it as a "questionable" practice). In the 2002 survey of the general public, the figures were generally the same, with slightly more (73 percent) rating the practice as unacceptable and slightly fewer (6 percent) deeming it acceptable. In our March 2000 survey, following the Super Tuesday primaries, likely voters were found to rate this practice acceptable more often than those less likely to vote—12 percent to 6 percent. Both groups deemed the practice unacceptable with the same frequency (about two in three); but more of those who were unlikely to vote rated it questionable—and this slight difference disappeared in the October study.

There was no significant partisan difference in the March 2000 survey, but in the October 2000 survey more members of the electorate who identified themselves as independents said that focusing on personal characteristics was unacceptable (69.4 percent) than did Democrats (65.2 percent) or Republicans (55.9 percent). Similar but smaller differences were uncovered in November 2002. One possible explanation for the differences is that independents (and even Democrats), after witnessing the conduct of the general election campaign, became frustrated with the conduct of candidates' campaigns.

It is probable that some Americans said they found this practice to be questionable (more than one in four did so in both surveys during 2000) rather than completely unacceptable because they find some of the personal characteristics that get disclosed to be important. Members of the

Table 5-3. *The Public's Assessment of the Ethics of Selected Campaign Practices*[a]

Percent

Practice	Acceptable	Questionable	Unacceptable	N
Focusing primarily on the negative personal characteristics of an opponent rather than on issues				
March 2000	7.8	26.1	66.0	983
October 2000	9.6	27.7	62.7	987
2002	6.0	21.0	73.0	1,113
Making statements that are factually untrue				
March 2000	3.1	9.2	87.7	991
October 2000	4.0	8.0	88.0	989
2002	1.0	7.5	91.5	1,107
Making promises that are impossible to keep				
March 2000	2.3	14.6	83.1	994
October 2000	3.8	16.1	80.1	990
2002	3.4	14.8	81.8	1,109
Making statements that are factually true but are taken out of context				
March 2000	9.3	37.9	52.8	983
October 2000	12.7	39.8	47.5	979
2002	8.3	34.7	57.1	1,102

a. The question asked was, "I'm going to read you several practices that sometimes occur during the course of a campaign. As I read, please tell me whether you believe that practice is acceptable, questionable, or unacceptable."

electorate are careful in distinguishing between what they see as permissible and what they see as intolerable. Some survey work conducted during 1999 by the Institute for Global Ethics (IGE) suggests how far the public is willing to go. Survey respondents said that it was fair for candidates to criticize their opponents for "not paying their taxes on time" (65 percent) and "current problems with substances like alcohol and marijuana" (58 percent) (in addition to standard criticisms such as "talking one way and voting another" [68 percent], "taking campaign money from special interests" [59 percent], and "their voting record" [57 percent]). Respondents did not think it was appropriate for a candidate to attack his or her opponent for "the actions of a candidate's family members" (84 percent), "lack of military service" (72 percent), "past personal financial problems" (71 percent), or "past personal troubles like alcoholism and smoking marijuana" (63 percent).[31] Clearly, the general public makes a distinction between personal issues that are current and those that are from a candidate's distant past.

The electorate is clearly less forgiving of candidates' lying than of their focusing on their opponents' negative personal characteristics. Asked whether making statements that were factually untrue was an acceptable, questionable, or unacceptable practice, the public was nearly unanimous. In all three measurements of the public's views, roughly 90 percent reported that lying was an unacceptable campaign practice. Here, there were no substantive differences between partisans in the electorate. Those likely and unlikely to vote were equally clear in their feelings about lying in a campaign, nearly 90 percent of each group deeming it unacceptable.

One recent example of the public's intolerance for candidates who are less than truthful is the case of former U.S. representative Wes Cooley (R-Ore.). Cooley was elected in 1994, claiming on the Oregon Voters' Pamphlet that he had served in the Korean War. During his first two years in Congress, however, questions arose about the truthfulness of this declaration. Military records from that time clearly showed that Cooley had not finished training for the U.S. Army Special Forces unit that he claimed to have served with until after the war was over; other documents indicate that he never left the United States during the war period.[32] Cooley claimed to have served in Korea under the command of a Sergeant Major Poppy, who had since passed away, but said he could not remember the names of any of the other men with whom he had served. One can assume that Cooley got his seat on the U.S. House's Committee on Veterans Affairs partly, if not solely, based on his alleged military service. Cooley, during the early parts of his 1996 reelection campaign, denied the allegations but dropped out of the race in early August, under a great deal of pressure. In December 1996, he was indicted by a grand jury on charges that he had lied to voters on the 1994 information pamphlet. Cooley was also "accused of lying about when he got married, enabling his second wife to fraudulently continue to collect benefits as the widow of a Marine who died in 1965."[33] By no means is Wes Cooley the only candidate who has ever lied about his record, resume, or life leading up to his candidacy.[34]

The public was also unambiguous in its assessment of candidates who make promises they will not be able to keep. In each survey, fewer than 4 percent of all Americans (2.3 percent in March 2000; 3.8 percent in October 2000; and 3.4 percent in November 2002) rated such behavior acceptable, and more than 80 percent in each measurement called it unacceptable. These data lend some empirical support to Maisel's claim that there are differences between the promises candidates make—those they can keep and those they know they are unable to keep. This conduct is not on the order of Wes Cooley's lie about his military service. Given the disdain in which the general public holds both practices, however, it may be that the public sees them as two sides of the same coin. If the candidate knows that his or her promise is unattainable, then to make the promise is a lie. (It can also be assumed a candidate who knows anything about the system in which he or she will be working should certainly know whether the promise is attainable.) There were, again, only small differences between Republicans, Democrats, and independents and between likely voters and those less likely to vote.

One final campaign practice we asked the general public about was making statements that were factually true but taken out of context. This happens frequently in campaigns, typically in thirty-second television ads. The ads run against John McCain in the 2000 GOP presidential primary are an example. Did he vote against the bill that continued funding for breast cancer research, as the ad stated? Yes. Was it taken out of context, implying something that was not true? Yes.

Sometimes what is said in a campaign amounts to splitting hairs that are already thin. Some early advertising by the Bush campaign focused on John Kerry's voting record on taxes during his nineteen-year career in the U.S. Senate. One ad in particular argued that Kerry had voted for higher taxes 350 separate times. In this ad, the announcer says,

> John Kerry's record on the economy: troubling. He opposed tax relief for married couples 22 times. Opposed increasing the child tax credit 18 times. Kerry supported higher taxes over 350 times. He even supported increasing taxes on Social Security benefits, and a 50-cent a gallon tax hike for gasoline. Now Kerry's plan will raise taxes by at least $900 billion his first hundred days. Kerry and the economy: troubling.[35]

The president made similar statements on the campaign trail, which were met with denials from the Kerry camp.

After one such comment by the president, Kerry's campaign immediately released a statement that the senator "has never sponsored or voted for a gas-tax increase of that magnitude" and that "Sen. Charles Robb introduced legislation in 1993 that phased in a 50-cent increase. John

Kerry did not vote for or co-sponsor this bill."[36] Moreover, according to the watchdog group FactCheck.org,

> Kerry has not voted 350 times for tax increases, something Bush campaign officials have falsely accused Kerry of on several occasions. On close examination, the Bush campaign's list of Kerry's votes for "higher taxes" is padded. It includes votes Kerry cast to leave taxes unchanged (when Republicans proposed cuts), and even votes in favor of alternative Democratic tax cuts that Bush aides characterized as "watered down."[37]

The Bush campaign, in turn, released a statement citing an article from the *Boston Globe* in 1994 in which Kerry said that a rating by a budget watchdog group "doesn't reflect my $43 billion package of cuts or my support for a 50-cent increase in the gas tax."[38]

Were the statements in the Bush ad factually true? Specifically, did John Kerry say at one point that he was in favor of a fifty-cent-a-gallon gas tax? Did Kerry vote on the specific votes as characterized by the ad? The answer to both questions is yes. Were they facts taken out of context? Yes. The gas tax referred to was a decade old, and, as noted by FactCheck.org, Kerry voted not in favor of raising taxes but in opposition to lowering them.

Democrats during the 2004 campaign were not immune to these sorts of contextual games. In April 2004 the Kerry campaign started airing an ad that said, in part, "While jobs are leaving our country in record numbers, George Bush says sending jobs overseas makes sense for America. His top economic advisors say moving American jobs to low-cost countries is a plus for the U.S."[39] In reality, however, Bush never said any such thing; the words were taken from a document written by the administration's economists, *The Economic Report of the President*. Since the words in question—the phrase about outsourcing "making sense"—appeared in something with the president's name on it, the Kerry campaign had some legs to stand on. However, according to FactCheck.org,

> the Kerry campaign claims that the report in which the words appear was "signed by President Bush." But that's also false. Actually, what Bush signed was *The Economic Report of the President*, which occupies only the first few pages of a 412-page volume that also contains the *Annual Report of the Council of Economic Advisers*, a separate document signed by the three members of the council, not by the President.

The President's signature appears on page 4, at the end of his economic report. The passage to which the Kerry ad refers appears on page 25, in the midst of the report by the President's economists.[40]

The electorate is not convinced that these practices do not have a place in today's campaigns. Although only roughly 10 percent of the general public in both waves of the 2000 survey reported that making statements that are factually true but taken out of context was an acceptable practice, and slightly more than 8 percent said the same in 2002, the results do not constitute a clear condemnation of the practice. Rather, a sizable portion of the public—more than a third in all three measurements—described taking an opponent's statements out of context as only a questionable campaign practice. The differences between Democrats, Republicans, and independents were negligible. In our survey early in the 2000 cycle, those identified as likely voters were more prone to say that this practice was unacceptable than were unlikely voters (60.6 percent to just under 49.8 percent), but still relatively few in each group (7.3 percent of likely voters and 10.0 percent of unlikely voters) considered the practice acceptable. The reason that campaigns engage in this behavior more so than the others mentioned earlier, save getting into the personal lives of an opponent, may lie in these data. The public does not accept candidates and campaigns that lie or make unattainable promises, but they are less sure about statements that are taken out of context. Candidates and their campaigns engage in the latter but not the former because they know they can get away with one but not the other.

Consultants' View of Campaign Tactics

Professional political consultants have a far different view of these campaign practices. In our 1999 survey of the industry, nearly 40 percent of all consultants reported that they thought focusing on the personal characteristics of a candidate was an acceptable campaign practice, only slightly less than 17 percent identified it as clearly unethical, and the remainder called it questionable (see table 5-4).[41] The consultants we interviewed in 2002 were also relatively comfortable with this practice; the same proportion (about 40 percent) felt it was all right to use this tactic, and nearly 50 percent said it was only questionable.

Few consultants see anything wrong with going on the attack against a candidate based on the candidate's personal life. Consultants are no

Table 5-4. *Consultants' Assessment of the Ethics of Selected Campaign Practices*[a]

Percent

Practice	Acceptable	Questionable	Clearly unethical	N
Focusing primarily on the negative personal characteristics of an opponent, rather than on issues[b]				
1999	38.1	45.2	16.7	496
2002	38.1	47.0	14.9	202
Making statements that are factually untrue				
1998	0.5	2.0	97.5	195
1999	0.8	5.0	94.2	504
2002	0.0	2.0	98.0	202
Making statements that are factually true but are taken out of context				
1998	13.1	61.1	25.8	198
1999	12.9	60.2	26.9	502
2002	9.4	62.4	28.2	202
Contrasting a candidate's issue stands with those of the opponent[c]				
1999	98.4	1.6	0.0	502
2002	99.0	1.0	0.0	203
Using push polls				
1998	7.2	21.0	71.8	195
1999	25.7	36.6	37.7	470
2002	19.8	29.2	51.0	192
Using negative ads to decrease turnout				
1998	22.7	29.4	47.9	194
1999	38.0	33.6	28.4	497
2002	31.3	41.3	27.4	201

a. The question asked was, "I'm going to read you several practices that sometimes occur during the course of a campaign. As I read each, please tell me whether you believe that practice is acceptable, questionable, or clearly unethical."

b. Because this question was asked slightly differently in 1998, we omit those data from this comparison table.

c. This question was not asked in 1998.

doubt behind some of the personal attack ads, such as the one that was aired during the 2002 Montana Senate race in which Republican Mike Taylor challenged incumbent senator Max Baucus. Controversy was stirred by a television spot run by the Democratic Party against Taylor insinuating, in the eyes of many observers, that he was a homosexual. Less than one month before Election Day, Taylor dropped out of the race.

> The 30-second spot begins with a disco beat and flashes Taylor's name in letters evocative of "Saturday Night Fever." It features old footage promoting Taylor's macramé-decorated beauty school. . . . In it, a much younger, thinner Taylor, wearing an open-front shirt and gold chains, administers skin care to a male client by massaging his cheekbones. At the end of the ad, as Taylor reaches down toward his client's lap, the announcer reads: "Mike Taylor. Not the way we do business here in Montana."[42]

In announcing he was leaving the race, Taylor said, "I'm willing to suspend my campaign because my opponent's lies about me are hurting my wife, my family, my friends, my party and most of all, Montanans from all walks of life."[43] He added, "Basically, I'm sending a message that if you've got to sink to these lows to win office, it's not worth it."[44] Taylor also said that he had dropped out of the race because he did not have enough money in his campaign to fight the sexual innuendo and wanted to make his situation a national example of the consequences of negative campaigning.[45]

The *Denver Post* noted in an editorial that "the ad deals with a legitimate issue: about $159,000 in questionable student loans at a Denver beauty school Mike Taylor ran in the early '80s."[46] The ad refers to U.S. Department of Education documents that reported Taylor's school had obtained federal loans for students enrolled in a program who were ineligible for financial aid. The ad accuses the school of failing to properly refund the loan money when students left the school. Taylor rebutted that charge, saying that the dispute with the Department of Education was over a total of $261 and was a result of a paperwork mistake by an employee who happened to be his wife. According to Taylor's campaign manager, a poll taken shortly after the ad aired showed that following broadcast of the ad, Baucus's lead over Taylor doubled to 33 points.[47] The Democratic Party saw nothing wrong with their spot: "Our ad was based entirely on the message of his abuse of the student loans while running a hair-care school in Colorado."[48] Two weeks before election day, Taylor got back in the race and was easily defeated by Baucus. We include this example in a discussion devoted to consultants because of the manner in which this attack took place—subtly, in a thirty-second ad. This ad was a result of a consultant's work, unlike the Weller example given earlier in this chapter, in which the candidate himself was explicitly attacked by his opponent.

In the 2002 survey, an interesting partisan split appeared. Consultants who reported that they were Republicans or Democrats were more likely to say that focusing on the negative personal characteristics of an opponent was an acceptable practice (about 40 percent in each party) than were consultants who did not align themselves with one of the two major parties (only 26 percent of independents). In addition, far more independents (three times as many as Democrats and twice as many as Republicans) said this was clearly unethical.[49]

Although campaign consultants and the general public do not see eye to eye on the ethics of using personal accusations as an issue in a campaign, they are very similar in their beliefs about telling untruths in a campaign. In this case, consultants were even more cohesive in their attitudes, as roughly 95 percent of all consultants in all three surveys— 97.5 percent in 1998, 94.2 percent in 1999, and 98.0 percent in 2002— said that making factually untrue statements was clearly unethical. In the latest measurement, not one political consultant described the practice as acceptable, and only 2 percent called it questionable. Clearly, this is a line that political consultants will not cross in a campaign.

Like the electorate, the consultants surveyed were rather indistinct in their opinions about using statements that are taken out of context. In 1998, 1999, and 2002 a strong majority, more than 60 percent, said this practice was questionable, but only about one in four described it as clearly unethical. Again, this should come as no surprise, since taking candidates' statements out of context happens quite often in today's campaigns. In the 2002 survey, a partisan split again appeared: more independents were clear in their dislike for this practice (nearly half said it was "clearly unethical") than Democrats (23.8 percent) or Republicans (27.8 percent).

With the exception of focusing on personality and negative personal characteristics rather than issues, political consultants and the general public have similar attitudes about certain campaign practices. They both draw the line at telling lies, and both are ambivalent as to the acceptability of taking statements that are true and using them out of context.

We also asked political consultants about some practices that are less likely to be well known among the general public and could be characterized as "inside baseball" in a campaign. We asked about contrasting candidates' issue stances, the ethics of push polls, and using negative ads to suppress voter turnout. Consultants were most clear in their attitudes about contrasting their candidates' stands on issues with those of the opponents. Here, in both 1999 and 2002, nearly all consultants (more than 98 percent in both instances and without any differences between Republicans, Democrats, and independents) said this was an acceptable practice; not one said it was something that should not be done.[50] Here we may be able to get a glimpse into what consultants believe about the purpose behind campaigns. In one sense, campaigns are battles about ideas, policy solutions, philosophies of government, and visions for the future. Voters are presented with a clear choice between candidates only if comparisons and contrasts of the candidates' records, public statements, and ideas are made. Consultants concur and see this as a sound way of campaigning.

Consultants were less certain about the use of two tactics that are considered particular ills of modern campaigns. During the 2000 Republican presidential primary campaign, "at a town hall meeting . . . in Spartanburg [South Carolina], Donna Duren told [Senator John] McCain that her 14-year-old son, Chris, took a call Wednesday from a 'push poller.' . . . Duren said her son admires McCain and was on the verge of tears after talking to the pollster, who described the candidate, in Duren's words, as 'a cheat, a liar and a fraud.'"[51] Push polls are not legitimate pieces of survey research but are "telemarketing techniques with the goal of influencing voter behavior,"[52] which "canvass potential voters, feeding them false or misleading information about a candidate under the pretense of taking a poll to see how this information affects voter preferences. The intent is to 'push' voters away from one candidate and toward the opposing candidate. Usually thousands of calls are made, and if questions are asked, the answers usually are not tabulated."[53] In the 2000 presidential primary, Senator McCain accused the Bush campaign of being behind these phone calls; Bush denied that his campaign had anything to do with it, and the source of the calls was never made clear.

The opinions of professional political consultants about the use of push polls are troubling. In the three measurements of their opinions, we found inconsistent attitudes. Seventy percent of the consultants we interviewed in 1998 said this was a clearly unethical practice; in 1999, however, slightly fewer than 38 percent said the same; in 2002 a majority of consultants (51 percent) again described push polls as unethical. Putting the varied responses aside for a moment, what is troubling about these data is that so many consultants find this to be either unobjectionable, or at the very least, questionable, behavior.[54] Even in 1998, when 70 percent of consultants described push polls as unethical, 30 percent thought them either questionable or acceptable. In 1999 one-quarter of all consultants said push polls were acceptable. As might be expected, given the closeness of the practice to their field, pollsters were the least likely of consultants to say that this was an acceptable practice (only 14.7 percent). Media consultants, too, outpaced other types of consultants in finding this to be an unacceptable practice.[55] Moreover, in 1999 and 2002 fewer Republicans than Democrats or independents called the use of push polls clearly unethical (see table 5-5). "It's unfortunate that this term 'push poll' ever achieved currency, because it's not a poll," notes Michael W. Traugott, a scholar of public opinion and the former head of the American Association of Public Opinion Research. "It makes people more cynical about politics, and that's something that the democracy can't afford."[56]

One criticism of modern campaigning is that campaigns do not strive to generate as much participation as possible. It is common knowledge among those who study campaigns as well as those involved in electioneering that near the end of a race, when the campaigns focus their work on get-out-the-vote (GOTV) efforts, that each side is only focused on its own supporters; for this reason, some feel the term should be GOYV (get-out-your-vote). In a typical campaign at any level of politics, on the last days before election day, everyone involved in the campaign—candidates' campaigns, parties, and interest groups—is focused on making sure that everyone who supports their candidate is going to participate and cast a ballot. They do not care about the other side's supporters. Although this tendency is open to criticism, it is far from the final tactic we asked consultants about—using negative advertising to try to decrease voter turnout either among certain groups of potential voters or in certain regions or areas of a district or state.

In an ambitious project, Stephen Ansolabehere and Shanto Iyengar present evidence that negative advertising, or a negative campaign tone, works to demobilize the electorate. What is more, they suggest that campaigns deliberately and purposefully use negative advertising to decrease turnout. In their book *Going Negative*, Ansolabehere and Iyengar argue that "negative 'attack' advertising actually suppresses voter turnout" and that campaigns use such advertising "strategically for this purpose."[57] They consider this tactic to be a fundamental arrow in a campaign's tactical quiver. Moreover, they argue, political consultants are the main pur-

Table 5-5. Consultants' Assessment of the Ethics of Selected Campaign Practices, by Party Affiliation[a]

Percent

Practice and rating	1999			2002		
	Republicans	Democrats	Independents	Republicans	Democrats	Independents
Using push polls						
Acceptable	36.4	17.6	25.0	24.6	16.3	18.2
Questionable	36.4	38.6	26.8	39.1	21.4	31.8
Clearly unethical	27.2	43.8	48.2	36.2	62.2	50.0
N	173	233	56	69	98	22
Using negative ads to decrease voter turnout						
Acceptable	47.0	33.1	28.3	36.1	26.9	40.9
Questionable	32.2	34.3	38.3	47.2	38.5	31.8
Clearly unethical	20.8	32.7	33.3	16.7	34.6	27.3
N	183	245	60	72	104	22

a. The question asked was, "I'm going to read you several practices that sometimes occur during the course of a campaign. As I read, please tell me whether you believe that practice is acceptable, questionable, or clearly unethical."

veyors of this strategy: "consultants brag about using negative advertising to depress turnout, when higher turnout may hurt their candidate."[58]

Here, too, consultants' attitudes are troubling. In both 1999 and 2002 sizable proportions (38 and 31 percent, respectively) said that using negative ads to try and decrease voter turnout was an acceptable practice; fewer than 30 percent called it clearly unethical (see table 5-4). More striking, and more important, however, are the numbers of consultants who reported that this actually happens. In both our 1999 and 2002 studies, roughly 20 percent of all consultants said that negative ads are fairly often used to decrease turnout, and 13 percent said this practice occurs very often. Although a plurality of consultants in both waves of the survey—44.7 percent in 1999 and 45 percent in 2002—said it happens "just sometimes," that it happens at all is a problem. Furthermore, roughly 46 percent of consultants (again in both waves) reported that the main factor in the decision to engage in this practice is the consultants' input—nearly three times as many as thought it was the candidate's input into the decision. Some of the claims made by Ansolabehere and Iyengar are confirmed—campaigns do run negative ads to chill voter turnout. Most consultants did not find this to be an unethical practice. Partisan differences again appeared: fewer Republicans than Democrats found this to be clearly unethical; see table 5-5.

This may be a case in which the eleventh-hour focus on getting out the vote has gone too far. Worrying about turning out voters who are on your side is one thing; trying to reduce the chances that voters in the opponent's camp turn out is quite another. Unfortunately, these data may feed the fire of consultants' critics, who often claim consultants have a "win-at-all-costs" mentality. We argue elsewhere that these practices are not the norm in the consulting industry or in campaigns and that a couple of bad apples do not spoil the bunch.[59]

On a few issues consultants see ethical questions as black or white—drawing contrasts on issues between candidates is clearly acceptable, making factually untrue statements clearly is not—but on the other campaign practices we asked about there was no clear consensus among the consultants. The lack of consensus on what is ethical behavior and what is not is consistent over time. The proportions of political professionals who found particular practices acceptable, questionable, or unethical were stable over the four years of our surveys. This suggests that though consultants may disagree about the acceptability of different campaign practices, they have thought about what is acceptable behavior and what is not. It is

Table 5-6. *Party Elites' Assessment of the Ethics of Selected Campaign Practices*[a]

Percent

Practice	Acceptable	Questionable	Clearly unethical	N
Focusing primarily on the negative personal characteristics of an opponent rather than on issues	39.2	52.9	7.8	102
Making statements that are factually untrue	0.9	12.0	87.0	108
Making statements that are factually true but are taken out of context	16.7	59.3	24.1	108
Contrasting a candidate's issue stands with the opponent	98.1	1.9	0.0	108
Using push polls	24.0	44.8	31.3	96
Using negative ads to decrease turnout	21.0	47.6	31.4	105

a. The question asked was, "I'm going to read to you several practices that sometimes occur during the course of a campaign. As I read each, please tell me whether you believe that practice is acceptable, questionable, or clearly unethical."

neither the case that the electioneering business is full of angels nor that consultants and party operatives will do whatever it takes to win.

Party Elites' View of Campaign Tactics

In our survey of state and national party elites, we asked the same questions about the ethics of campaign practices that we posed to consultants. The views of the party operatives we interviewed were in remarkable agreement with those of the consultants. As table 5-6 shows, most party operatives reported that focusing on a candidate's negative personal characteristics was either questionable (52.9 percent) or acceptable (39.2 percent). Among party operatives, Republicans and Democrats were equally likely to say that this practice was clearly unethical (about 10 percent of each group), but they differed on whether it was an acceptable practice, more Republicans (40.4 percent) than Democrats (29.3 percent) agreeing (see table 5-7). Party staffers showed similarly undivided agreement on

Table 5-7. *Party Elites' Assessment of the Ethics of Selected Campaign Practices, by Party Affiliation*[a]

Percent

Practice and rating	Republicans	Democrats
Focusing on the negative personal characteristics of a candidate		
Acceptable	40.4	29.3
Questionable	61.0	51.1
Clearly unethical	8.5	9.8
N	47	41
Using push polls		
Acceptable	28.9	18.4
Questionable	48.9	50.0
Clearly unethical	22.2	31.6
N	45	38
Is using negative ads to decrease voter turnout		
Acceptable	25.0	11.4
Questionable	54.2	45.5
Clearly unethical	20.8	43.2
N	48	44

a. The question asked was, "I'm going to read to you several practices that sometimes occur during the course of a campaign. As I read each, please tell me whether you believe that practice is acceptable, questionable, or clearly unethical."

two practices: making statements that are factually untrue—nearly 90 percent called this clearly unethical (similar to results among both the general public and professional consultants)—and contrasting candidates' stands on issues and policy alternatives with those of their opponents—98.1 percent deemed this an acceptable practice, and none called it unethical (similar to the results in the consultant studies). They also shared views with consultants and the electorate on using statements that are factually true but taken out of context. Party elites neither accepted nor rejected this practice outright: a strong majority of 59 percent called it questionable, while fewer than 17 percent said it was acceptable. Fewer party staffers than consultants said that using push polls was clearly unethical, and significant numbers said that push polls and using negative ads to decrease turnout were tolerable practices in today's campaigns.

Moreover, similar to the results from the consultant surveys, more Republicans than Democrats described these practices as acceptable. The difference between GOP and Democratic Party staffers' views on focusing on a candidate's personal characteristics was not in the numbers who said it was clearly unethical but in those who said it was acceptable versus questionable. The partisan differences on the use of push polls and negative ads to decrease turnout were more distinct: there was roughly a 10-point difference between Republicans and Democrats in their views of whether push polls were acceptable or clearly unethical and, with even larger differences, of using negative ads to decrease voter turnout (see table 5-7).

Candidates' View of Campaign Tactics

In his surveys of state legislative candidates Paul S. Herrnson, using a similar battery of questions about acceptable campaign conduct, has found some evidence that complements our own (see table 5-8).[60] When comparing Herrnson's data with ours, we find a good deal of agreement between political consultants, party operatives, the general public, and candidates on the acceptability of making statements that are factually untrue. All four groups overwhelmingly thought that making false statements was not appropriate. However, different campaign actors did not see eye to eye on every issue. Specifically, when asked if it was all right to make statements that are factually true but are taken out of context, the opinions of the general public, political professionals (consultants and party elites), and candidates diverged.[61] Approximately half of the general public thought such a practice was clearly unacceptable, whereas only one-quarter of the political professionals held such a view; more political professionals described such a practice as questionable. Candidates were the most likely to see the practice as objectionable; almost two-thirds (64 percent) of candidates thought making statements that were factually true but taken out of context was clearly unethical, and another one-third thought it was a questionable practice. Just 3 percent of candidates saw it as acceptable.

Many of the questions about campaign practices that we asked only of political professionals were also replicated in Herrnson's survey of candidates. Herrnson's candidates had mixed views about push polling. Almost one-third (31 percent) found it clearly unethical, and almost one-quarter

Table 5-8. *Candidates' Assessment of the Ethics of Selected Campaign Practices*[a]

Percent

Practice	Acceptable	Questionable	Clearly unethical
Focusing primarily on the negative personal characteristics of an opponent rather than on issues	7	28	65
Making statements that are factually untrue	0	1	99
Making statements that are factually true but are taken out of context	3	32	64
Contrasting a candidate's issue stands with the opponent	90	5	2
Using push polls	8	24	38
Using negative ads to decrease turnout	7	21	70

Source: Ronald A. Faucheux and Paul S. Hernnson, eds., *The Good Fight: How Political Candidates Struggle to Win Elections without Losing Their Souls* (Washington, D.C.: Campaigns & Elections, 2001), pp. 131–47.

a. Some rows do not add to 100 percent because those respondents who said "Don't know" or refused to answer the question were included in the tabulations.

(24 percent) found the practice questionable. Interestingly, 38 percent of candidates either said they did not know what they thought about push polling or refused to answer the question; this is a higher percentage (nearly threefold) who did not answer the question than we found in our surveys of either consultants or party elites. That such a high proportion of candidates for office do not know enough about push polling to give an opinion may illustrate two things: the nature of some modern campaign practices and the control that consultants have in campaigns today (see chapter 2) and the differences between federal and state legislative campaigns—push polling simply may not yet have found its way to lower-level campaigns.

One campaign practice that consultants, party officials, and candidates agreed was appropriate was contrasting candidates' stands on issues. As noted earlier, 98 percent of consultants and party elites in our surveys agreed that such a practice was acceptable, as did 90 percent of the candidates surveyed. On the other hand, candidates, in contrast to consultants and party operatives, were much more likely to think using negative ads to suppress turnout was clearly unethical. Seventy percent of candidates judged the practice clearly unethical, and another 21 percent found it questionable. Only 7 percent of candidates found using negative ads to suppress turnout acceptable, compared with roughly one-third of political consultants.

Herrnson's data indicate that the views of state legislative candidates are closer to the view of the general public than to those of consultants and party elites with respect to using negative personal information about a candidate. Sixty-five percent of candidates, a higher percentage than of consultants and party staffers, found such activity clearly unethical, whereas just 7 percent found focusing on one's opponent's negative personal characteristics acceptable.

Also, like the public, candidates reported that focusing on some negative personal information is permissible in campaigns, though other information is clearly off limits. Candidates said that information relating to a candidate's family or past personal life was out of bounds, whereas issues that could affect a candidate's ability to handle the office being sought or a recent transgression were fair game. Specifically, 97 percent of candidates reported that they thought using an unproven allegation about a candidate's spouse or family member was inappropriate, and 90 percent said the same about an unproven allegation from a lawsuit. Moreover, "73 percent said it would be inappropriate to use a youthful indiscretion such as shoplifting or smoking marijuana, and 71 percent said the same about a previously unpublicized homosexual relationship."[62] One issue that might relate to a candidate's ability to handle elective office—a recent bankruptcy—brought about a split reaction from candidates, 45 percent of whom said it was fair game and an equal proportion calling it unacceptable. However, solid majorities of candidates said that the following four areas of a candidate's personal life were all legitimate: a drunken driving conviction (59 percent), a documented allegation of sexual harassment (60 percent), failure to pay back property taxes (66 percent), and failure to pay child support or alimony (69 percent). Clearly, candidates also have an ethical line they will not cross; they simply draw it differently from professional campaigners and more like the general public. The attitudes of candidates on this point may be best summed up by U.S. representative Dennis Moore (D-Kans.), who, reflecting about his first run for Congress and what he wanted to say in the campaign compared with what his consultants wanted to say, remarked, "After those guys are gone, I'm still gonna be here living in this community, and I don't want to have a reputation as somebody who kinda shades the truth or bends the truth, and I'm trying to be accurate and truthful in this campaign."[63]

The Effects of Unethical Campaign Practices

No matter what consultants, party operatives, or candidates for office think about the ethics of certain campaign practices, if the public believes there is wrongdoing in campaigns, there are bound to be undesirable effects. For instance, consultants view the process of drawing distinctions between two candidates' records as an ethical tactic; given their near-unanimous response to this question, one might even make the case that consultants find it to be a necessary part of campaigns. However, the practice is often labeled (either by the media or the opponent) as negative campaigning, which the public does not like. In the end, it is the public perception of the tactics that is important. There are some things that the public finds acceptable and other things they will not tolerate. Our data illustrate that the public is clear in its disapproval of lying and candidates' making promises they know they cannot keep; they are less clear on things like taking true statements out of context and candidates' focusing on negative personal characteristics of their opponent. More important, however, is the finding that roughly two-thirds of all Americans believe that unethical practices occur frequently in today's campaigns. Whatever consultants or party staffers think about the ethics of certain campaign practices, it is the electorate's perception that matters, as it can have consequences that damage both the process itself and the outcomes of that process.

This is not to say that unethical practices do not happen in campaigns. Even political consultants and high-level party operatives agree than the ethics of some tactics are open to question. Some of the examples presented in this chapter are the use of push polls, focusing on an opponent's personal characteristics and beliefs, airing ads with overtones of racial bigotry, and challenging the patriotism of a candidate who served and was wounded in combat.

We also asked members of the electorate who was to blame for the campaign practices they disliked. The public's attitudes about who is responsible for undesirable campaign practices may be a microcosm of their attitude about the whole campaigning process; in short, no group of campaign actors escapes blame (this sentiment was fairly consistent from March 2000 to November 2002). Political parties were mentioned most often: in 2000 roughly 79 percent of all Americans said that parties were "a lot" or "somewhat" to blame for questionable campaign practices; in November 2002 that share increased to more than 86 percent. Candidates for office were not far behind: in March 2000, 80 percent of the electorate said candidates were responsible; in the fall of that year, the share dropped slightly, to 72 percent, but it rose again in November 2002 back to the 80 percent range. Approximately seven in ten members of the electorate in both waves in 2000 said that political consultants and interest groups were a lot or somewhat to blame for unacceptable campaign practices, but again there were increases in the 2002 measurement to nearly 80 percent for interest groups and more than 85 percent for consultants.

More members of the electorate are blaming each group of actors: the association of blame went up for each group, sometimes substantially (for example, consultants and interest groups), from 2000 to 2002. As we report in chapter 3, the public's sentiment about the major electoral actors did not stray far from an "average" rating. These data further illustrate the public's negative feelings about parties, candidates, and professional consultants. The public also is clear in saying that there is enough blame to go around for the campaign practices they dislike.

However, those most likely to vote on election day showed a few interesting differences from those not deemed likely to vote. In both March and October 2000, likely voters were more apt to assign "a lot" of blame for unethical campaign practices to interest groups and professional consultants than were unlikely voters. In the October study, nearly 43 percent of likely voters assigned "a lot" of blame to interest groups, whereas only about 31 percent of those less likely to vote did the same. One possible explanation for this is the higher level of engagement among likely voters. It may be that likely voters, because they are more tuned into the campaign, notice who is responsible for those things they find distasteful. Likely voters, for example, may have picked up on the fact that it was the NAACP National Voter Fund that ran the James Byrd ad against Bush in 2000. They may also be more likely to place blame at the feet of consultants because, having paid more attention to the campaign and the players involved, they have a clearer sense of who is responsible for what.

The data presented here raise the question, What happens as a result of such activities? We have some evidence that the general public sees these kinds of activities as damaging not only to our campaigns but to the democratic process in general. In the survey conducted by the Institute for Global Ethics noted earlier, respondents conveyed their concerns about today's campaigns. The survey finds that "most Americans (53 percent) think campaign 'values and ethics' have gotten worse in the last twenty years, with a quarter (27 percent) saying they have gotten much worse."[64] In addition, according to the IGE study, the electorate is also concerned about the performance of a candidate while in office—72 percent of Americans said that they were "very concerned" about candidates saying one thing and doing another once elected; and a solid majority—59 percent—said that all or most candidates deliberately twist the truth during campaigns. Moreover, 39 percent reported that they believed all or most candidates deliberately lie to voters. This adds up to an electorate that does not have confidence in the government that an election produces. The electorate also has a lower sense of political efficacy today, and it does not show high levels of trust of government (strong majorities of the general public in the same survey reported that they believe they can trust government to do the right thing only some of the time).[65]

In terms of measuring the tangible effects from the perspective of the public, we can examine further a selection of the practices outlined in this chapter. We know that negative and sometimes hurtful information about a candidate in the context of trying to "push" a potential voter away from supporting that candidate can upset the public (witness the phone call 14-year-old Chris Duren received during the 2000 Republican presidential primary campaign). The push poll may work in ways never intended by those who use the tactic: it is exactly the kind of action that pushes people away from politics and participation in the democratic process.

Now consider a practice that the public neither endorsed nor wholeheartedly condemned: taking statements that are true and using them out of context. Sizable portions of the electorate in all three waves failed to classify this as an unacceptable practice. Campaign communications that use statements taken out of context—for example, Senator Kerry voted 350 times for higher taxes and supported a fifty-cent-a-gallon gas tax; President Bush favors sending jobs overseas while losing "3 million jobs" in the United States—can be very effective. The National Annenberg Election Survey finds evidence that many in the electorate buy into these out-of-context statements. The Annenberg poll, conducted in the eighteen most competitive battleground states where the Bush and Kerry campaigns were showing commercials using these kinds of statements, finds that "61 percent of the public believe Bush 'favors sending American jobs overseas,' 56 percent believe Kerry 'voted for higher taxes 350 times,' and 72 percent say 3 million jobs have been lost in Bush's presidency"; in addition, "forty-six percent, including a majority of independents, agreed that 'John Kerry wants to raise gasoline taxes by 50 cents a gallon.'"[66] Furthermore, the survey finds that late in the campaign, after the Kerry campaign's ads about President Bush's alleged intention to reinstate the draft were aired, nearly one in three Americans, and about half of Americans aged 18 to 29, thought that Bush did want to restore the draft.[67] Careful investigations into those claims demonstrated that they were based on original statements that were at best taken out of context and at worst deliberate manipulations of the truth. In the end, the use of this tactic can lead to a misinformed electorate.

The political consultants we surveyed thought that one factor contributing to voter cynicism is the way money is raised in elections in the United States (see chapter 4). Other factors might also cause voter cynicism. Most relevant for our discussion here was the question of the impact of negative campaigning on voter cynicism. Consultants' views on this question were clear and consistent; as table 5-9 demonstrates, more than two-thirds of political consultants in 1998 thought that negative campaigning contributed a "great deal" or a "fair amount" to voter cynicism; in both 1999 and 2002, more than three-quarters of professional consultants said the same.

In our 1998 survey of the industry, we asked consultants if they thought the practice of "going negative" was itself unethical. Nearly unanimously, consultants responded that they believed going negative was not an unethical practice. A few anecdotes summarize the thoughts of many consultants:

> People say they hate negative advertising. But it works. They hate it and remember it at the same time. The problem with positive ads is that you have to run it again and again and again to make it stick. With negative, the poll numbers will move in three or four days."

> Voters will tell you in focus groups that they don't like negative ads, but they retain the information so much better than the positive ones. The point is: People like dirty laundry. Why do tabloids sell?

One of the professionals hired by Representative Dennis Moore for his 1998 congressional campaign elaborates on the ethics of going negative:

> There is no such thing as negative. You can only compare and contrast. . . . You can't get away with the sort of stuff that candidates

Table 5-9. *Consultants' Assessment of the Causes of Voter Cynicism*[a]

Practice and rating	1998	1999	2002
Negative campaigning			
A great deal	24.5	35.7	34.2
A fair amount	43.0	39.6	42.6
Not very much	29.5	19.3	20.8
None at all	3.0	5.4	2.5
N	200	502	202
Politicians' poor performance in office			
A great deal	27.1	39.1	40.6
A fair amount	46.7	40.1	38.1
Not very much	26.1	17.4	18.8
None at all	0.0	3.4	2.5
N	199	501	202
The way the news media report on politics			
A great deal	63.8	55.6	64.0
A fair amount	27.6	36.5	30.0
Not very much	7.0	7.4	4.4
None at all	1.5	0.6	1.5
N	199	502	203
The way money is raised in campaigns			
A great deal	24.6	33.8	31.9
A fair amount	36.7	32.2	36.8
Not very much	32.7	24.4	21.6
None at all	6.0	9.6	9.8
N	199	500	204

a. The question asked was, "Thinking now about voter cynicism and what causes it, please tell me whether you think each of the following has a great deal of impact in causing voter cynicism, a fair amount, not very much, or none at all."

and campaigns used to get away with, frankly, now. The public won't stand for it. It has to be based in fact. I mean you can't just go out and say, "Don't vote for the other guy because he's not very nice at all." You have to base your characterization of your opponent on the facts. And to say that it's negative to point out votes that your opponent cast that you disagree with, I think, does the whole process of running a campaign a disservice.[68]

This produces an intriguing paradox. Consultants report that they do not think "going negative" is unethical, yet they report with almost the

Table 5-10. *Consultants' Assessment of the Influence of*
Negative Campaigning on Voter Cynicism, by Party Affiliation[a]
Percent

Respondents	A great deal	A fair amount	Not very much	None at all	N
Consultants, 1999					
Republicans	29.7	39.5	24.3	6.5	185
Democrats	38.1	41.3	16.6	4.0	247
Independents	43.3	35.0	13.3	8.3	60
Consultants, 2002					
Republicans	18.3	49.3	26.8	5.6	71
Democrats	36.8	41.5	20.8	0.9	106
Independents	63.6	31.8	4.5	0.0	22

a. The question asked was, "Thinking now about voter cynicism and what causes it, please tell me whether you think negative campaigning has a great deal of impact in causing voter cynicism, a fair amount, not very much, or none at all."

same frequency that "negative campaigning" causes voter cynicism. What we may be seeing here is a two-pronged way of thinking about elections. On the one hand, when political consultants ask themselves, "What do I need to do to win?" they may decide that "going negative" is not unethical. On the other hand, when they take a step back and examine the broader picture it is also clear to them that the practice can increase cynicism among voters.[69] When push comes to shove, however, a consultant's job is to help his or her client get elected, and that goal is likely to win out in the end.

There were clear and large differences across partisan consultants in how much they thought negative campaigns contributed to cynicism in the electorate, especially in 2002. In 1999 more independents than Republicans or Democrats said that negative campaigning was a major cause of voter cynicism; in 2002 more than 63 percent of independents said the same, nearly twice the number of Democrats and nearly four times the number of Republicans (see table 5-10). Independents in the consulting business are likely to mirror independents among the general public—they simply are fed up with what they view as harmful elements of campaigns.

To put these findings into some perspective, we offer some data on other factors that might contribute to voter cynicism: politicians' performance in office and media coverage of politics. We have seen that consultants think the way money is raised and negative campaigning both contribute to voter cynicism: when consultants consider the topic of voter cynicism, they do lay blame at the feet of their own industry. However, their assessment of these factors as important causes of cynicism pales in comparison with how they view elected public officials and the media. As reported in chapter 3, approximately half of all the consultants we surveyed expressed regret over helping to elect at least one candidate during their careers, because they felt the candidate did not keep his or her campaign promises, engaged in unethical practices, or simply was not qualified for the position to which he or she was elected. All three of these factors relate to a politician's performance in office. We asked consultants what impact they thought politicians' poor performance in office might have in causing voter cynicism. Political consultants reported that politicians' performance in office, even more than negative campaigning and the way money is raised, contributed to voter cynicism. As table 5-9 shows, almost 80 percent of political consultants in both 1999 and 2002 thought that politicians' poor performance in office contributed a great deal or a fair amount to voter cynicism; in 1998 the percentage was only slightly less (almost 74 percent). Political consultants have a fairly negative view of journalists, particularly broadcast journalists, as reported in chapter 2. Consequently, it is not surprising that political consultants overwhelmingly cited the way the news media report on politics as contributing a great deal or a fair amount to voter cynicism. The media's coverage of politics was the number-one reason cited by consultants for voter cynicism in America today (see table 5-9). More than 90 percent of political consultants in all three surveys, 1998, 1999, and 2002, thought that the way the media covers politics contributes a great deal or a fair amount to voter cynicism.

Consultants' critics and those who take a more cynical look at the process might say, "Well, of course consultants place the blame at the feet of others." We, on the other hand, do not believe this to be self-serving on the part of consultants. In all our experiences, and as can be seen from other data presented here, consultants have been willing to take stock of their performance in campaigns in an honest manner. We do not believe that the consultants who participated in our studies were giving us anything but a candid assessment about what drives voters to become cynical about the process.

A Solution? Mandating Good Behavior

Given the negative aspects of our present system of campaigning, what can be done to move our electoral process toward healthier campaigns? The First Amendment to the Constitution forbids any sort of restrictions on speech during a campaign. Candidates, parties, and interest groups have the protected constitutional right to say just about whatever they like during a campaign, and the American electorate will just have to live with that. The ads aired by the Swift Boat Veterans for Truth during the 2004 campaign are a fine example of the impact the First Amendment has had on our campaigns. The Swift Boat Veterans questioned Senator Kerry's service, said he lied to get his medals in Vietnam, and challenged his patriotism for testifying before a U.S. Senate committee about the atrocities he had seen while serving. It is difficult to quarrel with the feelings of the Swift Boat Veterans, who felt betrayed by Kerry's testimony (just as it is difficult to quarrel with the feelings of Rene Mullings, James Byrd's daughter, who was part of the NAACP's ad against Bush in 2000), but the ad about Kerry's medals simply could not be backed up by evidence. If restrictions on this type of speech are not possible (and we are not arguing that they ever should be), what else can be done to raise the debate to ensure high-quality, information-rich campaigns?

One idea that has been floated, and even tested, is the use of codes of conduct, or codes of ethics, for campaigners and candidates. In our research for this book, we explored the use of such codes and whether they would limit some of the unethical activity that occurs in campaigns. We asked professional consultants and party operatives about codes of conduct for campaigners; we asked the general public about their views on codes of conduct for candidates during a race, and whether they would be more or less likely to vote for a candidate who refused to sign a code of conduct.

First, consider codes of ethics for those running campaigns—most notably, professional political consultants. It is a little-known fact—even among students of campaigns, but less so among the general population—that the national organization of political consultants, the American Association of Political Consultants (AAPC), has a code of ethics already in place that it requires its members to sign every year (see box 5-1). This is good news; however, there are a few important caveats. First, not all political consultants are members of the AAPC; we estimate

---

Box 5-1. *The American Association of Political Consultants'*
Code of Ethics

As a member of the American Association of Political Consultants, I believe there are certain standards of practice which I must maintain. I, therefore, pledge to adhere to the following Code of Professional Ethics:

— I will not indulge in any activity which would corrupt or degrade the practice of political consulting.

— I will treat my colleagues and clients with respect and never intentionally injure their professional or personal reputations.

— I will respect the confidence of my clients and not reveal confidential or privileged information obtained during our professional relationship.

— I will use no appeal to voters which is based on racism, sexism, religious intolerance or any form of unlawful discrimination and will condemn those who use such practices. In turn, I will work for equal voting rights and privileges for all citizens.

— I will refrain from false or misleading attacks on an opponent or member of his or her family and will do everything in my power to prevent others from using such tactics.

— I will document accurately and fully any criticism of an opponent or his or her record.

— I will be honest in my relationship with the news media and candidly answer questions when I have the authority to do so.

— I will use any funds I receive from my clients, or on behalf of my clients, only for those purposes invoiced in writing.

— I will not support any individual or organization which resorts to practices forbidden by this code.

Source: American Association of Political Consultants, "Code of Ethics" (www. theaapc.org/content/aboutus/codeofethics.asp [July 15, 2004]).

---

the figure to be less than half of all consultants. Therefore, the existing code is not signed on a yearly basis by every political consultant. Second, the enforcement of the existing code is rather weak: only recently did the AAPC actually begin to censure its members for violations of the code.

Our surveys of consultants and party elites bear out these problems with the current AAPC code of ethics. Although most of the consultants we interviewed were familiar with the code, a sizable proportion had no idea it existed. In all three of our measurements, more than 60 percent of all consultants were familiar with the AAPC code of ethics; in fact, that share increased between the time of the first survey in 1998 (64 percent) and the second and third (roughly 75 percent were familiar with the code

Table 5-11. *Consultants' Assessment of the Effectiveness of the AAPC Code of Ethics*[a]

Percent

Rating	1998	1999	2002
A great deal	0.0	1.1	1.2
A fair amount	12.6	14.9	8.6
Not very much	48.7	43.4	54.9
None at all	38.7	40.6	35.2
N	119	362	162

a. The question asked was, "How much of an effect do you think the AAPC (American Association of Political Consultants) code has on the behavior of political consultants?" This question was asked only of those consultants who said that they were familiar with the AAPC code.

in both 1999 and 2002). More important, there was widespread support among political consultants for a code of ethics for professionals who work on campaigns. Eighty-one percent of the consultants surveyed in 1998 said they supported a code, nearly 70 percent in 1999, and almost six out of ten consultants in 2002.[70] There was great consensus among Democrats, Republicans, and independents in support of the code. In addition, almost two-thirds of the consultants surveyed thought that a professional association should be able to censure those campaign professionals who violate a code of ethics.[71] Party elites agreed that there should be some kind of code of ethics for professional campaigners (63 percent said there should be a code, and 12 percent noted that one already existed) and that the profession's main organization should be able to censure those who violate the code (nearly 70 percent supported censure).

However, when asked how much effect the AAPC code of ethics has on the behavior of political consultants, an overwhelming percentage of the consultants surveyed—87 percent in 1998, 84 percent in 1999, and 90 percent in 2002—agreed that the code had little or no effect on consultant behavior (see table 5-11). This probably reflects the enforcement problems associated with the current AAPC code.[72]

Political consultants are supportive of a code of ethics, yet they do not really think the present code is effective in influencing consultant behavior. The general public similarly sends mixed messages as to the importance of a code of ethics stipulating acceptable campaign behavior. In our

Table 5-12. *The Public's Support for a Code of Conduct for Candidates and Its Effect on Their Vote Choice*
Percent

Factor	March 2000	October 2000
Support for code[a]		
Favor	79.1	78.5
Oppose	20.9	21.5
N	892	905
Impact on vote choice[b]		
Less likely	46.9	42.5
More likely	9.9	10.6
Wouldn't make any difference	43.3	46.9
N	943	944

a. The question asked was, "In some places, candidates are asked to sign a code of campaign ethics. Do you favor or oppose candidates' signing such a code?"

b. The question asked was, "Would you be less likely or more likely to vote for a candidate that refused to sign such a code, or wouldn't it make any difference?"

surveys, more than three-quarters of the public (nearly 80 percent in both March and October 2000) said they supported the idea of a code of ethics for candidates (see table 5-12). In both surveys slightly more Republicans and independents (more than 80 percent of each) than Democrats (just over 70 percent) expressed a desire to see candidates sign a code, but as in other cases, the important point here is the high proportion of Americans supporting the idea of candidate codes. Although there was no difference by propensity to vote in March 2000, likely voters in October were more prone to say that they favored a code of ethics for candidates (83 percent) than their nonvoting counterparts, though 74 percent of those deemed unlikely to vote reported the same.

However, when we asked if they would be more or less likely to vote for a candidate who refused to sign a code of ethics, the public was equally divided in how important having signed a code would be. Approximately 45 percent said they would be less likely to vote for a candidate who refused to sign a code, and roughly the same percentage said it would make no difference in their vote (see table 5-12). In October 2000, again more Republicans and independents (49.5 and 46.0 percent, respectively) than Democrats (35.2 percent) said they would be less likely to vote for a candidate who did not sign such a code.

Codes of this sort have actually been implemented in a few select past campaigns. The Institute for Global Ethics has tried to encourage candidates to adopt codes of ethics in their campaigns. The institute's efforts have not involved mandated codes of conduct; rather, the candidates in a particular race crafted the wording of a code and then pledged to uphold that code. The idea behind the IGE's work was not to impose a code of conduct on candidates from the outside but to have the participants agree on the language and engage with voters to work toward a higher standard of conduct. The IGE worked with candidates in select states between 1996 and 2002 to develop codes that emphasized "honesty, fairness, respect, responsibility, and compassion."[73]

The success of the IGE-sponsored codes is difficult to judge. From our own survey work, we know that voters are in favor of some kind of code of conduct but are not likely to punish candidates who do not sign. Once signed, the codes are difficult to enforce: although it could be damaging to their campaigns, there are no formal repercussions to candidates who violate the codes. A broader difficulty is getting candidates to sign in the first place. Few candidates are interested in a code that is likely to be vague, open to interpretation in terms of its conditions, and therefore potentially limiting of the kinds of activities they could engage in during the campaign. The code initiative begun by IGE had limited success mainly because some candidates who participated did not see the project through to the end; they either showed initial interest but did not follow through to develop a code, or did not sign a code they had taken a part in developing, or did not sign the code until late in the campaign. This illustrates the difficulties with a code of conduct—either a candidate-composed code or one developed by an organization, such as the AAPC code of ethics. If a change in behavior from candidates' campaigns is going to come about, citizens must get involved and start to demand the kind of behavior they want to see from those involved in our political campaigns.

CHAPTER 6

The Health of
U.S. Campaigning
after the 2004 Election

From the Howard Dean scream to the Swift Boat Veterans for Truth ads to the references to Vice President Cheney's daughter's sexual orientation, the 2004 election provided many opportunities to examine the health of American campaigns. In the preceding chapters we have looked at major players both inside and outside American campaigns to assess their views of campaign successes and problems of the past and the difficulties campaigns face at the beginning of the twenty-first century. Throughout this book, we have combined empirical data we have collected on these major electoral actors with examples from recent campaigns to illustrate both aspects of our system of campaigning that are working well and those that may be in need of help. As noted in chapter 1, the 2004 election season included elements that made it both the best of campaigns and the worst of campaigns. That election was, we believe, a microcosm of our system in general. Some portions of the system are working well; others are not. In this conclusion, through the lens of the 2004 campaign, we offer our assessment of what seems to be functioning well and where there seems to be some trouble.

What Is Healthy about Our Campaigns

After our examination presented in the previous chapters, we are convinced that our system of campaigning is not completely broken. Critics of modern campaigns would have us believe, among other things, that parties have become irrelevant because of campaign professionals and outside interests and that the electorate is uninterested and incapable of taking an active role in politics. We believe these claims are overstated and that there are several positive signs in regard to the health of American campaigning.

Campaigns Matter

We think that in addition to detailing some specific aspects that we think are working well in our system of campaigning, it is also important to illustrate a larger point. Campaigns matter. We agree with the conclusions reached by Thomas Holbrook in his important work, *Do Campaigns Matter?*[1] More specifically, for our purposes here, the way campaigns are waged matters. Aspects of campaigns and candidates' campaign organizations can drive the outcome of elections. Factors such as the campaign message, how it is developed, how it is communicated, and how it resonates with potential voters, as well as the individuals creating and communicating the message, are all crucial to the success of a campaign. Strategic decisionmaking within a campaign and how the campaign is prosecuted can make a significant difference in the eventual outcome of an election. This is important in an adversarial system, in which each campaign is expected to make its own case to the electorate. The 2004 campaign was a clear indicator that this system is functioning—neither George W. Bush nor John Kerry expected his opponent to make his case for him. In the end, the organization and tactics of the Bush and Kerry campaigns helped determine the outcome of the 2004 election.

Once John Kerry had captured the Democratic Party's nomination in early March 2004, scholars and pundits alike agreed there were competing dynamics in the 2004 presidential election. One dynamic—the difficulties plaguing the war effort in Iraq and the weak U.S. economy— favored the challenger and the Democratic Party, whereas the other— Bush was a wartime president dealing with the issues of domestic security and the war on terrorism—favored Bush and the Republicans. In other words, an argument could have been made that the 2004 election was Kerry's to lose—while the nation was at war and incumbents tend to benefit from this, the war was not going well, and the economy had not rebounded as quickly as had been hoped. On the other hand, Bush was in a strong position because of his advantage on the security issue and by virtue of being commander in chief during a conflict. Most observers agreed at the time that if the election were fought on the success of the war in Iraq and Bush's handling of the economy, Kerry would be the likely winner, but if the election were more generally about the war on terrorism and security at home in a time of war, Bush had a good chance of being reelected. The candidate who did a better job of making his case to and connecting with the American public would win the race.

The 2004 presidential election illustrated the roles of key campaign actors discussed in preceding chapters. As noted in chapter 2, who controls today's campaigns is an important topic to consider when assessing the health of our system, and it was at the heart of the 2004 election in a number of respects. The campaigns of Bush and Kerry could not have been more different in several ways. The two campaigns differed in the individuals who were leading their respective charges through the campaign. They differed in their approaches to communicating to the electorate. They differed, of course, in their stands on the issues. Finally, however, there was a similarity between the two—in how each candidate's respective party organization got involved in the individual campaigns and what they contributed to it.

Most observers agree that Bush ran the better campaign in 2004. His campaign team did a better job of connecting with the voters and fighting the battle on the issues that advantaged its candidate. Exit polls conducted on election day illustrate this clearly. Fifty-one percent of those interviewed on election day 2004 said that they supported the war in Iraq, and 54 percent said they were safer from terrorism than they had been four years ago. More important, 55 percent said that the war in Iraq was part of the larger war on terror. The Kerry campaign had hoped to tap the opposite sentiments. As these exit poll results indicate, it was the Bush campaign team that successfully framed the election on its terms.[2]

Part of the reason for Bush's success lies in who was at the helm of the campaign and how they executed the strategy developed before the campaign even started. The Bush and Kerry campaigns both had well-respected teams of political consultants, who had successfully and collectively won elections in the past. The difference was in the organization and management of the two campaigns. The Bush campaign was managed by a seasoned group of campaign professionals who had worked with Bush since his days as governor of Texas. Karl Rove, the lead strategist, had known Bush for thirty years.[3] Karen Hughes, senior strategist, also knew Bush from his days as Texas governor. Mark McKinnon, Bush's media consultant in 2000, reprised that role in 2004. Other key campaign staff and consultants—including campaign manager Ken Mehlman and pollster Matthew Dowd—also had worked with Bush on past campaigns. In short, Bush's team comprised experienced professionals who had worked with the president and with one another in the past.

The Kerry campaign, on the other hand, was guided by three different campaign teams in trying to create an effective strategy and message. When his primary campaign was failing in the fall of 2003, Kerry fired his campaign manager, Jim Jordan, and brought on board Mary Beth Cahill, Senator Edward Kennedy's chief of staff. After a disastrous month in August 2004, Kerry shuffled his campaign team once again, only two months before the election, bringing in veterans of Bill Clinton's presidential campaigns—Joe Lockhart and Mike McCurry—as well as longtime Massachusetts political operative John Sasso. Although Lockhart, McCurry, and Sasso were given credit for rejuvenating the Kerry campaign in the last two months before the election, there continued to be tension between the new campaign operatives and those who had been with Kerry through the primaries and the summer. Unlike Bush's campaign, Kerry's had no consistent tight control.

The issue of control is central to our point that campaigns matter. We believe that this control had an important effect on a more important aspect of the campaign. Because the core group of advisers on the Bush team was solid from the beginning, it was in a much better position to develop and carry out a plan to win the election. The Bush team was in place well before the campaign began, whereas Kerry's team was in flux throughout the primary and general election season. The successive, and different, Kerry campaign teams found it difficult to agree on one message—let alone communicate it—that would carry them through the campaign. The Bush campaign, in contrast, "was run to ensure that every dollar went to fulfill core strategies, that resources were allocated to capitalize on Bush's strengths and Kerry's vulnerabilities, and that the money necessary to finance research, technological advance, television and the ground war was available when needed."[4] This has important implications for the notion of control of campaigns, as well as the role of professional political consultants.

Although both were run by some of the most respected political pros in the country, the two campaigns could not have been more different in how they were run and were managed. The *Washington Post,* in July of 2004, illustrated this difference clearly:

From a tight-knit group of experienced advisers, John F. Kerry's presidential campaign has grown exponentially in recent months to include a cast of literally thousands, making it difficult to manage an increasingly unwieldy policy apparatus. The campaign now includes 37 separate domestic policy councils and 27 foreign policy groups, each with scores of members. The justice policy task force alone includes 195 members. The environmental group is roughly the same size, as is the agriculture and rural development council. Kerry counts more than 200 economists as his advisers. In contrast, President Bush's campaign policy shop is a no frills affair. . . . Fewer than a dozen outside task forces, with five to 10 members, . . . help out on education, veterans' issues, the economy, and energy, environment and natural resources.

The result for the Kerry campaign, the *Post* article continues, was a "muddled campaign message."[5]

The Kerry campaign struggled with this muddled message for much of the campaign—its revolving door of advisers being only one reason. From the official announcement of his candidacy in late 2003 to the primary campaign to the summer months and the Democratic National Convention and finally to the general election campaign, the Kerry team struggled to find its message. In April 2004, after Kerry had wrapped up the nomination, one of the consultants to the campaign, Michael Donilon, noted that "the essence of the upcoming campaign message" would be biographical and focus on his life story, including his service during the Vietnam War.[6] All well and good; but the campaign should already have settled on its message long before then.

During the summer, as the Kerry campaign floundered from message to message, the Bush campaign focused on security at home and the more general war on terrorism. For instance, as pointed out in chapter 1, Kerry's service during the Vietnam War was prominently on display during the Democratic National Convention, when the goal was to reintroduce the candidate to the public and to convey the message that Kerry would "make America stronger at home and respected in the world." This message, too, was biographical. By this point in the campaign, the Kerry team should already have accomplished the task of telling Americans who John Kerry was. Clearly, the Kerry campaign, in having to introduce their candidate to the American public during the late summer, never accomplished what it had intended.

Moreover, when former Clinton White House spokesman Joe Lockhart was added to the staff in September 2004, he was brought in to oversee "Kerry's efforts to shape his themes against Bush and sharpen his defense against Republican attacks."[7] If the campaign had not found its message by Labor Day, however, it was never going to find it. This was certainly a recurring theme in the Kerry camp. As early as November 2003, observers were asking, "What, exactly, is Kerry's message? What is the essence of his campaign?"[8] Unfortunately for John Kerry, his campaign team—all three of his campaign teams—could never figure this out. In stark contrast, the Bush campaign "kept the same campaign team and, despite shifting public opinion, the same message from the beginning."[9]

The contrasting models of campaign organization drive home an important point. Professional political consultants are heavily involved in modern campaigns at the federal level and can affect the outcome of a race (see chapter 2). Although some may argue that this is a sign of problems for our system of campaigning because it means that candidates are no longer in control of their campaigns, we would argue otherwise for three reasons. First, candidates have never really been in control of their campaigns. During the golden age of parties, the party elite controlled every aspect of the campaign. As the parties began to lose their grip on electioneering, candidates found that they needed help running campaigns, so they turned to those who had the skills and knowledge to provide the services they demanded.

Second, and more important, even if consultants' control in individual campaigns is high, it is not universal, and simply hiring a consultant does not in itself result in victory. The Kerry campaign in 2004 clearly illustrates this. Despite the high-powered and well-known consultants among his staff, "people both inside and outside the Kerry brain trust say Kerry himself ultimately bears the responsibility for his sometimes fuzzy message. But they also suggest that he has not always been well served by his multiple advisers and consultants."[10] Moreover, "Kerry has a reputation of relying heavily, some say too heavily, on the advice of strategists, pollsters, and close advisers and friends to guide his campaigns."[11] Consultants cannot get anyone elected; they can only advise on what they see to be the strategy most likely to bring success. Candidates bear ultimate responsibility for guiding their own ships and communicating the message developed by the consultants.

Third, we do not believe the central role consultants play in most campaigns today is a negative aspect of the system because parties still do play a significant role; 2004 may be the best example yet of the division of labor and partnership developed by consultants and parties. This aspect of our system, we believe, is functioning well.

Parties Still Matter

We learned lessons about the role of parties in presidential races during 2004 on two main fronts—fundraising and mobilization efforts—both of which were key to the final outcome of the race. Both the Democratic and Republican Parties, through their fundraising efforts, played key roles in the campaign; and they were as successful as they had ever been in this area, raising $1.2 billion.[12] However, a new dimension was added to the party fundraising story in 2004: it was the first election contested under the Bipartisan Campaign Reform Act (BCRA) of 2002. When the BCRA was passed, there was considerable speculation as to what effect it would have on the role of political parties in American elections. The Republican Party committees had always raised more hard money than their Democratic counterparts, but in both the 2000 and 2002 elections, the Democratic Party committees reached parity with the Republicans in soft-money receipts. With the BCRA's ban on soft money at the national party level, the ability of the Democratic Party committees to compete with the Republicans was called into question.

Following the 2000 election, the Democratic National Committee realized that it needed to revamp its fundraising program. When Terry McAuliffe took over as chair in 2001, there was no voter file at the committee, and most of the committee's direct mail donors were 65 years and older. During the 2001–02 election cycle, the Democratic National Committee focused its efforts on building its direct mail and Internet solicitation programs, and by the 2004 election cycle, it had significantly expanded its contribution bases from both sources.[13] The committee recruited 2.3 million new direct mail donors in 2004 and received 4 million contributions online.[14]

With the BCRA's prohibition on large soft-money donations, the parties had to change their fundraising strategies. Both the Democratic and Republican National Committees began to focus more on direct mail, telemarketing, and Internet fundraising, particularly targeting small donors, as the Dean campaign had done, and to use their large-donor programs to take advantage of the BCRA's increase in the amount of hard money individuals could donate to the party committees. As Anthony Corrado points out, the partisan political environment surrounding the 2004 election created a favorable atmosphere for party fundraising. In large part as a result of the increase in new donors, both party committees raised more hard money in 2004 than they had raised in hard and soft money combined in either 2000 or 2002.[15] At least financially, the Democratic and Republican Parties continued to be strong players in the 2004 elections. The parties' financial strength played a key role in the air and ground wars in the 2004 presidential election.

Parties also left their mark on the campaign through their efforts to get voters to the polls. Traditionally, the assumption has been that the Republican Party, and Republican candidates, have more money to spend, so the Republicans spend more money on paid advertising, whereas the Democratic Party, and Democratic candidates, rely more on volunteer field programs to provide a margin of victory. In the 2004 election the opposite was the case. The Democratic Party and the Kerry campaign spent $80 million on the so-called ground war; the Republican National Committee and the Bush campaign spent $125 million on their field and get-out-the-vote (GOTV) efforts. Whereas the Democratic Party spent $128 million on independent expenditures from August 1 to election day, the Republican Party spent just $18 million over the same time period.[16] In the 2004 election, as in 2002, the two major political parties reached parity with respect to funding of GOTV operations. While the amounts raised and spent were not exactly equal, both parties agreed that they had ample resources to meet their vote goals—the Democrats, in part, because of the help of 527 organizations.

In both the Bush and Kerry campaigns it was the political consultants who provided the strategic guidance to the campaigns, did the polling, created the television ads, and designed the direct mail pieces. The party organizations, however, in addition to their massive fundraising efforts, provided much of the personnel for the get-out-the-vote operations (more so for the Bush campaign than the Kerry campaign). This generally reflects the partnership between consultants and parties noted in chapter 2: consultants have assumed responsibility for the tasks that are centered on message creation and delivery, and parties focus on tasks that are more heavily reliant on staff and time resources.

However, the division of labor between the campaign team and the party organization was more seamless on the Republican side than on the

Democratic side. In addition to the core of the Bush team—Rove, Mehlman, Hughes, McKinnon, and Dowd—having been together for four years, they were also working with a party chair who had been handpicked by Bush. The Democrats, not knowing who their candidate would be until the election year, did not have those same luxuries. In addition, their party chair, Terry McAuliffe, though a fabulous fundraiser, was a holdover from the Clinton years and may not have been fully in step with the consultants running the Kerry campaign (whichever team was in place). Because of these differences, the Bush team had the advantage of planning a reelection campaign for four years and developing and road testing its GOTV plan in 2001 and 2002. As a result, the Bush and Kerry campaigns had different relationships with their respective party organizations.

Mobilization was also key to voter turnout. Steven Rosenstone and John Mark Hansen argue in *Mobilization, Participation, and Democracy in America* that the decline in mobilization efforts in the 1970s and 1980s explains more than half of the decline in turnout over that period.[17] More recently, Donald Green and Alan Gerber, in studies aimed at finding ways to increase turnout, argue that "the more personal the interaction between campaign and potential voter, the more it raises a person's chance of voting." They conclude that "door-to-door canvassing by friends and neighbors is the gold-standard mobilization tactic."[18] This was exactly the technique employed by the Republican Party, with great success; the same cannot be said, however, for the Democrats. The results were predictable, given Green and Gerber's findings.

The Republican Party focused on a large volunteer effort—a neighbor-to-neighbor strategy in which local Republicans encouraged their friends and neighbors to vote for President Bush. The Democrats did have some of their traditional supporters, such as organized labor, active in neighbor-to-neighbor GOTV efforts, but they mainly relied on 527 organizations such as America Coming Together to bring Kerry voters to the polls.[19] In the words of Jack Oliver, the national finance vice chair for the Republican National Committee's Victory 2004 (the committee's effort to elect Republicans up and down the ticket), "the Democrats chose to outsource their ground game to 527s."[20] Howard Dean has come to the same conclusion, arguing that though the Democrats did a sound job of turning out voters, the GOP did better: "We ran the best grassroots campaign that I've seen in my lifetime. They ran a better one. Why? Because we sent

14,000 people into Ohio from elsewhere. They had 14,000 people from Ohio talking to their neighbors, and that's how you can win."[21]

The effects of this difference in strategy were felt on two levels. First, as Green and Gerber illustrate empirically, voter contact is more effective when it connects people who are familiar with one another. The *Washington Post* relayed the experience of one America Coming Together worker, who was paid eight dollars an hour to canvass for the group in Ohio: "At many houses, people poked their heads out groggily, like hibernating bears, and mumbled sullenly that they were not interested in registering to vote or answering his questions about 'what two national issues matter most to you.'"[22] Second, the new BCRA provisions also made it more difficult for outside groups to be as effective as the GOP effort. Part of the reason that the Democrats' outsourcing of their GOTV efforts did not work as well as planned was that the new environment created by the BCRA did not allow coordination between the groups—America Coming Together, for example—and the Kerry campaign. This "left them with a message out of harmony with the Kerry campaign." Although both parties seemed satisfied that they had met their vote goals, the Republican Party argued that their focus on local, volunteer activists was more effective than the Democratic Party's largely outsourced and paid GOTV effort. At the end of the day, they were proved right; even Terry McAuliffe later admitted that Republicans "were much more sophisticated in their message delivery."[23]

The Republican Party not only expanded its GOTV operations, it also targeted potential Bush voters through unprecedented voter research. The Republican National Committee's mobilization tactics are best described by Matthew Dowd, the pollster for the Bush campaign, who directed much of what the Republican National Committee did:

Republican firms . . . delved into commercial databases that pinpointed consumer buying patterns and television-watching habits to unearth such information as Coors beer and bourbon drinkers skewing Republican, brandy and cognac drinkers tilting Democratic; college football TV viewers were more Republican than those who watched professional football; viewers of Fox News were overwhelmingly committed to vote for Bush; homes with telephone caller ID tended to be Republican; people interested in gambling, fashion, and theater tended to be Democratic.

Surveys of people on these consumer data lists were then used to determine "anger points" (late-term abortion, trial lawyer fees, estate taxes) that coincided with the Bush agenda for as many as 32 categories of voters, each identifiable by income, magazine subscriptions, favorite television shows and other "flags." Merging this data, in turn, enabled those running direct mail, precinct walking and phone bank programs to target each voter with a tailored message.[24]

Moreover, Karl Rove, building on the success of the 72-Hour Project in 2002 (see chapter 3), used the resources of the Republican Party to identify, target, and mobilize likely Bush supporters. Based on the assumption of an extremely polarized electorate, as a result of the 2000 election and the war in Iraq, the Republican Party invested its resources not on undecided voters, as it had in the past, but on voters "inclined to vote for Bush, but who were either unregistered or who often failed to vote—'soft' Republicans." Estimates are that the Republican Party spent about $125 million on this ground war in 2003 and 2004. While the Republicans were targeting likely voters in 2003 and early 2004, the Democratic Party was trying to coalesce around a nominee. Comparing the Democratic and Republican Parties' ground games, one Democrat involved in the party's get-out-the-vote effort said the Republicans "did a lot of stuff really well. They were ahead of us. . . . They had a strategy set by the beginning that they were going to live and die by. And we didn't."[25]

The Bush campaign also perceived another dynamic in the 2004 election, one that was largely ignored by both the Kerry campaign and the media until after the election. Although the issues at the national level were the economy and jobs, the war in Iraq, and the war on terror, state initiatives were also driving voter attention to the election. The most controversial of these state propositions were initiatives to ban gay marriage. Gay marriage initiatives were on the ballot in eleven states in 2004, including the key battleground states of Ohio and Michigan; Karl Rove and the GOP understood that evangelical Christians, a key Republican voting bloc, could be mobilized to vote around this issue, and the Republican Party mounted an extensive ground effort to turn out these voters. In fact, turning out evangelicals in 2004 was one of the main pillars of Rove's strategy, developed soon after President Bush was sworn into office in 2001. This plan made the difference in the end. Although hundreds of millions of dollars were spent on television ads over the course of the campaign, it was the mobilization of voters that made the key difference in the final few battleground states.

The parties' fundraising and mobilization successes in 2004 illustrate that the political parties are part of a sound partnership with political consultants in the execution of campaigns. Each group of actors focuses on the aspects of electioneering that it is best equipped to provide to each candidate's campaign. In fact, party elites argue that this system works well for them and helps them achieve electoral success. Parties may not do as much as they once did in campaigns, or as much as some would like, but that does not mean that they are irrelevant. This is an important positive aspect of our system of campaigning.

Signs of Life in the Electorate

The successes of the parties and outside groups in getting voters to the polls (more people voted in 2004 than in any election in history) is linked to another important aspect of the 2004 election cycle that we also believe is a healthy sign in our campaigns. Some might argue that the 2004 campaign for the presidency began on December 12, 2000, when the United States Supreme Court, in its now-famous case *Bush* v. *Gore,* ordered that the manual recounting of ballots in Florida be stopped. The Supreme Court decision ensured that George W. Bush, who was ahead in the ballot count at that time, would get Florida's twenty-five electoral votes and thus a majority of the Electoral College vote. Democrats, who felt that Al Gore, the popular vote winner, had lost the election because of a series of ballot mishaps and missed opportunities, were determined to capture what they felt was their rightful claim on the presidency in 2004. Republicans were similarly determined to prove President Bush's legitimacy as president with a majority of both popular votes and Electoral College votes in 2004. Although the tragic events of September 11, 2001, momentarily suppressed the partisan rancor that followed the 2000 presidential election, the ferocity of partisans on both sides was not far from the surface of the American psyche and returned with a vengeance in 2004.

Despite the view of candidates, consultants, and journalists that the level of political information the American public possesses is rather low—a view shared by the public, in self-described evaluations—2004 seemed to illustrate a slight departure from this conventional wisdom in major ways. First, voters were activated by the candidates, parties, outside groups, and other factors to head to the polls. Turnout was at its highest point since 1968, and at many polling locations voters waited in long lines for more than an hour. This may have been owing, in part, to the importance that the electorate placed on the outcome of the election. Voters were clearly engaged with the 2004 presidential election. Although the campaigns, at least the Kerry campaign, focused on "undecided" voters, few voters, in fact, were undecided in 2004. Seventy-eight percent of voters had made up their minds about whom they would vote for more than a month before the election. In addition, record numbers of Americans watched the presidential and vice presidential debates, even though almost eight in ten voters had already chosen a candidate.

Second, more members of the public seemed to have more political information in 2004 than in previous election cycles. Measures of the public's interest and attention to the campaign showed an increase relative to past presidential election cycles.[26] Studies conducted during the summer of 2004 illustrate that the electorate was more interested in politics and the election during 2004 than in the summer of 2000 or 1996, nearly 60 percent of all Americans reporting that they had given a lot of thought to the election.[27] By late in the campaign, this was expressed by 71 percent of Americans surveyed.[28]

Although our data, which measure different electoral actors' attitudes about the public's information levels from past elections, suggest a more pessimistic view, we believe 2004 is a positive sign for our system of campaigning. The American public in 2004 showed that it is capable of becoming engaged and getting itself to the polls. Part of the reason for this increased interest was the candidates and their campaigns. In 2004 George W. Bush and John Kerry gave the public a clear choice in terms of the direction in which they would take the nation. The *Washington Post* has noted that "whatever mistakes . . . Bush and . . . Kerry may have made during the campaign, they did a spectacular job of energizing the electorate."[29] By April, nearly nine months before election day, the campaigns, the parties, and the outside groups on both sides had registered tens of thousands of new voters and recruited thousands as volunteers.[30] Is there room for improvement? Certainly. But is this a good sign? Absolutely. The key will be how the public responds in the 2006 midterm elections, the 2008 presidential election, and in future campaigns.

As noted in chapter 3, the political science literature and the actors around the campaign agree that the voters are able to make a sound choice on election day. Interestingly, the public does not seem to share this optimism. Although there is no direct evidence from the 2004 campaign that would further the argument that voters are able to make a sound decision on election day—half of the voters undoubtedly think they made a wise decision, but the other half almost certainly disagree[31]—we believe the prior evidence from scholarly study is an indication that Americans can form opinions and make sound decisions through whatever shortcuts they may use.

In 2004 the candidates gave the electorate clear choices on several important issues in the campaign—the economy, the war in Iraq, homeland security, and the war on terror. How these issues would play out during the campaign, and the relative importance of each issue, was less clear early in 2004. As the campaign unfolded in the summer and fall, voters became engaged with the issues and with the campaign. In the end, voters saw clear differences between the candidates and voted accordingly.[32] Those who saw the war on terror as the most important issue and who linked Iraq to the overall war on terror voted for President Bush; those voters who cited the economy and the war in Iraq as the most important issues and separated Iraq from the war on terror voted for Kerry. Another set of issues, what came to be called moral values, also surfaced in exit polls; in fact, more voters (22 percent) listed moral values as the most important issue of the campaign. Among those voters who reported moral values as their primary concern, 80 percent voted for President Bush, confirming the wisdom of Karl Rove's targeting strategy.

Finally, as we note in chapter 4, the candidates and parties raised a great deal of money during this election season. However, to an unprecedented extent these donations were made in small-dollar amounts ($200 or less), showing that Americans were willing to participate in the electoral system not only by voting in record numbers but also by contributing to the campaigns and parties. Both candidates raised roughly $78 million in small-dollar donations. This, we believe, is a strong sign of a more engaged electorate. Whether it carries through to future campaigns remains to be seen.

What Is Not Healthy about Our Campaigns

As we note early on in chapter 1, it would simply be naïve to argue that all is well with our system of campaigning. We certainly do not wish to make such an argument. Just as the 2004 campaign illustrated what is working well in our system, it can also illustrate more problematic areas.

Candidate Alternatives

Democratic partisans entered the 2004 election united around one purpose—the defeat of President Bush. When Howard Dean captured much of the energy of the party in 2003, Democrats wondered whether Dean, a former governor of Vermont with no foreign policy experience, could compete against Bush in a time of war. "Electability" became a key issue within the Democratic Party, and when the Dean campaign imploded in Iowa and New Hampshire, John Kerry, thanks to his Vietnam War record and nineteen-year Senate career, seemed eminently electable in a campaign against a wartime president. After his wins in Iowa and New Hampshire, Kerry quickly sewed up the Democratic nomination and became the presumptive nominee of his party.

Howard Dean's experience in the early portions of the primary campaign cast the question of candidate quality in a different light. Although his support was waning in Iowa during the last few days leading up to the caucuses, Dean lost, in part, because he was seen as unelectable. We believe this says a lot about the quality of candidates in our system and how a quality candidate is identified and chosen. Dean was responsible for motivating the Democratic base with his fierce criticism of President George W. Bush early in the campaign. Through his impassioned speeches about issues and his Republican rival, he also helped create the atmosphere that led to an excitement and enthusiasm among Democrats that continued until election day. Yet he was not chosen to represent the party because many Democrats did not think he could win in November.[33] Did the Democratic Party choose a qualified candidate to run against George W. Bush? Yes; John Kerry, a Vietnam War veteran and a longtime U.S. Senator, had a resume as good as anyone the Democrats could have chosen. However, if the choice of nominee is based, even partially, on the notion of electability, are Americans choosing from the best possible set of alternatives?

There are no truly objective data that can inform us as to the quality of a candidate; different people will apply different standards in reaching their own conclusions. One indication of this is the importance of a candidate's ability to raise money. A candidate who cannot motivate people to provide financial backing is not likely to have much of a chance of winning elective office. Moreover, candidates must be able to raise significant sums of money early on, to get their campaigns off to a good start and to signal to other elites that they are capable of waging a viable campaign. For lesser-known candidates, this is a nearly insurmountable challenge. Howard Dean was able to rise from relative obscurity to a position of prominence in the Democratic primaries, but he is certainly the exception to the rule. Most potential candidates who are not tied into a large fundraising network either realize that they cannot afford to wage a campaign and decide not to run or run anyway and get wiped out by their more cash-rich opponents. This is not purely a presidential problem, either. Many great potential candidates at the congressional level do not run for office because they cannot raise the requisite funds. A congressional candidate in a competitive race today who cannot raise $1 million is up against odds that are seemingly impossible to overcome. If those inside and outside campaigns are going to change the kind of candidates that are running for office in the United States, the quality of candidates needs to be judged on the merits of their ideas rather than exclusively on how electable they are.

Campaign Funding

Despite the efforts of the Bipartisan Campaign Reform Act to remove soft money from the electoral process, at least at the federal level, the 2004 election was the most expensive in history (the total cost of the presidential campaign in 2004 was roughly $2.2 billion).[34] Although the number of small contributions increased to record levels, the number of large contributions to both candidates and parties also increased. More important, because of the increase in the individual contribution limit from $1,000 to $2,000, the large-dollar contributions to candidates were larger.

The cost of campaigns continues to rise. The amount of money needed to pursue a bid for the White House will soon be so high—if it is not already—that it will prohibit many qualified candidates from running. As noted in chapter 4, Americans believe that campaigns are affected by the ways in which money is raised and spent. Large majorities (more than 80 percent) of the electorate we surveyed believe that good candidates choose not to run for public office because they are daunted by the amount of money needed for a campaign and that to have a chance of winning, candidates are sometimes forced to go against the public interest to support special interests who make campaign contributions. This is problematic on several levels. First, if good candidates are not running because of the amount of money it takes to run, Americans are not choosing from the best set of possible alternatives—which is consistent with our findings on the quality of candidates today. Second, this chilling effect on potential candidates may be related to the regrets expressed by political consultants and the electorate about having helped candidates get elected, either by working on their campaigns or voting for them on election day, as reported in chapter 3 of this book. If the choice of candidates were not so severely restricted by the need to raise large sums of money, perhaps these important electoral actors would be happier with the outcomes.

The status of the partial public funding system is another development in the 2004 presidential election that suggests a caution about the health of American campaigning in terms of the way campaigns are financed.[35] In 2004 both the Democratic and Republican nominees chose to privately fund their nomination campaigns, as did George W. Bush in 2000. Given the large sums of money raised by both campaigns, compared with the amounts available to be raised and spent by candidates participating in partial public funding of the primary process, it seems likely that, unless the primary funding system is changed, candidates seeking to be competitive in 2008 will also forgo partial public funding. The level playing field envisioned when the Federal Election Campaign Act was passed may well be a thing of the past, and we may see candidates in 2008 thinking seriously about privately funding the general election as well.

In addition to eliminating soft money from federal elections, the BCRA also sought to limit the influences of issue advocacy by interest groups and advocacy organizations. Yet advocacy groups continued to play a major role in the 2004 election; only the form of their participation changed. Democrats, concerned about the effect of the BCRA's soft-money ban on their party's ability to compete effectively with the GOP and President Bush's assumed financial advantage, formed two 527 organizations, America Coming Together and the Media Fund, early in 2004 to provide advocacy for the Democratic Party's eventual nominee. Republicans first tried to get the Federal Election Commission to rule that such organizations violated the spirit if not the letter of the BCRA. When the commission refused to act, Republican-leaning 527 organizations were quickly created to support President Bush's candidacy.

Although the 527s formed in 2004 provided a way for soft-money contributors to continue to participate in the electoral system at high financial levels, donors to 527s in 2004 did not entirely replace soft-money contributors to the political parties in 2000 and 2002. A study by the Campaign Finance Institute has found that there was a $302 million decrease in soft money between the 2002 and 2004 election cycles. The study also finds that individual donors to 527 organizations, most of whom had been soft-money donors to the parties, gave more money to 527s in 2004 than they had given to the political parties in earlier election cycles. It is difficult to know to what extent the momentum to contribute to 527 organizations was driven by the dynamics of the 2004 presidential election, but to the extent that such support for 527s can be sustained, the study concludes, there is "a large potential for expansion of 527 activities in '06 and '08 based on increasing donor generosity and the large universe of thus far untapped ex-party soft money donors."[36]

What is more, it can be argued that the transparency of money in elections has decreased since the passage of the BCRA. The parties who raised and spent soft money were a known quantity. Today, however, since passage of the act, it is hard for voters to know who is behind an advertising campaign that is financed by Progress for America or America Coming Together. Who can argue with a group promoting unity in America or progress for the nation? The ambiguous and even misleading names of some 527 organizations give the public less information, and possibly more misinformation, than they had before the reform. When it was the parties spending millions on issue ads, the public at least knew who was behind the spending. Thanks to other research indicating that the public uses party labels as shortcuts to information gathering, we can assume that when a citizen comes across a message sent by a party organization, the party label carries with it some additional information. In other words, the public has a better chance to know who and what is behind a party message than one coming from a 527 with a name created to appeal to everyone and implying that it is only out to educate the public or do some altruistic deed. Late in the 2004 campaign, for example, Progress for America, a GOP-leaning group, spent $14 million on one series of television ads that depicted "President Bush hugging a teenage girl whose mother died in the September 11, 2001, attacks."[37] Was this a public service announcement or a campaign ad? Who can tell? Of course, that the spot was run in October of an election year and featured one of the candidates should provide a hint.

A similar argument could be made about the Swift Boat Veterans for Truth. The name of the organization would seem to indicate that the intentions of the group were above reproach. However, we know from press reports throughout the 2004 campaign that this was not the case. What is more, it is clear from the 2004 campaign that these groups had a major impact not only on the information potential voters received during 2004 but also on what potential voters thought about each of the candidates.

It is likely that this ambiguity will only increase in size and scope. Certainly, there is ample room for growth among these groups. Although 527s have existed for quite some time, the 2004 campaign was the first in which they played a major role. This is probably the reason for the soft-money gap between what the parties raised in 2000 and what 527s received in 2004. When the donors who did not give in 2004 engage in the process again, not only will there likely be more 527s, but they will be better funded to engage in the same kinds of activities. The influence of 527s may even extend to congressional races. According to Michael Toner, a commissioner of the Federal Elections Commission, "Without congressional action, 527 organizations will become even more important in the 2006 election. In a [U.S.] Senate or House contest, a group that can raise $10 million has the ability to drive the entire election by spending that kind of money."[38]

Early in 2005 Senator John McCain and others who were instrumental in seeing that the BCRA became law noticed the same problems. In response, they drafted legislation to curb some of the difficulties with 527s. McCain and his allies hope to have the new proposal in place before the 2006 elections get under way.[39] The proposal would require 527s to register with the Federal Election Commission and abide by the same limits imposed on hard-money contributions, but it would do little to affect the information asymmetry created by the misleading or manipulative names of some of these organizations.

The Issue of Ethics

The 2004 elections raised a host of ethical questions. From the Bush campaign's use of 9/11 images in January to Senator Kerry's October reference to the sexual orientation of Vice President Cheney's daughter, ethical issues surfaced repeatedly during the 2004 presidential elections. The candidates themselves, the parties, outside groups, and the media all came under ethical scrutiny. What are ethical questions, how best to deal with them, and the role of the media in examining these issues were all raised in the 2004 election. However, to raise an issue is one thing, to know what to do about it is entirely another.

Although crossing the ethical line in campaigns can create a backlash against the offender, the line is ill defined. In most cases, when an ethical line is hazy, most observers would probably search for a definition as Justice Potter Stewart did in his concurring opinion on pornography in a 1964 Supreme Court decision: "I shall not today attempt further to define the kinds of material I understand to be embraced within that shorthand description; and perhaps I could never succeed in intelligibly doing so. But I know it when I see it."[40] In other words, what crosses the ethical line that everyone "knows" is out there is a judgment call. It has not been our intention to speak for others as to what is ethical and what is not, either in detailing examples of questionable conduct from past elections or in our descriptions of how different electoral actors viewed certain activities that could be defined as unethical. However, what is clear from our findings is that there are certain lines that some will not cross. In our research, consultants drew the line at lying, whereas the public was more dubious of more activities, and candidates were arguably the most careful.

Ethically questionable actions have consequences. Statements taken out of context can lead to misinformed voters. The 2004 presidential election was replete with examples, from both the Kerry and Bush campaigns as well as outside groups, of using statements out of context. Many Americans who heard the claims that the president supported the outsourcing of jobs or that Kerry had supported a fifty-cent-a-gallon gas tax believed them. In response to the multitude of instances from past campaigns, and as a way to combat these kinds of practices, FactCheck.org was formed, an organization whose sole purpose was to check the accuracy of statements made by candidates, their campaigns, and outside groups.

Our data show that two-thirds of the general public thinks that ethical violations occur in campaigns; the 2004 election is not likely to change those opinions. We have discussed in great detail the ethical issues raised in 2004; suffice it to say that ethics continues to be an issue in campaigns and continues to influence the health of American campaigning. It is not our intention to argue that the ethics of campaigning signals doom for our electoral process. The perception and reality of unethical practices is unquestionably worrisome. It is likely that future elections will include activities that raise ethical questions and that the system will nonetheless survive.

We have described in this book the way elections in the United States have evolved over the past several years, and the roles various actors—candidates, political consultants, party elites, the general public, organized interests, and the media—have played in ever-changing campaign dynamics. The 2004 elections continued to illustrate changes in the American campaigns, and we have seen examples of both the health of and the challenges to our system of campaigning. The increase in voter turnout and other forms of participation in the 2004 elections, coupled with the important activities of political parties, are certainly things to give the American public some optimism about their system of campaigning. The issues of money and what it means for potential candidates, voters, parties, and outside interests, as well as the knowledge that ethical questions continue to surface, on the other hand, should give us pause.

Moreover, we do not pretend that either list—those aspects that are healthy and those that are not—is exhaustive. Rather, we have tried to lay out some issues over which scholars, journalists, and the public have expressed some concern, and we have tried to illustrate that while some of those concerns have merit, others do not. The system of campaigning in the United States is neither perfect nor completely broken. Certainly, there is more to study on this important topic. We hope that readers will use our work as a starting point and will build on our findings to take the next step. As we said at the beginning, we view this book not as a hypothesis-testing exercise but as a hypothesis-generating exercise.

We wish we could leave the reader with a stronger statement. But our work and the stories from the 2004 election season suggest that the health of American campaigning is still uncertain and very much evolving.

Details of Survey Sample Selection and Administration

1998 Survey of Political Consultants

The sample for the 1998 political consultants' survey was drawn by Princeton Survey Research Associates, with the help of American University's Center for Congressional and Presidential Studies. It was a stratified sample, drawing on experienced firms in four major sectors of the consulting industry (survey research, media, fundraising, and general consulting).

The final sample comprised two hundred principals in major consulting firms, with whom in-depth telephone interviews were conducted between November 1997 and March 1998. The firms and individuals were selected through a two-stage process. First, because there is no agreed-upon universe of consultants, the closest substitute was used. A list of 302 political consulting firms (including general consulting, media, survey research, and fundraising firms) was created by searching *Campaigns & Elections* magazine's postelection reports from 1992, 1994, and 1996. These firms were identified as being associated with one or more campaigns for president or Congress in any of the three preceding election cycles.

Second, the 302 firms were divided into two groups. The first group consisted of firms that had been involved in one or more presidential campaigns, five or more Senate campaigns, or thirty or more congressional campaigns during the past three election cycles. The second group was made up of all the other firms. Each firm in the first group was contacted for an interview. In addition, a subset of firms from the second group was randomly selected for interviews.

Individual consultants were selected from firms in each group and were identified from the principals or partners listed in the 1996 edition of *The Political Resource Directory*, an annual publication that allows consultants of all types to list the services they offer and to advertise in their given area of specialization. For firms of two or more principals, one of the principals was selected at random to be interviewed first. When an interview was completed with the first principal at each firm, that person was asked for the names of the firm's other principals or senior associates who work on political campaigns. These individuals were then contacted for interviews. Therefore, though firms were used to create the initial list, the unit of analysis is the individual.

Each individual selected for an interview was sent a letter requesting his or her participation in the study. Subsequently, every person was contacted (several times, if necessary) to complete an interview.

1999 Survey of Political Consultants

The 1999 political consultants' survey consisted of 505 thirty-minute telephone interviews with senior-level political consultants, conducted by Yankelovich Partners, Inc., in conjunction with American University's Center for Congressional and Presidential Studies. The sample of consultants was drawn through a multistep process. We built on our experiences in the 1998 study and turned again to *The Political Resource Directory* to obtain the best estimate of the names of all known consulting firms and their principals. A complete list of principals was obtained from *The Political Resource Directory* and supplemented with names obtained from *Campaigns & Elections* magazine's "Political Pages." This yielded a master list of principals whose firms offered services in seven different areas, from full campaign services and survey research to media buying or rental of voter lists. However, only general consultants, media consultants, and those who specialized in survey research and focus group services, fundraising, and opposition research were included in the final sample. Again, we built on our earlier study and expanded the list to include a broader range of consultant types. This yielded a total of 2,587 individuals from whom to draw the sample.

To ensure that respondents were currently working as political consultants in the areas identified, two screen questions were utilized during the interviews. First, respondents were asked if they currently worked as a consultant, or if they had worked as a consultant in the past year (any other answer led to termination of the interview). Second, respondents were asked to identify the campaign service in which they specialized. Only those answering either general consultant, field operations, polling, media specialist, fundraiser, direct mail specialist, or research were included.

Interviews were conducted between April 5 and May 14, 1999, by Yankelovich's Executive Council of interviewers, who are specially trained to conduct high-level interviews with hard-to-reach individuals. The margin of error for the total sample is ±4.4 percent.

2002 Survey of Political Consultants

The 2002 political consultants' survey was a panel study in which we returned to a subset of consultants who were interviewed in 1999 and who said they were willing to be recontacted at a later date for further questions. The final sample of 204 individuals was interviewed between November 6 and December 12, 2002. Respondents qualified for this survey if they had previously participated in the 1999 study, currently worked as a political campaign consultant or had done so in the past year, and did not work exclusively in media production or for a telephone bank.

The margin of error for the total sample is ±6.9 percent.

2002 Survey of Party Elites

The results of the 2002 survey of party elites are based on telephone interviews with ninety-three state party officials and fifteen national party committee staffers. To obtain the sample of participants, we first called each state party headquarters to obtain the name of the person serving as executive director or the most equivalent position. Because state parties vary in the extent of their professionalization, some contacts were made at the state party office, and others were made at individuals' residences. Interviews were conducted from March 18 to April 17, 2002, and multiple attempts were made to contact an individual from each state party.

To ensure that the most appropriate person was interviewed, the initial contact was asked a series of screening questions, including whether he or she was still in the position. More important, initial contacts were asked whether they were "fully responsible," "partly responsible," or "not at all responsible" for selecting political consultants for their party organizations (because this activity was at the heart of many of the survey questions). Those who answered "fully responsible" or "partly responsible" qualified for the survey. A follow-up question was posed to those who did not have any role in this activity, asking them to identify who was responsible for selecting consultants for their state party organization during the 2000 election. We then contacted the individual mentioned in the follow-up.

The margin of error for the total sample is ±4.9 percent.

March 2000 Survey of the General Public

For the March 2000 survey of the general public, we again turned to Yankelovich Partners, Inc., who completed 1,005 telephone surveys between March 15 and March 27, 2000. Respondents were selected through an unrestricted random-digit dial technique that significantly reduces serial bias and ensures that both respondents with listed numbers and those with unlisted numbers are reached. Respondents had to be at least 18 years old and could not work for a market research firm, the media, a political party, or a political campaign.

The margin of error for the total sample is ±3.1 percent.

October 2000 Survey of the General Public

For the October 2000 survey of the general public, Yankelovich Partners, Inc., again completed all telephone interviews (1,002). The survey was administered between October 19 and October 29, 2000. Respondents were again selected through an unrestricted random-digit dial technique. Respondents had to be at least 18 years old and could not work for a market research firm, the media, a political party, or a political campaign.

The margin of error for the total sample is ±3.1 percent.

November 2002 Survey of the General Public

The November 2002 survey of the general public was conducted by the Survey Research Center at the University of Kansas between November 6 and December 18, 2002. This survey, again, selected participants through random-digit dial. A total of 1,163 interviews were completed.

The margin of error for the total sample is ±1.4 percent.

Additional information about each of the surveys can be obtained from the authors.

Notes

Chapter One

1. Jodi Wilgoren, "The 2004 Campaign: The Former Governor; Little Familiar with Setbacks, Dean Stumbles," *New York Times,* January 20, 2004, p. A1.

2. More important, the Dean example illustrates the overwhelming importance of expectations and momentum in our primary process. Although he was slipping in support at the polls, Howard Dean was not out of the race for the Democratic nomination at the time of his impassioned speech. In fact, coming out of the Iowa caucuses, Dean was trailing John Kerry, the eventual nominee, by only thirteen delegates. This is not so large a number as it might seem: the total number of delegates needed to win the nomination was 2,162. Kerry garnered twenty delegates in his caucus performance, John Edwards eighteen, and Dean seven; John Kerry's twenty delegates were less than 1 percent of the number needed to win the nomination. (Dean could have easily overcome this "defeat" and continued to amass delegates had his loss in Iowa not been seen as a crushing blow to his chances. The Iowa caucuses certainly started Campaign 2004 off with a bang and gave all observers something to remember. However, the campaign continued to produce story lines and outcomes that, when one looks back at the campaign in its entirety, illustrate the different identities of the campaign.

3. We recognize that other candidates were on the ballot in states across the United States, including Ralph Nader, Michael Badnarik, and David Cobb. However, each of these candidates failed to garner a significant portion of the national vote.

4. Donald Lambro, "It's the Turnout, Stupid," *Washington Times*, October 31, 2004, p. A1.

5. Down-ballot races are listed farther down on the ballot and are for offices—both the offices themselves and the candidates—that are less familiar to voters.

6. We explore this point in more detail in chapter 6.

7. Lambro, "It's the Turnout, Stupid."

8. Dan Balz and Mike Allen, "Four More Years Attributed to Rove's Strategy; Despite Moments of Doubt, Adviser's Planning Paid Off," *Washington Post*, November 7, 2004, p. A1.

9. Pew Research Center, "Voters Liked Campaign 2004, but Too Much 'Mud-Slinging,'" November 11, 2004 (http://people-press.org/reports/display.php3?ReportID=233 [accessed December 16, 2004]). These individuals reported that they had been contacted either by phone, by e-mail, or in person.

10. Peter Slevin and Dan Keating, "Both Parties Claim Registration Success: But Despite Fierce Get-Out-the-Vote Efforts, Neither Has Gained Major Advantage," *Washington Post*, October 19, 2004, p. A4.

11. June 2004 figures are based on survey respondents who reported they were registered voters; the June 2000 and 2004 figures are from Pew Research Center, "Voters More Engaged, but Campaign Gets Lukewarm Ratings," July 8, 2004 (http:// people-press.org/reports/display.php3?ReportID=218 [accessed July 12, 2004]); the September 2004 figure is from Pew Research Center, "Kerry Support Rebounds, Race Again Even," September 16, 2004 (http://people-press.org/reports/display.php3?ReportID=224 [accessed December 16, 2004]).

12. Pew Research Center, "Voters More Engaged"; Pew Research Center, "Kerry Support Rebounds."

13. Pew Research Center, "Voters Liked Campaign 2004, but Too Much 'Mud-Slinging.'" This figure is based on those who reported having voted in the election.

14. Pew Research Center, "Voters More Engaged."

15. The survey cited here was a survey by CBS News and the *New York Times* conducted between July 11 and July 15, 2004. However, in surveys dating back to 1995, findings have been consistent, as more than 30 percent of Americans have said that there is no real difference between the two parties. See, for example, the survey by the Cable News Network, *USA Today*, and Gallup Organization, October 3–6, 2002; the survey conducted by CBS News/*New York Times*, November 20–24, 2002; the survey by the *Washington Post*, Henry J. Kaiser Family Foundation, August 2–September 1, 2002; the survey conducted by Princeton Survey Research Associates, August 2–September 1, 2002; the survey by *Time*, the Cable News Network, and Yankelovich Partners, January 5–6, 2000; the survey by CBS News/*New York Times*, September 8–10, 1998; and the survey conducted by ABC News/*Washington Post*, September 28–October 1, 1995. The survey results reported here were obtained from searches of the iPOLL

Databank and other resources provided by the Roper Center for Public Opinion Research, University of Connecticut (www.ropercenter.uconn.edu/ipoll.html). All survey data were retrieved from iPOLL on December 11, 2004.

16. We know that we will not be able to convince everyone that there actually were important differences between Kerry and Bush in 2004. It is likely, however, that this is because those who see no differences between the two candidates would argue that the set of issues that are generally examined in discussions about the differences between the two candidates is not inclusive enough.

17. Pew Research Center, "Kerry Support Rebounds."

18. "How He Did It," *Newsweek,* November 15, 2004, p. 110.

19. Pew Research Center, "Kerry Support Rebounds."

20. Annenberg Public Policy Center, "Voters Learned Positions on Issues since Presidential Debates," National Annenberg Election Survey, October 23, 2004 (www.annenbergpublicpolicycenter.org/naes/2004_03_%20Voters-and-the-issues_10-23_pr.pdf [accessed December 10, 2004]).

21. We cannot say that the debates were the causal variable here, but they were one of the variables at play, and with the large audience and high level of interest, they certainly played a part in informing the public of the policy positions of the candidates.

22. Larry Nobel, executive director of the Center for Responsive Politics, "The Role of Money and Fundraising in Lobbying," presentation to the Public Affairs and Advocacy Institute, American University, January 2005.

23. Center for Responsive Politics, "2004 Election Overview Stats at a Glance" (www.opensecrets.org/overview.stats.asp?Cycle=2004 [accessed February 12, 2005]).

24. For perspectives on money in politics as an unethical occurrence, see, for instance, James A. Thurber, "From Campaigning to Lobbying, " in *Shades of Gray: Perspectives on Campaign Ethics,* edited by Candice J. Nelson, David A. Dulio, and Stephen K. Medvic (Brookings, 2002), or Larry Makinson, "What Money Buys," in Nelson, Dulio, and Medvic, *Shades of Gray.*

25. The alternate view is that the total spending in all campaigns across the United States amounts to only about three times the amount that advertisers spent on commercials during the 2005 Super Bowl. *Advertising Age* magazine reported on its web site (www.adage.com) the companies that were scheduled to purchase ads during the February 6, 2005, game as of February 4, 2005. The site also noted that the Fox network was charging $2.4 million for a thirty-second ad. Roughly fifty such ad segments were listed on the site, which, at $2.4 million each, is $1.2 billion (www.adage.com/news.cms?newsId=42286 [accessed February 2005]).

26. David M. Farrell, "Campaign Strategies and Tactics," in *Comparing Democracies: Elections and Voting in Global Perspective,* edited by Lawrence LeDuc, Richard G. Niemi, and Pippa Norris (Thousand Oaks, Calif.: Sage Publications, 1996).

27. Lambro, "It's the Turnout, Stupid."

28. Chris Cillizza, "Senate Hopefuls Pump in $60M," *Roll Call,* October 21, 2004; Center for Responsive Politics, "2004 Election Overview Most Expensive Races" (www.opensecrets.org/overview/topraces.asp [accessed February 12, 2005]).

29. Center for Responsive Politics, "New This Week: Total 527 Receipts and Expenditures, 2003–2004" (www.opensecrets.org/527s/527new.asp?cycle=2004 [accessed February 12, 2005]); Center for Responsive Politics, "Top PACs: Top 20 PAC Contributors to Federal Candidates, 2003–2004" (www.opensecrets.org/pacs/topacs.asp?txt=A&Cycle=2004 [accessed February12, 2005]).

30. Center for Responsive Politics, "Top Individual Contributors to 527 Committees 2004 Election Cycle" (www.opensecrets.org/527s/527indivs.asp?cycle=2004 [accessed February 12, 2005]).

31. Dana Milbank and Jim VandeHei, "From Bush, Unprecedented Negativity," *Washington Post,* May 31, 2004, p. A1.

32. Milbank and VandeHei, "From Bush, Unprecedented Negativity."

33. Dan Balz, "Bush Appears Close to Victory as Kerry Considers Ohio Fight, *Washington Post,* November 3, 2004, p. A1.

34. Quoted in "Wisconsin: Feingold Camp Warns of Coming Attacks," *Roll Call,* September 22, 2004.

35. Meg Kinnard, "MoveOn Goes after Bush's Service Record," *National Journal Ad Spotlight,* April 24, 2004 (nationaljournal.com/members/adspotlight/2004/04/0427moveon1.html [accessed December 7, 2004]).

36. Bill Sammon, "White House Accuses Kerry of 'Coordinating' Guard Attacks," *Washington Times,* September 10, 2004, p. A1.

37. Mike Allen and Jim VandeHei, "Kerry Hopes to Cement Image with New Ads," *Washington Post,* April 16, 2004, p. A1.

38. Charles Hurt, "Kerry Calls for 'Birth of Freedom,'" *Washington Times,* July 30, 2004, p. A1.

39. Howard Kurtz, "Rather Concedes Papers Are Suspect," *Washington Post,* September 16, 2004, p. A1.

40. More coverage, however, was provided on PBS, as well as the cable news networks, and ABC did offer gavel-to-gavel coverage over its digital television signal as well as its website (CBS and NBC also provided more coverage on their websites).

41. Quoted in Jennifer Harper, "Cable Sees 'Big Story' in Political Conventions; but the Networks Will Offer Viewers Only an Hour Each Day," *Washington Times,* July 14, 2004, p. A18.

42. Dan Balz, "The GOP's Challenge: Softening the Edges," *Washington Post,* September 1, 2004, p. A1.

43. Howard Kurtz, "Voters Chew over Dissected Debates," *Washington Post,* September 29, 2004, p. C1.

44. Albert Eisele and Jeff Dufour, "The Last Word on Bush's Bulge," *The Hill,* November 4, 2004, p. 41.

45. Our intention in the preceding discussion is not to provide a comprehensive recap of the 2004 presidential election but simply to remind the reader of several of the highlights of the 2004 election cycle.

46. Dan Balz and Mike Allen, "Four More Years Attributed to Rove's Strategy.

47. Paul Farhi, "Consultant Works His Magic on Kerry," *Washington Post,* January 27, 2004, p. A5.

48. Lambro, "It's the Turnout, Stupid."

49. Quoted in Farhi, "Consultant Works His Magic on Kerry."

50. How campaigns approach this task is beyond the scope of this book; see, for example, Stephen K. Medvic, *Political Consultants in U.S. Congressional Elections* (Ohio State University Press, 2001), especially the sections on his theory of deliberate priming; David A. Dulio, *For Better or Worse? How Professional Political Consultants Are Changing Elections in America* (State University of New York Press, 2004); James A. Thurber and Candice J. Nelson, eds., *Campaigns and Elections American Style,* 2nd ed. (Boulder, Colo.: Westview Press, 2004); Daniel M. Shea and Michael John Burton, *Campaign Craft: The Strategies, Tactics, and Art of Political Campaign Management,* rev. and exp. ed. (Westport, Conn.: Praeger, 2001).

51. Quoted in Ralph Z. Hallow, "Terrorism, Iraq War Shaped Campaigns," *Washington Times,* November 3, 2004, p. A1.

52. There is disagreement among scholars, commentators, and pundits on whether political consultants invent positions for candidates to take in the simple hopes of identifying the position that will get their candidate the most votes. The cynical view is that consultants manipulate the American people by saturating "the mass electorate with partisan and image propaganda" (Dan Nimmo, *The Political Persuaders: The Techniques of Modern Election Campaigns* [New Brunswick, N.J.: Transaction Publishers, 2001], p. 222); see also Karen S. Johnson-Cartee and Gary A. Copeland, *Manipulation of the American Voter: Political Campaign Commercials* (Westport, Conn.: Praeger, 1997); Stanley Kelley Jr., *Professional Public Relations and Political Power* (Johns Hopkins University Press, 1956); Larry J. Sabato, *The Rise of Political Consultants: New Ways of Winning Elections* (New York: Basic Books, 1981); and Nicholas J. O'Shaughnessey, *The Phenomenon of Political Marketing* (New York: St. Martin's Press, 1990); others, however, view what consultants do as a process that primes the electorate to think about certain issues in a certain way (Medvic, *Political Consultants*).

53. Interestingly, although 2004 was deemed to be one of the most negative campaigns ever, it also saw the largest number of people participate on election day. The conventional wisdom, in the popular press and to some extent in political science, is that negative campaigning drives down turnout (for a review of this literature, see Richard R. Lau and Lee Sigelman, "Effectiveness of Political Advertising," in *Crowded Airwaves: Political Advertising in Elections,* edited by

James A. Thurber, Candice J. Nelson, and David A. Dulio [Brookings, 2000]). This clearly was not the case in 2004 and is an interesting question that should be studied.

54. John F. Harris, "Reintroducing the Candidate," *Washington Post*, July 14, 2004, p. A1.

55. Ken Fireman, "President's Vow: A Time for Hope," *Newsday*, September 3, 2004, p. W3.

56. Mike Allen, "Kerry vs. the Format, Bush vs. His Temper," *Washington Post*, October 1, 2004, p. A8.

57. Mark P. Petracca, "Political Consultants and Democratic Governance," *PS: Political Science and Politics* 22, no. 1 (1989), p. 11.

58. This is undoubtedly far from an exhaustive list of topics that could be covered in this type of exercise. The same can be said for the brief list of broader topics that could be included in an examination of the health of our electoral system in general. It would be unwise to attempt to provide an exhaustive list of questions to consider as we would be hard pressed to identify such a list; around every corner would be another question that we or the reader would consider integral to the discussion. Therefore, we limit ourselves to the questions that we have been investigating over the course of our long-term project.

59. Details concerning the administration of each survey, including the sampling procedures, can be found in the appendix. Copies of the questionnaires and other details may be obtained from the authors.

60. Those surveyed include political consultants (1998, 1999, 2002), political party elites (2002), and the general public (March and October 2000 and November 2002).

61. For instance, Paul S. Herrnson reports on his surveys of candidates in *Party Campaigning in the 1980s* (Harvard University Press, 1988) and the 2nd, 3rd, and 4th editions of *Congressional Elections: Campaigning at Home and in Washington* (Washington: CQ Press, 1998, 2000, and 2004); reports on surveys of political consultants are found in Petracca, "Political Consultants and Democratic Governance"; Mark Petracca and Courtney Wierioch, "Consultant Democracy: The Activities and Attitudes of American Political Consultants" (paper prepared for the annual meeting of the Midwest Political Science Association, Chicago, 1988); Kerwin C. Swint, *Political Consultants and Negative Campaigning: The Secrets of the Pros* (Lanham, Md.: University Press of America, 1998); and Robin Kolodny and Angela Logan, "Political Consultants and the Extension of Party Goals," *PS: Political Science and Politics* 31, no. 2 (1998): 155–59; and Robin Kolodny ("It's the System, Stupid!" in Nelson, Dulio, and Medvic, *Shades of Gray*) reports on a survey of party officials. This is only a small sampling of other studies based on surveys of campaign actors. Of course, the studies that use survey research to study the public and voters are too voluminous to attempt to list here.

62. As we note in chapter 2, there is some debate about when the first consultants arrived on the scene in the United States, but the 1930s seems to be a consensus opinion for the appearance of the first modern consultants.

63. Stanley Kelley Jr., *Professional Public Relations and Political Power* (Johns Hopkins University Press, 1956), p. 205.

64. See Petracca, "Political Consultants and Democratic Governance."

65. Henry E. Brady, "Contributions of Survey Research to Political Science," *PS: Political Science and Politics* 33, no. 1 (2000): 47.

Chapter Two

1. We focus in this book on federal campaigns (that is, for the presidency of the United States, the U.S. House of Representatives, and the U.S. Senate) and other statewide campaigns (for example, governor). Down-ballot races for offices such as state house, state senate, county commissioner, and city council are different creatures on a number of levels. For a complete discussion of the differences between these two kinds of campaigns, see L. Sandy Maisel, *Parties and Elections in America,* 3rd ed. (Lanham, Md.: Rowman and Littlefield, 1999).

2. In many cases these calls for reform are well founded. The U.S. electoral system has seen changes in some areas (for example, campaign finance regulation); but in many others (for example, election administration), further reform is needed. For instance, even after Congress passed the Help America Vote Act, which was designed to fix administrative problems on election day, questions about how elections are administered remain. Many counties around the nation had planned on using new computer touch-screen voting machines to replace the outdated punch-card systems that gained such notoriety in the Florida recount during the 2000 election. Changing from the antiquated systems would bring states and counties into compliance with the new law. However, questions about the reliability of the systems, not to mention the possibility of fraud by hackers who gain access to the computers, caused several states to delay their changes (see Julie Carr Smyth, "Blackwell Blocks Use of New Voting Machines," *Cleveland Plain Dealer,* July 17, 2004, p. B1; and Leslie Parrilla, "Counties Choose Scan Machines until Touch Screen Proves Reliable," Associated Press state and local wire, July 12, 2004). Several recent examples confirm these worries. In Miami-Dade County, ironically, detailed electronic records of the 2002 gubernatorial primary election, which used the high-tech touch-screen voting machines, were lost because of computer crashes in May and November 2003. With no paper trail, these kinds of problems are cause for concern. Moreover, after election day in 2004, more questions were raised in Ohio as "an error with an electronic voting system gave President Bush 3,893 extra votes in suburban Columbus, election officials said. Franklin County's unofficial results had Bush receiving 4,258 votes to Democrat John Kerry's 260 votes in a precinct in Gahanna. Records show only

638 voters cast ballots in that precinct. Bush's total should have been recorded as 365" (John McCarthy, "Voting Machine Error Gives Bush 3,893 Extra Votes in Ohio," Associated Press state and local wire, November 5, 2004).

3. The notion of control in campaigns is broader and more complex than as presented here. Other aspects of control are beyond the scope of this book, however.

4. A complete review of this literature is beyond the scope of this chapter and book. For a description of these changes, see Robert J. Dinkin, *Campaigning in America: A History of Election Practices* (Westport, Conn.: Greenwood Press, 1989).

5. Frank J. Sorauf, "Political Parties and Political Action Committees: Two Life Cycles," *Arizona Law Review* 22 (1980): 445–64; see also Harold R. Bruce, *American Parties and Politics: History and Role of Political Parties in the United States* (New York: Henry Holt, 1927); Charles E. Merriam, *The American Party System* (New York: Macmillan, 1923); and Edward M. Sait, *American Parties and Elections* (New York: Century Company, 1927).

6. Among the former, see Larry J. Sabato, *The Rise of Political Consultants: New Ways of Winning Elections* (New York: Basic Books, 1981); for an example of the latter, see Mark P. Petracca, "Political Consultants and Democratic Governance," *PS: Political Science and Politics* 22, no. 1 (1989): 11–14.

7. David S. Broder, "No Way to Choose a President," *Washington Post*, December 31, 2003, p. A19. We should note, however, that this can be said for the vast majority of campaigns, since the standard method of picking general election candidates in the United States is a primary election.

8. William N. Chambers, *Political Parties in a New Nation: The American Experience, 1776–1809* (Oxford University Press, 1963); Paul F. Boller, *Presidential Campaigns* (Oxford University Press, 1984).

9. Stephen K. Medvic, "Is There a Spin Doctor in the House? The Impact of Political Consultants in Congressional Campaigns," Ph.D. dissertation, Purdue University, 1997.

10. Ibid.; Alan Ware, *The Breakdown of Democratic Party Organization, 1940–1980* (Oxford University Press, 1985); Dinkin, *Campaigning in America*.

11. Paul S. Herrnson, *Party Campaigning in the 1980s* (Harvard University Press, 1988), p. 13.

12. Mosei Ostrogorski, *The United States*, vol. 2 of *Democracy and the Organization of Political Parties*, edited by Seymour Martin Lipset (Garden City, N.Y.: Anchor Books, 1964).

13. Boller, *Presidential Campaigns;* Dinkin, *Campaigning in America.*

14. In addition, in 1939 Congress passed the Hatch Act, which prohibited civil service employees from actively participating in political activities, including political management and political campaigns. Congress amended the Hatch Act in 1993, loosening the restrictions on forbidden activity.

15. Herrnson, *Party Campaigning*, p. 12.

16. Ibid., p. 18.

17. Ibid.

18. Ibid., p. 26.

19. For more on Whitaker and Baxter and the development of the consulting industry, see David A. Dulio, *For Better or Worse? How Professional Political Consultants Are Changing Elections in America* (State University of New York Press, 2004); Medvic, "Is There a Spin Doctor in the House?"; Dan Nimmo, *The Political Persuaders: The Techniques of Modern Election Campaigns* (New Brunswick, N.J.: Transaction Publishers, 2001); and David L. Rosenbloom, *The Election Men: Professional Campaign Managers and American Democracy* (New York: Quadrangle Books, 1973).

20. Nimmo, *The Political Persuaders*, p. 33.

21. Rosenbloom, *The Election Men*, p. 50.

22. Dulio, *For Better or Worse*.

23. Herrnson, *Party Campaigning*, p. 20.

24. Ibid. This may seem like an unimportant point. However, as the voting-age population increased, parties were still trying to campaign as they always had—with the traditional vote-getting methods of handshakes and canvassing. The increase in the number of voters was important because parties found that they could no longer reach everyone in this way. This caused campaigns to look to other means of campaigning.

25. Ibid.

26. Robert Agranoff, *The New Style in Election Campaigns* (Boston: Holbrook Press, 1972); Herrnson, *Party Campaigning*; Sabato, *The Rise of Political Consultants*.

27. Agranoff, *The New Style in Election Campaigns*, p. 63.

28. Herrnson, *Party Campaigning*, p. 29.

29. Herrnson, *Party Campaigning*, and Xandra Kayden and Eddie Mahe Jr., *The Party Goes On: The Persistence of the Two-Party System in the United States* (New York: Basic Books, 1985), discuss resurgence, whereas revitalization is examined in John A. Aldrich, *Why Parties? The Origin and Transformation of Political Parties in America* (University of Chicago Press, 1995).

30. Herrnson, *Party Campaigning*.

31. Ibid.; Kayden and Mahe, *The Party Goes On*; Aldrich, *Why Parties*; and David B. Menefee-Libey, *The Triumph of Campaign-Centered Politics* (New York: Chatham House, 2000).

32. Herrnson, *Party Campaigning*.

33. Dulio, *For Better or Worse*; also, David A. Dulio and James A. Thurber, "The Symbiotic Relationship between Political Parties and Political Consultants: Partners Past, Present and Future," in *The State of the Parties: The Changing Role of Contemporary American Parties,* edited by John C. Green and Rick Farmer, 4th ed. (Lanham, Md.: Rowman and Littlefield, 2003).

34. Herrnson, *Party Campaigning*.

35. Menefee-Libey, in *The Triumph of Campaign-Centered Politics*, credits Barbara Salmore and Stephen Salmore (*Candidates, Parties, and Campaigns* [Washington, D.C.: Congressional Quarterly Press, 1985]) for being among the first to note that the political context in the United States is campaign centered rather than candidate centered.

36. Menefee-Libey, *The Triumph of Campaign-Centered Politics*, pp. 3 and 5. Emphasis in original.

37. Ibid., p. 25.

38. Burdett A. Loomis, "Kansas's Third District: The 'Pros from Dover' Set Up Shop," in *The Battle for Congress: Consultants, Candidates, and Voters*, edited by James A. Thurber (Brookings, 2001), p. 142.

39. Menefee-Libey, *The Triumph of Campaign-Centered Politics*, p. 23.

40. Jim VandeHei, "Old-School Team to Sell Kerry as Modern Centrist," *Washington Post*, April 21, 2004, p. A1.

41. Ibid.

42. Dulio, *For Better or Worse*; Dulio and Thurber, "The Symbiotic Relationship"; Robin Kolodny and Angela Logan, "Political Consultants and the Extension of Party Goals," *PS: Political Science and Politics* 31, no. 2 (1998): 155–59; Robin Kolodny and David A. Dulio, "Political Party Adaptation in U.S. Congressional Elections: Why Political Parties Use Coordinated Expenditures to Hire Political Consultants," *Party Politics* 9, no. 6 (2003): 729–46.

43. The respondents from the national parties and party committees were from the highest levels of those organizations. They included executive directors, communications directors, and political directors of the Democratic National Committee and the Republican National Committee as well as their campaign committees—the Democratic Congressional Campaign Committee, the Democratic Senatorial Campaign Committee, the National Republican Congressional Committee, and the National Republican Senatorial Committee.

44. Herrnson, *Party Campaigning*; Aldrich, *Why Parties?*

45. Herrnson, *Party Campaigning*.

46. Quoted in ibid., p. 63.

47. Ibid.

48. Quoted in Dulio, *For Better or Worse*, p. 111.

49. This is an example of the ebb and flow of party power that would be noticed by a consultant who had many years of experience and would not be noticed by someone new to a party organization. For a lengthier discussion of party adaptation during this time, see Dulio, *For Better or Worse*; Robin Kolodny, "Electoral Partnerships: Political Consultants and Political Parties," in *Campaign Warriors: Political Consultants in Elections*, edited by James A. Thurber and Candice J. Nelson (Brookings, 2000); and Robin Kolodny, "Towards a Theory of Political Party Institutional Capacity, or Why Parties

Need Political Consultants to Remain Viable in the C20th" (paper prepared for the Elections, Parties and Opinion Polls working group of the Political Studies Association, Edinburgh, Scotland, September, 8–10, 2000); and Kolodny and Dulio, "Political Party Adaptation."

50. Dulio, *For Better or Worse.*

51. Martin Hamburger, "Lessons from the Field: A Journey into Political Consulting," in *Campaign Warriors,* edited by Thurber and Nelson, pp. 58–59.

52. Quoted in Dulio, *For Better or Worse,* pp. 127 and 128.

53. Federal Election Commission, "Presidential Prenomination Campaign Receipts through August 31, 2004," September 9, 2004 (www.fec.gov/press/ bkgnd/pres_cf/documents/presreceiptsm92004.pdf [accessed May 26, 2005]).

54. Center for Responsive Politics, "Political Parties: 2003–2004 Totals" (http://opensecrets.org/parties/index.asp [accessed February 12, 2005]).

55. "How He Did It," *Newsweek,* November 15, 2004, p. 108.

56. Donald Lambro, "Gearing Up for Battle at RNC," *Washington Times,* July 28, 2003, p. A21.

57. Morton Kondrake, "Advice to Kerry: Steal Bush's 2000 'Uniter' Theme," *Roll Call,* May 13, 2004.

58. Peter Slevin and Dan Keating, "Both Parties Claim Registration Success: But Despite Fierce Get-Out-the-Vote Efforts, Neither Has Gained Major Advantage," *Washington Post,* October 19, 2004, p. A4.

59. Donald Lambro, "It's the Turnout, Stupid," *Washington Times,* October 31, 2004, p. A1.

60. Some consulting firms do provide opposition research or fieldwork services. However, they are few in number compared with firms that handle polling, media, and mail services. See Dennis Johnson, *No Place for Amateurs: How Political Consultants Are Reshaping American Democracy* (New York: Routledge, 2001), appendix B.

61. Dulio and Thurber, "The Symbiotic Relationship."

62. These data are taken from Paul S. Herrnson, "2002 Congressional Candidate Study," in *Congressional Elections: Campaigning at Home and in Washington,* 4th ed. (Washington: CQ Press, 2004). Incumbents in jeopardy were defined as those candidates who won by less than 20 percent of the vote, and hopeful challengers were defined as those who lost by less than 20 percent of the vote. This may seem like a large margin, but both operational definitions correspond to a two-party vote split of 60-40.

63. The first to investigate this relationship were Kolodny and Logan, "Political Consultants." The evidence presented here confirms much of what they report in their work, which is also based on a survey of consultants, albeit a smaller and more limited survey. For more on this aspect of the relationship, see Dulio, *For Better or Worse.*

64. Herrnson, *Party Campaigning.*

65. On the 2002 campaign, see Jim VandeHei and Dan Balz, "In a GOP Win, a Lesson in Money Muscle, Planning," *Washington Post*, November 10, 2002, pp. A1 and A6; on the 2004 campaign, see Lauren W. Whittington, "Committees Carry Dept into '06 Cycle," *Roll Call*, December 6, 2004.

66. See James A. Thurber and Carolyn Long, "Brian Baird's 'Ring of Fire': The Quest for Campaign Funds and Votes in Washington's 3rd Congressional District," in *The Battle for Congress*, edited by Thurber.

67. Quoted in Dulio, *For Better or Worse*, pp. 126 and 127.

68. Parties are not the only force that can muddy the water for candidates' campaign messages. Outside interest groups can also become major players in communicating messages in campaigns. See Jeff Gill, "One Year and Four Elections: The 1998 Capps Campaign for California's Twenty-Second District," in *The Battle for Congress*, edited by Thurber. See also David B. Magleby, ed., *Outside Money: Soft Money and Issue Advocacy in the 1998 Congressional Elections* (Lanham, Md.: Rowman and Littlefield, 2000); and David B. Magleby and J. Quin Monson, eds., *The Last Hurrah? Soft Money and Issue Advocacy in the 2002 Congressional Elections* (Brookings, 2004).

69. Robin Toner, "Where Candidates May Fear to Tread, National Parties Stampede In," *New York Times*, September 30, 2002, p. A18.

70. Instead, consultants may have to shift their worry to nonparty groups—the so-called 527 organizations—because these groups are not affected by the BCRA law and can send communications to potential voters without regard to what the candidates want them to say. Early in the 2004 cycle, this was not a problem for either George Bush or John Kerry. There was little, if any activity by conservative 527 groups at this point in the campaign—they did not need to be active because of Bush's large fundraising advantage; and those on the Democratic side—most notably, MoveOn.org and the Media Fund—seemed to be in lockstep with the Kerry message. Of course, later in the campaign, the Swift Boat Veterans for Truth appeared and began attacking Senator Kerry's service in Vietnam. The Kerry campaign tried to tie this group and their message to the Bush campaign, which could have put Bush in a difficult position, since the ads were seen as over the top by most reasonable observers. However, the Bush camp was quick to point out that they were not responsible for the ads in question and did not support the message of the Swift Boat Veterans. Of course, this is all in light of the fact that the ads run by the Swift Boat Veterans did the Bush campaign a big favor by damaging Senator Kerry. See chapters 4 and 5 for a further discussion of these points. For more detail on the change in the law, its effects, and consultants' attitudes toward it, see our discussion of the BCRA in chapters 4 and 6.

71. For more on consultants' career history, see James A. Thurber, Candice J. Nelson, and David A. Dulio, "Portrait of Campaign Consultants," in *Campaign Warriors*, edited by Thurber and Nelson, as well as Dulio, *For Better or Worse*, and Kolodny and Logan, "Political Consultants."

72. Kolodny, "Electoral Partnerships," provides evidence that is similar to that presented below. Kolodny also conducted a survey of state parties and found that they hired consultants to provide certain services. For more on this point as it relates to national parties, see also Kolodny and Dulio, "Political Party Adaptation."

73. We have confidence that these results reflect the hiring practices of both state and national party committees. At the beginning of the telephone interview, each respondent was asked a screening question to confirm that he or she was responsible for making these types of decisions. Interviews with those who were not responsible were terminated. These individuals were asked who in their organization was responsible, and those individuals were contacted.

74. See the Alliance for Better Campaigns, "Gouging Democracy: How the Television Industry Profiteered on Campaign 2000" (http://bettercampaigns. org/reports/display.php?ReportID=4 [accessed February 12, 2005]).

75. This may not be as clear in the post-BCRA world, since the reform law has taken a big arrow out of the party's quiver of tactics in restricting the kinds of ads parties can run. However, it is unlikely that parties will cease demanding this service from consultants completely.

76. Thomas B. Edsall, "An 'Independent' Spending Blitz; Democrats to Use Novel Approach to Finance Advertising," *Washington Post,* July 30, 2004, p. A1; "Morning Business," *Roll Call,* October 7, 2004.

77. For more on this point, see Dulio, *For Better or Worse,* as well as Kolodny and Dulio, "Political Party Adaptation," who illustrate that one way the national parties engage in this activity is through coordinated expenditures.

78. Kolodny and Logan, "Political Consultants"; Kolodny, "Electoral Partnerships"; Kolodny and Dulio, "Political Party Adaptation"; Dulio, *For Better or Worse.*

79. Paul S. Herrnson, *Party Campaigning in the 1980s* (Harvard University Press, 1988), p. 28.

Chapter Three

1. See, for instance, Jonathan S. Krasno and Donald Philip Green, "Preempting Quality Challengers in House Elections," *Journal of Politics* 50, no. 4 (1988): 920–36.

2. Dan Balz, "In Debate, Kerry Touts Experience and Edwards Stresses Electability," *Washington Post,* February 27, 2004, p. A1.

3. Allison Vekshim, "Corzine Eases into New Role as Senator," States News Service, April 6, 2001; Betsy Rothstein, "Senate Chiefs of Staff Took Diverse Paths to Power," *The Hill,* January 17, 2001; Zev Chafitz, "Crazy Lessons from an Election," *New York Daily News,* November 9, 2000, p. 31.

4. Quoted in Balz, "In Debate, Kerry Touts Experience and Edwards Stresses Electability."

5. Different officeholders are often expected to do different things. For instance, U.S. House members may be expected, by their constituents, to handle casework and local issues, whereas U.S. senators may be looked to for more national and certainly statewide issues. The president, on the other hand, is expected to address national issues, certainly, but also international issues, which House members typically are not. The differences in what we expect elected officials to do are probably only greater at lower-level offices such as mayor and city council.

6. E. J. Dionne, "Should Our Leaders Be Amateurs?" *Washington Post*, September 21, 2003, p. B1.

7. For more on consultants as players in campaign crises, see R. Sam Garrett, "Campaigns, Crises, and Communication: Crisis Management in House and Senate Campaigns," paper prepared for the annual meeting of the American Political Science Association, Chicago, September 2-5, 2004; and R. Sam Garrett, "Adrenalized Fear: Crisis Management in U.S. House and Senate Campaigns," Ph.D. dissertation, American University, 2005.

8. The scale of responses in 1998 and in 1999 were slightly different; therefore we do not report the 1998 data in table 3-1.

9. James A. Thurber, Candice J. Nelson, and David A. Dulio, "Portrait of Campaign Consultants," in *Campaign Warriors: Political Consultants in Elections*, edited by James A. Thurber and Candice J. Nelson (Brookings, 2000); David A. Dulio, *For Better or Worse? How Professional Political Consultants Are Changing Elections in America* (State University of New York Press, 2004).

10. The rating was based on a scale in which 1 = very poor, 2 = poor, 3 = average, 4 = good, and 5 = excellent.

11. Pew Research Center, "Campaign 2000 Highly Rated," 2000 (people-press. org/reports/display.php3?ReportID=23 [December 21, 2004]). "Voters" are those respondents who reported voting in the 2000 election.

12. Pew Research Center, "Democratic Primary Campaign Impresses Voters," February 19, 2004 (http://people-press.org/reports/display.php3?ReportID=203 [accessed July 12, 2004]).

13. Pew Research Center, "Voters More Engaged, but Campaign Gets Lukewarm Ratings," July 8, 2004 (http://people-press.org/reports/display.php3? ReportID=218 [accessed July 12, 2004]). These results are of self-reported registered voters.

14. Pew Research Center, "Voters Liked Campaign 2004, but Too Much 'Mud-Slinging,'" November 11, 2004 (http://people-press.org/reports/display. php3? ReportID=233 [accessed December 16, 2004]). "Voters" are those respondents who reported voting in the 2004 election.

15. Likely voters were determined with the help of Yankelovich Partners. They were identified based on their responses to a series of questions measuring their attention to the campaigns, how confident they were that they would actually cast ballots in the November election, and their level of political involvement.

Specifics about how these individuals were identified can be obtained from the authors. In the March 2000 survey, 277 respondents were identified as likely voters; in October 2000, 475. The smaller numbers in March compared with October reflect the fact that many Americans do not pay attention to electoral politics until much later in the election cycle. This difference derives not from a flaw in the likely-voter model but rather from the fact that fewer individuals met the criteria in March than in October.

16. "Political Ticker: Always Time to Get in a Dig," Cox News Service, October 13, 2000.

17. Quoted in Jennifer Harper, "Understudies' Style, Civility Impressive," *Washington Times*, October 7, 2000, p. A2.

18. On Kerry as a bad candidate, see Joe Hallett, "Unlike Kerry, Bush Makes His Positions Clear," *Columbus (Ohio) Dispatch,* September 5, 2004, p. 1C; and Ben Smith, "Kerry's Backers a Little Panicky as Bush Surges," *New York Observer,* September 13, 2004, p. 1. On Gore as a bad candidate, see Chris Weinkopf, "Recycled Repertoire: Gore Campaign Suffers from Old Thinking," *Daily News of Los Angeles,* July 16, 2000; and Don Van Natta Jr. and Katharine Q. Seelye, "Gore Gets a Lukewarm Greeting in Comeback Pitch to Big Donors," *New York Times,* September 2, 2001, p. 1.

19. Pew Research Center, "Voters Impressed with Campaign, but News Coverage Gets Lukewarm Ratings," October 24, 2004 (http://people-press.org/reports/print.php3?PageID=900 [accessed December 21, 2004]).

20. Pew Research Center, "Voters More Engaged."

21. Ibid.

22. John R. Hibbing and Elizabeth Theiss-Morse, *Congress as Public Enemy: Public Attitudes toward American Political Institutions* (Cambridge University Press, 1995).

23. Consultants cited other reasons as well, including that candidates had changed their political philosophies, that they had sold out to special interests, and that they could not be trusted or had lied. Multiple responses were allowed for this question.

24. For more on consultant motivations, see chapter 4 in this volume as well as Dulio, *For Better or Worse.*

25. For a broader description of the industry, the choices that consultants have to make when taking on clients, and the factors that go into those decisions, see Dennis Johnson, *No Place for Amateurs: How Political Consultants Are Reshaping American Democracy* (New York: Routledge, 2001); Dulio, *For Better or Worse;* and Thurber, Nelson, and Dulio, "Portrait of Campaign Consultants."

26. Stephen K. Medvic, *Political Consultants in U.S. Congressional Elections* (Ohio State University Press, 2001).

27. Although the vast majority of consultants in the three surveys we have done reported that they were either Democrats or Republicans, some 12 percent

did not tie themselves to one of the major political parties. For more on the partisan division between consultants in this survey, see Dulio, *For Better or Worse,* and Thurber, Nelson, and Dulio, "Portrait of Campaign Consultants."

28. For more on this point, see Dulio, *For Better or Worse.*

29. Robin Kolodny, *Pursuing Majorities: Congressional Campaign Committees and American Politics* (Norman: University of Oklahoma Press, 1988).

30. Quoted in Dale Russakoff, "Democrats' Switch to Lautenberg Paying Off; Republican Seems Headed for Defeat," *Washington Post,* November 6, 2002, p. A27.

31. Bernard R. Berelson, Paul F. Lazarsfeld, and William N. McPhee, *Voting: A Study of Opinion Formation in a Presidential Campaign* (University of Chicago Press, 1954), p. 308.

32. Larry M. Bartels, "Uninformed Votes: Information Effects in Presidential Elections," *American Journal of Political Science* 40, no. 1 (1996): 194–230, p. 194.

33. Paul M. Sniderman, "The New Look in Public Opinion Research," in *Political Science: The State of the Discipline II,* edited by Ada W. Finifter (Washington: American Political Science Association, 1993), p. 219.

34. See, for example, Norman H. Nie, Sidney Verba, and John R. Petrocik, *The Changing American Voter* (Harvard University Press, 1979).

35. Sniderman, "The New Look in Public Opinion Research," p. 220.

36. Russel J. Dalton and Martin P. Wattenberg, "The Not So Simple Act of Voting," in *Political Science,* edited by Finifter, p. 196.

37. Ronald A. Faucheux and Paul S. Herrnson, *The Good Fight: How Political Candidates Struggle to Win Elections without Losing Their Souls* (Washington: Campaigns & Elections, 2001), p. 141.

38. Pew Research Center, "Bottom-Line Pressures Now Hurting Coverage, Say Journalists," May 23, 2004 (http://people-press.org/reports/display.php3?ReportID= 214 [accessed July 2, 2004]).

39. Ron Hutcheson, "Poll: More Voters Following Race," *Detroit Free Press,* July 9, 2004 (www.freep.com/news/politics/pols9_20040709.htm [accessed July 10, 2004]); Richard Morin and Dan Balz, "Bush Loses Advantage in War on Terror," *Washington Post,* June 22, 2004, p. A1.

40. Pew Research Center, "Voters More Engaged."

41. Pew Research Center, "Kerry Support Rebounds, Race Again Even," September 16, 2004 (http://people-press.org/reports/display.php3?ReportID=224 [accessed December 16, 2004]).

42. Ibid.

43. Pew Research Center, "Voters More Engaged."

44. We believe that our surveys of individuals in the electorate and their own estimation of their level of knowledge is evidence of this point, but we also encourage the reader to look at other studies that deal with the level of political information and knowledge in the electorate. See, for instance, Benjamin I. Page

and Robert Y. Shapiro, *The Rational Public: Fifty Years of Trends in Americans'
Policy Preferences* (University of Chicago Press, 1992); Richard Nadeau and
Richard G. Niemi, "Educated Guesses: The Process of Answering Factual Knowl-
edge Questions in Surveys," *Public Opinion Quarterly* 59, no. 3 (1995): 323–44;
Michael X. Delli Carpini and Scott Keeter, "Measuring Political Knowledge:
Putting First Things First," *American Journal of Political Science* 37, no. 4
(1993): 1179–206.

45. Michael X. Delli Carpini and Scott Keeter, "Stability and Change in the
U.S. Public's Knowledge of Politics," *Public Opinion Quarterly* 55, no. 4 (1991):
583–612; Dalton and Wattenberg, "The Not So Simple Act of Voting," p. 196.

46. Richard D. McKelvey and Peter C. Ordeshook, "Sequential Elections with
Limited Information," *American Journal of Political Science* 29, no. 3 (1985):
480–512; Page and Shapiro, *The Rational Public*; Philip E. Converse, "Popular
Representation an the Distribution of Information," in *Information and Demo-
cratic Processes*, edited by John A. Ferejohn and James Kuklinski (University of
Illinois Press, 1990).

47. Samuel L. Popkin, *The Reasoning Voter: Communication and Persuasion
in Presidential Campaigns* (University of Chicago Press, 1991); Paul M. Sniderman, Richard A. Brody, and Philip E. Tetlock, *Reasoning and Choice: Explo-
rations in Political Psychology* (Cambridge University Press, 1991); Page and
Shapiro, *The Rational Public*.

48. W. Russell Neuman, *The Paradox of Mass Politics: Knowledge and Opinion in the American Electorate* (Harvard University Press, 1986); Popkin, *The
Reasoning Voter*.

49. This figure combines those whose responses were "a great deal" and "a
fair amount."

50. Pew Research Center, "Bottom-Line Pressures Now Hurting Coverage,
Say Journalists."

51. Page and Shapiro, *The Rational Public*, p. 387.

52. For a discussion of the decline in voter turnout, see, for example, Walter
Dean Burnham, *The Current Crisis in American Politics* (Oxford University Press,
1982); Paul R. Abramson, John H. Aldrich, and David W. Rhode, *Change and
Continuity in the 1996 Elections* (Washington: CQ Press, 1998); Paul R. Abram-
son, John H. Aldrich, and David W. Rhode, *Change and Continuity in the 1996
and 1998 Elections* (Washington: CQ Press, 1999); Paul R. Abramson, John H.
Aldrich, and David W. Rhode, *Change and Continuity in the 2000 and 2002
Elections* (Washington: CQ Press, 2003); Ruy A. Teixeira, *The Disappearing
American Voter* (Brookings, 1992); Steven J. Rosenstone and John Mark Hansen,
Mobilization, Participation, and Democracy in America (New York: Macmillan,
1993); Frances Fox Piven and Richard A. Cloward, *Why Americans Don't Vote*
(New York: Pantheon Books, 1988); Frances Fox Piven and Richard A. Cloward,
Why Americans Still Don't Vote: And Why Politicians Want It That Way (Boston:
Beacon Press, 2000); Martin P. Wattenberg, *Where Have All the Voters Gone?*

(Harvard University Press, 2002); Thomas E. Patterson, *The Vanishing Voter: Public Involvement in an Age of Uncertainty* (New York: Knopf, 2002); William H. Flanigan and Nancy H. Zingale, *Political Behavior of the American Electorate*, 10th ed. (Washington: CQ Press, 2002).

53. Of the 1,002 individuals in the original sample, 225 of those least likely to vote were asked questions about why they would probably not vote in the November 2000 election.

54. We limit this to January and February 2004 because John Kerry had become the presumptive nominee by March 3, when his main rival, John Edwards (who later went on to be the vice presidential nominee), suspended his campaign.

55. Joe Hallett, "Caucusgoers Sure of One Thing: They Want Bush Out," *Columbus Dispatch* (Ohio), January 19, 2004, p. 1A.

56. Craig Gilbert, "Kerry Wins Iowa," *Milwaukee Journal Sentinel*, January 20, 2004, p. A1.

57. Erin Kelly, "Voter Turnout Low for Presidential Primaries," *USA Today*, March 9, 2004 (www.usatoday.com/news/politicselections/nation/president/2004-03-09-voter-turnout_x.htm [accessed May 21, 2004]).

58. Center for Responsive Politics, "Political Parties, 1999–2000 Totals" (http://opensecrets.org/parties/index.asp?type=R&cycle=2000 [accessed December 21, 2004]); Center for Responsive Politics, "Republican National Committee, 1999– 2000 Election Cycle" (http://opensecrets.org/parties/total.asp?Cmte= RNC& cycle=2000 [accessed December 21, 2004]); Howard Kurtz, "Candidates' Ads Take High Road; Parties Go Low," *Washington Post*, October 21, 2000, p. A15. See also Ceci Connolly, "Gore Is $6 Million Ahead in Campaign Cash," *Washington Post*, October 21, 2000, p. A10; and Andrew Cain, "Negative Campaign Ads not the Norm, Study Finds," *Washington Times*, September 20, 2000, p. A12.

59. Ralph Hallow, "Bush Bet His Popularity, and GOP Hit the Jackpot," *Washington Times*, November 7, 2002, p. A1; Ralph Hallow, "GOP Eyed Big Win but Declined to Let On; Bush Campaign Reversed Lead in Close States to Republican Side," *Washington Times*, November 14, 2002, p. A4; Stephen Dinan, "It's Anybody's Game: Conflicting Polls Find Control of Congress Too Close to Call," *Washington Times*, November 5, 2002, p. A1; Dan Balz and David S. Broder, "Close Election Turns on Voter Turnout," *Washington Post*, November 1, 2002, p. A1.

60. Pew Research Center, "Voters Liked Campaign 2004."

61. In 2000 only 11 percent of Americans in March and 13 percent in October failed to give consultants a rating; this number did increase substantially to nearly 30 percent in 2002.

62. Pew Research Center, "Voters Liked Campaign 2004."

63. For reviews in the popular press, see Paul Farhi, "Consultant Works His Magic on Kerry," *Washington Post*, January 27, 2004, p. A5; Susan B. Glasser,

"Hired Guns Fuel Fundraising Race," *Washington Post,* April 30, 2000, p. A1; Susan B. Glasser, "In Costly California Race, Control Was Key," *Washington Post,* May 1, 2000, p. A1; Susan B. Glasser, "Consultants Pursue Promising Web of New Business," *Washington Post,* May 3, 2000, p. A1; Bill Ainsworth, "Critics See a Conflict in Davis Advisors' Roles," *San Diego Union-Tribune,* August 25, 1999, p. A1. For reviews in the scholarly literature, see Larry J. Sabato, *The Rise of Political Consultants: New Ways of Winning Elections* (New York: Basic Books, 1981); Mark P. Petracca, "Political Consultants and Democratic Governance," *PS: Political Science and Politics* 22, no. 1 (1989): 11–14; Nicholas J. O'Shaughnessey, *The Phenomenon of Political Marketing* (New York: St. Martin's Press, 1990). For a comprehensive review and critique of these criticisms, see Dulio, *For Better or Worse.*

64. "How He Did It," *Newsweek,* November 15, 2004, p. 92.

65. Ibid., p. 98.

66. In presidential elections, attention to the "horse race" often does less of a service to potential voters than originally appears. Coverage of the latest poll, like it or not, does convey some information. However, in presidential years the national polls are nearly meaningless because of the Electoral College's role in selecting the president. To provide relevant information from polling data, the news media would have to provide data state by state.

67. This attention to Clark's high poll numbers was also premature, given how those same poll numbers began to slide by the end of October 2003.

68. Stephen J. Farnsworth and S. Robert Lichter, *The Nightly News Nightmare: Network Television's Coverage of U.S. Presidential Elections, 1988–2000* (Lanham, Md.: Rowman and Littlefield, 2003).

69. Ibid.

70. Quoted in Edwin Diamond and Stephen Bates, *The Spot: The Rise of Political Advertising on Television,* 3rd ed. (MIT Press, 1992), p. 390.

71. NBC News ran a series of stories on the content of ads by both Bush and Kerry, but Jackson's individual reporting was much more comprehensive and included examinations of many different ads from different sources.

72. Quoted in Brian Williams, "A Reality Check on Campaign Ads: John Kerry" (www.msnbc.com/id/4671352 [accessed May 21, 2004]).

73. Quoted in ibid. We return to a discussion of the content of these types of ads in chapter 5. Here the point is simply that the media write and talk about them.

74. An example of this latter scenario can be found in the 1996 campaign of John Warner for one of Virginia's U.S. Senate seats. Warner's campaign doctored a photograph of an event featuring President Clinton and a number of other Democrats, including Warner's opponent, Mark Warner. The John Warner campaign moved Mark Warner's picture (specifically, his head) to another place in the photo, closer to that of President Clinton, to suggest Mark Warner's ties to Clinton and

paint him as a liberal. On this example, see chapter 5 of this volume as well as Candice J. Nelson, David A. Dulio, and Stephen K. Medvic, *Shades of Gray: Perspectives on Campaign Ethics* (Brookings, 2002).

75. Karen S. Johnson-Cartee and Gary A. Copeland, *Inside Political Campaigns: Theory and Practice* (Westport, Conn.: Praeger, 1997), p. 34; Diamond and Bates, *The Spot*.

76. Thomas E. Patterson, *Out of Order* (New York: Knopf, 1993), p. 200.

77. Howard Kurtz, "New Bush Ad Assails Kerry on Taxes, War," *Washington Post*, March 12, 2004, p. A1.

78. Johnson-Cartee and Copeland, *Inside Political Campaigns*, p. 14.

79. Pew Research Center, "Striking the Balance: Audience Interests, Business Pressures, and Journalists' Values" (1999) (www.people-press.org/press99rpt.htm [accessed May 12, 2004]); Pew Research Center, "Bottom-Line Pressures."

80. Pew Research Center, "Bottom-Line Pressures."

81. Pew Research Center, "Striking the Balance."

82. There was no difference on this question between those more and less likely to vote.

83. Pew Research Center, "Voters Liked Campaign 2004."

84. These rankings were based on a scale of 1 to 5 in which 1 = very poor, 2 = poor, 3 = average, 4 = good, and 5 = excellent.

85. Howard Kurtz, "39% See Bias in Reporting on Campaign; Nontraditional Media Gain Ground, Poll Finds," *Washington Post*, January 12, 2004.

86. "What Do People Want from the Press? National Poll of Public Attitudes toward the News," Center for Media and Public Affairs, *Media Monitor* 11, no. 2 (1997): 1–6.

87. Pew Research Center, "Media Seen as Fair, but Tilting to Gore," 2000 (http://people-press.org/reports/display.php3?ReportID=29 [accessed May 12, 2004]).

88. Dulio, *For Better or Worse*; Thurber, Nelson, and Dulio, "Portrait of Campaign Consultants."

89. Quoted in Howard Kurtz, "In the Lead, Howard Dean Finds He Can't Outrun Media," *Washington Post*, January 14, 2004, p. C1.

90. Dan Balz and Howard Kurtz, "Kerry Vies for Screen Time," *Washington Post*, May 19, 2004, p. A5.

91. Quoted in Kurtz, "In the Lead."

Chapter Four

1. Thomas B. Edsall and Sarah Cohen, "Kerry's Loan Was Key to His Revival," *Washington Post*, February 2, 2004, p. A6. Bush's ability to attract large numbers of donors, as he did in 2000, was not the only cause of this fundraising discrepancy. Certainly, it was not from the Kerry campaign's lack of effort. The reader should remember that Kerry's fundraising was off to a terrible start in 2003. In fact, he loaned his campaign nearly $6.5 million after mortgaging his Boston man-

sion (Edsall and Cohen, "Kerry's Loan Was Key to His Revival"). More important, however, Kerry had been through a lengthy primary season (beginning in 2002, after he formed an exploratory committee to test the waters as a candidate) that left his campaign strapped for cash. Bush faced no primary challenge and was therefore able to build up this great fundraising advantage.

2. On Bush's fundraising, see Candice J. Nelson, "Spending in the 2000 Elections," in *Financing the 2000 Elections,* edited by David B. Magleby (Brookings, 2002).

3. John C. Green and Nathan S. Bigelow, "The 2000 Presidential Nominations: The Costs of Innovation," in *Financing the 2000 Election,* edited by Magleby, p. 54.

4. Edsall and Cohen, "Kerry's Loan Was Key to His Revival."

5. Thomas B. Edsall and Jim VandeiHei, "Kerry Aims to Accept Federal Funding," *Washington Post,* July 12, 2004, p. A4.

6. A study conducted by the Campaign Finance Institute has recommended a series of changes to the current funding system. See Campaign Finance Institute, "Distinguished Task Force Recommends Revamping Public Financing of Presidential Elections," September 22, 2003 (www.cfinst.org/presidential/index.html [accessed July 7, 2004]).

7. Nelson, "Spending in the 2000 Elections."

8. Thomas B. Edsall, "Liberals Form Fund to Defeat President," *Washington Post,* August 8, 2003, p. A3.

9. Nelson, "Spending in the 2000 Elections."

10. Larry Nobel, executive director of the Center for Responsive Politics, "The Role of Money and Fundraising in Lobbying," presentation before the Public Affairs and Advocacy Institute, American University, January, 2005; Thomas B. Edsall and James V. Grimaldi, "On Nov. 2, GOP Got More Bang for Its Billion, Analysis Shows," *Washington Post,* December 30, 2004, p. A1.

11. Center for Responsive Politics, "2004 Election Overview Most Expensive Races" (www.opensecrets.org/overview/topraces.asp [accessed February 12, 2005]).

12. Ibid.

13. Federal Election Commission, "Presidential Prenomination Campaign Receipts through May 31, 2004" (June 6, 2004) (www.fec.gov/press/bkgnd/pres_cf/documents/presreceiptsm62004.pdf [accessed January 21, 2005]).

14. Campaign Finance Institute, "CFI Analysis of the Presidential Candidates' Financial Reports Filed June 20" (June 30, 2004) (www.cfinst.org/pr/063004.html [accessed July 18, 2004]).

15. Center for Responsive Politics, "2004 Election Overview Stats at a Glance" (www.opensecrets.org/overview/stats.asp?Cycle=2004 [accessed February 12, 2005]); Green and Bigelow, "The 2000 Presidential Nominations"; Anthony Corrado, "Financing the 2000 Presidential General Election," in *Financing the 2000 Election,* edited by Magleby.

16. Federal Election Commission, "Congressional Funding Continues to Grow" (May 11, 2004) (www.fec.gov/press/press2004/20040511canstat/20040511canstat.html [accessed January 21, 2005]).

17. Center for Responsive Politics, "2004 Election Overview Stats at a Glance."

18. Federal Election Commission, "Party Fundraising Continues to Grow" (August 6, 2004) (www.fec.gov/press/press2004/20040526party/20040526pty.stat.html [accessed January 21, 2005]); Corrado, "Financing the 2000 Presidential General Election."

19. In March 2000 and November 2002 more than three-quarters of those surveyed saw a relationship between special interests and campaign contributions, compared with slightly less than two-thirds of those surveyed in October 2000, just before the presidential election. We see no obvious explanation for this difference, but it may be that the public perceives the relationship between special interests and money to be more closely tied to congressional candidates than to presidential candidates. Although, clearly, congressional candidates were on the ballot in October 2000, the greater focus of the media, and perhaps the public, was on the presidential election.

20. Gregory Wawro, "A Panel Probit Analysis of Campaign Contributions and Roll-Call Votes," *American Journal of Political Science* 25, no. 3 (2001): 563–79; James M. Snyder, "Campaign Contributions as Investments: The U.S. House of Representatives, 1980–1986," *Journal of Political Economy* 98, no. 6 (1990): 1195–227; John R. Wright, "Contributions, Lobbying, and Committee Voting in the U.S. House of Representatives," *American Political Science Review* 84, no. 2 (1990): 417–38; Janet M. Box-Steffensmeier and J. Tobin Grant, "All in a Day's Work: The Financial Rewards of Legislative Effectiveness," *Legislative Studies Quarterly* 24, no. 4 (1999): 511–27.

21. We interpret these results to mean that consultants do not think money plays a major role in influencing policy. However, a different interpretation is also possible, namely, that consultants see that money does influence policy but that they do not see it as a problem. We reject the latter view, based on our other work on consultants.

22. Susan B. Glasser, "Hired Guns Fuel Fundraising Race," *Washington Post,* April 30, 2000, p. A1; Susan B. Glasser, "In Costly California Race, Control Was Key," *Washington Post,* May 1, 2000, p. A1; Susan B. Glasser, "Consultants Pursue Promising Web of New Business," *Washington Post,* May 3, 2000, p. A1.

23. See, for instance, Larry J. Sabato, *The Rise of Political Consultants: New Ways of Winning Elections* (New York: Basic Books, 1981).

24. David B. Magleby and Candice J. Nelson, *The Money Chase: Congressional Campaign Finance Reform* (Brookings, 1990); Diana Dwyre and Victoria Farrar-Meyers, *Legislative Labyrinth: Congress and Campaign Finance Reform* (Washington: CQ Press, 2001).

25. Anthony Corrado, Thomas E. Mann, and Trevor Potter, eds., *Inside the Campaign Finance Reform Battle: Court Testimony on the New Reforms* (Brookings, 2003); Michael J. Malbin, ed., *Life after Reform: When the Bipartisan Campaign Reform Act Meets Politics* (Lanham, Md.: Rowman and Littlefield, 2003); Charles Lane, "Justices Split on Campaign Finance," *Washington Post*, September 9, 2003, p. A1; Linda Greenhouse, "Justices, in 5-to-4 Decision, Back Campaign Finance Law That Curbs Contributions," *New York Times*, December 11, 2003, p. A1.

26. Center for Responsive Politics, "Political Parties: 2003–2004 Totals" (http://opensecrets.org/parties/index.asp [accessed February 12, 2005]).

27. Ibid.

28. David B. Magleby and J. Quin Monson, eds., *The Last Hurrah? Soft Money and Issue Advocacy in the 2002 Congressional Elections* (Brookings, 2004), p. 64.

29. The Supreme Court, in a footnote in its decision in *Buckley* v. *Valeo*, ruled that only advertising that contained words expressly advocating the election or defeat of a candidate—words such as "vote for," "support," "oppose," or "vote against"—were subject to hard-money contribution limits. Because political issue advocacy does not contain such words but rather uses phrases such as "call Senator X and tell him or her your views," the ads could be funded with unlimited soft money.

30. Quoted in Ruth Marcus and Dan Balz, "Democrats Have Fresh Doubts on 'Soft Money' Ban; Some Fear GOP Would Gain Edge in Campaign Finances," *Washington Post*, March 5, 2001, p. A1.

31. Campaign finance reform is not an issue that is of great concern to the American public. When a *Washington Post* survey asked the public how closely they were following the campaign finance reform debate near the height of the BCRA battle in Congress, almost two-thirds (62 percent) responded "not too closely" or "not closely at all" (*Washington Post* poll, February 2002). Not long after the *Washington Post* poll, Fox News asked how likely individuals were to read an article about campaign finance reform, and only one in five Americans said they would read the article (Fox News–Opinion Dynamics poll, April 2002). In the same Fox News poll, when asked what issues were most important for Congress to be working on, only 3 percent of the public mentioned campaign finance reform, compared with the economy (19 percent), education (15 percent), Social Security (14 percent), and homeland security (12 percent). The survey results reported here were obtained from searches of the iPoll databank and other resources provided by the Roper Center for Public Opinion Research, University of Connecticut. The polls cited in the following five notes were also accessed from the Roper Center.

32. CBS News–*New York Times* poll, 2000.

33. Gallup–CNN–*USA Today* poll, 2000.

34. State of the First Amendment 2001 survey by the Freedom Forum and the Center for Survey Research and Analysis, University of Connecticut, May 16–June 6, 2001.

35. ABC News–*Washington Post* poll, 2001; News Interest poll, 2002.

36. CBS News poll, 2002.

37. Campaign Finance Institute, "CFI's Wrap-Up Analysis of Primary Funding," October 4, 2004 (www.cfinst.org/pr/100404.html [accessed February 7, 2005]).

38. Campaign Finance Institute, "CFI Analysis of the Presidential Candidates' Financial Reports."

39. Campaign Finance Institute, "CFI's Wrap-Up Analysis."

40. Ibid.

41. Ibid.

42. Center for Responsive Politics, "Political Parties: 2003–2004 Totals."

43. Ibid.

44. James V. Grimaldi and Thomas B. Edsall, "Super-Rich Step into Political Vacuum; McCain-Feingold Paved Way for 527s," *Washington Post*, October 17, 2004, p. A1.

45. Ibid.

46. Ibid.

47. Ibid.

48. Dan Balz and Thomas B. Edsall, "Democrats Forming Parallel Campaign," *Washington Post*, March 10, 2004, p. A1.

49. Thomas B. Edsall and Sarah Cohen, "Kerry Campaign Relying on Help of Groups' Ads," *Washington Post*, March 22, 2004, p. A4.

50. Edsall, "Liberals Form Fund to Defeat President."

51. Center for Responsive Politics, "New This Week: Total 527 Receipts and Expenditures, 2003–2004" (www.opensecrets.org/527s/527new.asp?cycle=2004 [accessed February 12, 2005]).

52. Grimaldi and Edsall, "Super-Rich Step into Political Vacuum."

53. Thomas B. Edsall, "After Late Start, Republican Groups Jump into the Lead," *Washington Post*, October 17, 2004, p. A15.

54. Ibid.

55. Ibid.

56. Center for Responsive Politics, "New This Week."

57. Ibid.

58. Ibid. These are figures for all 527 organizations.

59. Center for Responsive Politics, "Top Individual Contributors to 527 Committees 2004 Election Cycle" (www.opensecrets.org/527s/527indivs.asp?cycle=2004 [accessed February 12, 2005]).

60. Ibid.

61. Mark H. Rodeffer, "Stand by Your Ad," *Campaigns & Elections* (June 2004): 17–19.

62. Ibid.

63. Campaign Finance Institute, "CFI Analysis of the Presidential Candidates' Financial Reports."

64. Dana Milbank and Jim VandeHei, "From Bush, Unprecedented Negativity," *Washington Post,* May 31, 2004, p. A1.

65. Rodeffer, "Stand by Your Ad."

66. Ibid.

Chapter Five

1. Quoted in Michael Laris, "Mention of Gay Daughter a Cheap Trick, Lynne Cheney Says," *Washington Post,* October 14, 2004, p. A6.

2. Dana Milbank and Jim VandeHei, "From Bush, Unprecedented Negativity," *Washington Post,* May 31, 2004, p. A1; Howard Kurtz, "Ads Push the Factual Envelope," *Washington Post,* October 20, 2004, p. A1; Charles Babington, "Crude or Refined, It's Many Barrels of Money," *Washington Post,* July 18, 2004, p. A6.

3. Quoted in Milbank and VandeHei, "From Bush, Unprecedented Negativity."

4. Pew Research Center, "Voters More Engaged, but Campaign Gets Lukewarm Ratings," July 8, 2004 (http://people-press.org/reports/display.php3? ReportID= 218 [accessed July 12, 2004]).

5. Ibid.

6. Kurtz, "Ads Push the Factual Envelope."

7. Stephen Ansolabehere and Shanto Iyengar, *Going Negative: How Political Advertisements Shrink and Polarize the Electorate* (New York: Free Press, 1995); Stephen Ansolabehere, Shanto Iyengar, Adam Simon, and Nicholas Valentino, "Does Attack Advertising Demobilize the Electorate?" *American Political Science Review* 88, no. 4 (1994): 829–38; Wendy M. Rahn and Rebecca Hirshorn, "Political Advertising and Public Mood: A Study of Children's Political Orientations," *Political Communication* 16, no. 4 (1999): 387–407; Paul Freedman and Kenneth M. Goldstein, "Measuring Media Exposure and the Effects of Negative Campaign Ads," *American Journal of Political Science* 43, no. 4 (1999): 1189–208.

8. Paul R. Babitt and Richard R. Lau, "The Impact of Negative Political Campaigns on Political Knowledge," paper prepared for the annual meeting of the Southern Political Science Association, Atlanta, November 7–9, 1994; Kim Fridkin Kahn and Patrick J. Kenney, "Do Negative Campaigns Mobilize or Suppress Turnout? Clarifying the Relationship between Negativity and Participation," *American Political Science Review* 93, no. 4 (1999): 877–89; Martin P. Wattenberg and Craig L. Brains, "Negative Campaign Advertising: Demobilizer or Mobilizer?" *American Political Science Review* 93, no. 4 (1999): 891–99. On increasing voter turnout, see Craig L. Brains and Martin P. Wattenberg, "Campaign Issue Knowledge and Salience: Comparing Reception from TV Commer-

cials, TV News, and Newspapers," *American Journal of Political Science* 40, no. 1 (1996): 172–93; Gina M. Garramone, Charles T. Atkin, Bruce E. Pinkelton, and Richard E. Cole, "Effects of Negative Political Advertising on the Political Process," *Journal of Broadcasting and Electronic Media* 34, no. 3 (1990): 299–311; John G. Geer and Richard R. Lau, "Modeling Campaign Effects: Does Attack Advertising Depress Turnout?" paper prepared for the annual meeting of the American Political Science Association, Boston, September 3–6, 1998; Kahn and Kenney, "Do Negative Campaigns Mobilize or Suppress Turnout?"; Richard R. Lau, Gerald Pomper, and Grace Ann Mumoli, "Effects of Negative Campaigning on Senate Election Outcomes: 1998, '90, '94, and '96," paper prepared for the annual meeting of the Midwest Political Science Association, Chicago, April 18–20, 1998.

9. Kathleen Hall Jamieson, Paul Waldman, and Susan Sherr, "Eliminate the Negative? Categories of Analysis for Political Advertisements," in *Crowded Airwaves: Campaign Advertising in Elections,* edited by James A. Thurber, Candice J. Nelson, and David A. Dulio (Brookings, 2000).

10. Clifford J. Levy, "The 2000 Campaign: The Ad Campaign; Making Breast Cancer a Political Issue against John McCain," *New York Times,* March 4, 2000, p. A10. See also Edward Walsh and Terry Neal, "Bush Begins N.Y. Swing Talking Breast Cancer," *Washington Post,* March 4, 2000, p. A6; Adam Nagourney and Frank Bruni, "Bush and McCain Battle for Support on Tuesday in High-Stakes Territory," *New York Times,* March 4, 2000, p. A10; Dick Polman, "McCain Raps Bush Tactics on Cancer Ad," *Milwaukee Journal Sentinel,* March 6, 2000, p. A6.

11. Ken Fireman and William Douglass, "'Rats' Nest for Bush," *Newsday,* September 13, 2000, p. A5.

12. Ibid.

13. The text of this ad was accessed through the ad archive housed by *National Journal* magazine at www.nationaljournal.com.

14. Whit Ayers, "Can Campaign Advertising Be on the Level?" *Campaigns & Elections* (October 2000): 20–24, p. 20.

15. R. Sam Garrett, "Campaigns, Crises, and Communication: Crisis Management in House and Senate Campaigns," paper prepared for the annual meeting of the American Political Science Association, Chicago, September 2–5, 2004; R. Sam Garrett, "Adrenalized Fear: Crisis Management in U.S. House and Senate Campaigns," Ph.D. dissertation, American University, 2005.

16. Ibid.

17. Kathleen Hall Jamieson, *Dirty Politics: Deception, Distraction, and Democracy* (Oxford University Press, 1992).

18. Paul Farhi, "Bush Ads Using 9/11 Images Stir Anger," *Washington Post,* March 5, 2004, p. A1.

19. L. Sandy Maisel, "Candidates: Promises and Persuasion," in *Shades of Gray: Perspectives on Campaign Ethics*, edited by Candice J. Nelson, David A. Dulio, and Stephen K. Medvic (Brookings, 2002), p. 46.

20. Alfred Tella, "Kerry, Jobs, and Misery," *Washington Times*, April 25, 2004, p. B4; John DiStaso, "Kerry Plans Return Trip to Seacoast," *Manchester (N.H.) Union Leader*, April 6, 2004, p. A1.

21. www.johnkerry.com/pressroom/releases/pr_2004_0330d.html (accessed June 21, 2004).

22. Included in this research is Nelson, Dulio, and Medvic, eds., *Shades of Gray*, a volume that addresses the question of ethical campaigns head-on and in detail; it is also a much more theoretical examination of the topic. Our purposes in this chapter are not to repeat what has been done in that volume. Rather, we aim simply to outline what we have found in our empirical research on different campaign actors.

23. For more on specific criticisms, see Mark P. Petracca, "Political Consultants and Democratic Governance," *PS: Political Science and Politics* 22, no. 1 (1989): 11–14; Larry J. Sabato, *The Rise of Political Consultants: New Ways of Winning Elections* (New York: Basic Books, 1981); and Nicholas J. O'Shaughnessey, *The Phenomenon of Political Marketing* (New York: St. Martin's Press, 1990).

24. The survey questions we asked the different groups of campaign actors differed slightly. In the 1999 consultants survey' and the 2002 party elites' survey, respondents were asked, "In your view, how common are unethical practices in the political consulting business? Do unethical practices happen very often, fairly often, sometimes, rarely or not at all?" Respondents in the 2002 consultants' survey were asked, "In your view, how common were unethical practices in the political consulting business for this election cycle? Do you think unethical practices happened very often, fairly often, sometimes, rarely or not at all?" In the surveys of the general public in both 2000 (March and October) and 2002, respondents were asked, "In your view, how common are unethical practices in the campaigns? Do unethical practices happen very often, fairly often, sometimes, rarely or not at all?" Consultants were asked about their business specifically because of its intimate link with the conduct of the campaign on an everyday basis. This has both advantages and disadvantages. It is advantageous in that it focused the respondents on the kind of occurrences we were interested in—those that happen inside the campaign as it is being run by the professionals—rather than what might be construed as extraneous events—the behavior of other actors such as the media or interest groups, for instance. This wording, however, also could lead consultants to think about their business in just that sense—from a financial perspective. We have developed a typology of activities gleaned from an open-ended question in the 1999 survey that asked consultants to describe an example of a serious ethical

problem they had experienced or knew about from contact with others during a recent political campaign. The responses to this question were varied and sometimes focused on the business practices of consultants rather than a tactical or strategic maneuver that occurred in the everyday workings of the campaign. For the typology, see Candice J. Nelson, Stephen K. Medvic, and David A. Dulio, "Political Consultants: Hired Guns or Gatekeepers of Democracy?" in Nelson, Dulio, and Medvic, *Shades of Gray*. The general public was asked generally about campaigns because we wanted their view of how the process was operating on the whole. We felt that to appropriately and carefully measure the phenomenon we were interested in, we had to ask consultants and party elites about the business of campaigns, since that is what rules the day in how modern campaigns are run (see chapter 2). However, to ask the general public about the business of political consulting and what some might deem "inside baseball" would quite likely yield unreliable results, given that not all Americans are familiar with what it is that political consultants do and even fewer are familiar with the business of political consulting. Although the wording is slightly different, we believe that each question reliably and validly gets at the appropriate phenomenon we were exploring.

25. Consultants were also asked this question in 1998. However, there was a different format in the response set: they were asked to put the frequency of unethical practices in the consulting business on the scale of "very often," "sometimes," "not very often," "rarely," or "never." In this measurement, 9.6 percent said unethical practices occurred very often, which is consistent with the findings in 1999 and 2002; the same is true for the nearly 42 percent who reported that unethical practices sometimes occurred. Moreover, few consultants said that unethical practices were rare in the consulting business and campaigns: only slightly more than 12 percent said they happened rarely, and only 0.5 percent said they never happen.

26. We address this last point later.

27. For a fuller discussion of the partisan split in the industry and the presence of consultants who do not align themselves with either major party, see David A. Dulio, *For Better or Worse? How Professional Political Consultants Are Changing Elections in America* (State University of New York Press, 2004).

28. Jim VandeHei, "Focus on Values and the Economy," *Washington Post,* July 8, 2004, p. A1; Patrick O'Connor, "'This Is a Fight about Creating Jobs in America,' Candidate Tells Supporters," *The Hill,* July 7, 2004, p. 1; Jim Vande-Hei and Dan Balz, "Kerry Picks Edwards as Running Mate," *Washington Post,* July 7, 2004, p. A1.

29. Jim VandeHei and Mike Allen, "Rhetoric on Values Turns Personal," *Washington Post,* July 10, 2004, p. A1.

30. Lois Romano, "In Oklahoma, GOP Race Not a Given," *Washington Post,* July 12, 2004, p. A4.

31. Institute for Global Ethics, "Poll Shows Voters Want Greater Civility, Ethical Behavior in Campaigns," December 15, 1999 (www.globalethics.org/news/cvs.htm [accessed July 12, 2004]).

32. "Rep. Cooley Denies He Lied about Army Record," *Seattle Post-Intelligencer*, May 29, 1996, p. A3; "Congressman Says He Didn't Lie to Voters about Military Service," *Seattle Post-Intelligencer*, December 17, 1996, p. B2.

33. "Rep. Cooley Denies He Lied about Army Record."

34. For an example of candidates' lying on their resumes, see Michael S. Gerber, "Kansas GOP Primary Turning Nasty," *The Hill*, July 31, 2002, p. 27.

35. The text of this ad was accessed through the ad archive housed by *National Journal* magazine at www.nationaljournal.com.

36. Quoted in Joseph Curl, "Bush Accuses Kerry of Seeking Higher Taxes," *Washington Times*, March 26, 2004, p. A1.

37. FactCheck.Org, "Bush Accuses Kerry of 350 Votes for 'Higher Taxes.' Higher than What?" March 24, 2004 (www.factcheck.org/article.aspx?docid=159 [accessed May 5, 2004]).

38. Quoted in Curl, "Bush Accuses Kerry of Seeking Higher Taxes."

39. The text of this ad was accessed through the ad archive housed by *National Journal* magazine at www.nationaljournal.com.

40. FactCheck.Org, "Outsourcing Jobs: The PRESIDENT Said That?" April 3, 2004 (www.factcheck.org/article 168 [accessed May 5, 2004]).

41. In our surveys, the wording for the response set for political consultants and party elites was slightly different from the wording for the general public. We asked consultants and party elites whether campaign practices were acceptable, questionable, or clearly unethical; the general public was asked if campaign practices were acceptable, questionable, or unacceptable.

42. Susan Green, "Baucus Rival Quits Montana Race: Ex-Denverite Says Ad Made Him 'Look Gay,'" *Denver Post*, October 11, 2002, p. B1.

43. Quoted in Bob Anez, "Republican Candidate Drops out of Montana Senate Race, Complains Ad Made Him Look Gay," Associated Press state and local, October 10, 2002.

44. Quoted in Green, "Baucus Rival Quits Montana Race."

45. Ibid.

46. "Right Issue; Sleazy Tactic," *Denver Post*, October 14, 2002, p. B7.

47. Anez, "Republican Candidate Drops out of Montana Senate Race."

48. Dore Schwinden, quoted in "Right Issue; Sleazy Tactic."

49. The number of independents in the 2002 survey was relatively small, so we are hesitant to draw any conclusions from these data and caution the reader to take care when interpreting these findings. It is interesting to note that this split did not appear in the 1999 survey. Because of slightly different question wording, we do not report the data from 1998.

50. This question was not asked in 1998.

51. Glen Johnson, "'Push Poll' Angers McCain," *Chicago Sun-Times*, February 11, 2000, p. 35.

52. Rob Daves, "'Push Polling' Controversy Muddies the Field for Public Opinion Surveyors," *(Minneapolis) Star Tribune*, February 17, 2000, p. 28A.

53. Ibid.

54. Complicating matters here is the fact that many reputable pollsters use the term *push poll* in their everyday business, but not with the same meaning as the push polls discussed here. Respectable pollsters use the term in the context of testing a candidate's message. Sound survey research that tries to identify the best way for a candidate to talk about an issue can "push" a respondent to provide researchers with an answer that helps achieve this goal.

55. Because there were seven types of consultants in our survey, cell sizes are small, making comparisons among types of consultants difficult. For this reason, we did not include other comparisons of this sort. However, because of the nature and name of this tactic, we felt a comparison was necessary. In addition, we report numbers only from the 1999 study here because the sample size in the 2002 panel study was smaller, which made comparisons with these many groups even more difficult.

56. Quoted in Daves, "'Push Polling' Controversy Muddies the Field."

57. Ansolabehere and Iyengar, *Going Negative*, p. 9.

58. Ibid., p. 102.

59. See Nelson, Dulio, and Medvic, *Shades of Gray*; and Dulio, *For Better or Worse?* The typology of unethical practices mentioned earlier (Nelson, Medvic, and Dulio, "Political Consultants: Hired Guns or Gatekeepers of Democracy?"), based on research in which consultants were asked about unethical practices they had either experienced or were familiar with from a recent campaign, provides more detail on the kinds of practices that consultants considered to be unethical; many of these had to do with business practices in the industry, such as taking on too many clients or working for more than one party (candidate, political party, or interest group) in the same race.

60. Here we stray from our focus on federal races to bring in the opinions of those whose names appear on the ballot. Although we cannot make a direct connection to federal races, the data are still informative. For the study referenced in this section, Herrnson and his colleagues surveyed 364 state legislative candidates. The results presented here are from that survey and can be found in Ronald A. Faucheux and Paul S. Herrnson, eds., *The Good Fight: How Political Candidates Struggle to Win Elections without Losing Their Souls* (Washington: Campaigns & Elections, 2001).

61. For the following comparisons, see tables 5-3, 5-4, 5-6, and 5-8.

62. Faucheux and Herrnson, *The Good Fight*, p. 132.

63. Quoted in British Broadcasting Company, "Mr. Moore Runs for Washington," 1999 (www.american.edu/academic.depts/spa/ccps/video.html [accessed December 20, 2004]).

64. Institute for Global Ethics, "Poll Shows Voters Want Greater Civility, Ethical Behavior in Campaigns."

65. In the IGE poll, 67 percent said that they could trust the government in Washington only some of the time or never. Many polls support this finding: 51 percent said the same in a poll conducted by the *Los Angeles Times*, August 22–25, 2002; 52 percent in a Gallup poll conducted September 2–4, 2002; and 57 percent in a poll conducted by CBS News/*New York Times*, September 2–5, 2002; 59 percent said they could trust the government only some of the time in a poll conducted by the *Washington Post*, September 3–6, 2002; 60 percent in a CBS News/*New York Times* poll, July 13–27, 2003; and 58 percent in a Gallup poll conducted October 24–26, 2003. The survey results reported here were obtained from searches of the iPOLL Databank and other resources provided by the Roper Center for Public Opinion Research, University of Connecticut.

66. Annenberg Public Policy Center, "Americans Say They Don't Learn from Ads but They Believe Strained Campaign Ads Anyway, Annenberg Data Show," National Annenberg Election Survey, May 12, 2004 (www.annenbergpublicpolicy center.org/naes/2004_03_%20kerry-and-bush_05-12_pr.pdf [accessed July 9, 2004]).

67. Annenberg Public Policy Center, "Majority of 18- to-29-Year-Olds Think Bush Favors Reinstating the Draft," National Annenberg Election Survey, October 8, 2004 (www.annenbergpublicpolicycenter.org/naes/2004_03_reinstate-the-draft_10-08_pr.pdf [accessed December 20, 2004]).

68. Jill Buckley, Democratic consultant, quoted in Alan Ehrenhalt, "Technology, Strategy Bring New Campaign Era," *Congressional Quarterly Weekly Report*, December 7, 1985, p. 2560; Roger Stone, Republican consultant, quoted in Steven W. Colford, "Polls Accentuated Negative," *Advertising Age*, November 10, 1986, p. 104. Mark Nevins, Dennis Moore's consultant, quoted in British Broadcasting Company, "Mr. Moore Runs for Washington."

69. In our experience with consultants over the seven years of this project, a great many showed an interest in the broader question of elections and the democratic process. We know this goes against how many popular accounts describe consultants, but we have seen that consultants are both willing and able to engage the ideas presented by political scientists with regard to larger questions of campaigning and elections.

70. These figures should not be immediately read as a decrease in the number of consultants who support a code of ethics. It is likely that the latter two numbers are understated. In the 1998 survey, two questions were asked about the appropriateness of a code. The first asked consultants whether there should be a

code of conduct for campaigners. Some consultants volunteered that one already existed; those who offered this response were presented with a follow-up question, asking again whether they thought there should be some kind of code. The responses to both of these questions yielded the 81 percent reported in text. However, in 1999 and 2002, because of time constraints in the survey (other questions were added that were not included in 1998, so parts of the original survey were dropped), the follow-up to the question about whether there should be a code was not asked. Therefore we were not able to gauge the thoughts of those consultants who volunteered that a code already existed on the appropriateness of a code.

71. There were slight partisan differences in the responses to this question, as fewer Republicans (59 percent) than either Democrats (69.7 percent) or independents (63.6 percent) said the industry's professional organization should be able to censure violators of the code.

72. For a further discussion of the enforcement difficulties associated with the AAPC code, see Nelson, Medvic, and Dulio, "Political Consultants."

73. Institute for Global Ethics, "Pew Charitable Trusts Provide Support for Ethical Elections," July 13, 1996 (http://globalethics.org/news/pew.html [accessed July 12, 2004]).

Chapter Six

1. Thomas Holbrook, *Do Campaigns Matter?* (Thousand Oaks, Calif.: Sage Press, 1996).

2. Exit poll data were collected by two polling firms, Mitofsky International and Edison Media Research, on behalf of the National Election Pool, a consortium of six national media organizations (AP, ABC, CBS, CNN, Fox, and NBC). Data reported here were reported on CNN.com (www.cnn.com/ELECTION/2004/pages/results/states/US/P/00/epolls.0.html [accessed February 10, 2005]).

3. Evan Thomas, *Election 2004: How BushCheney'04 Won and What You Can Expect in the Future* (New York: Public Affairs, 2005), p. 189.

4. Thomas B. Edsall and James V. Grimaldi, "On Nov. 2, GOP Got More Bang for Its Billion, Analysis Shows," *Washington Post,* December 30, 2004, p. A1.

5. Jonathan Weisman, "Kerry's Inner Circle Expands," *Washington Post,* July 14, 2004, p. A1.

6. Jim VandeHei, "Old-School Team to Sell Kerry as Modern Centrist," *Washington Post,* April 21, 2004, p. A1.

7. Mark Leibovich and Jim VandeHei, "New Blood at Heart of Kerry Campaign," *Washington Post,* September 17, 2004, p. A1.

8. Howard Kurtz, "Kerry Goes to the Bullpen," November 11, 2003 (www.washingtonpost.com/wp-dyn/articles/A25629-2003Nov11.html [accessed January 20, 2005]).

9. Dale Russakoff and Jim VandeHei, "Lifelong Collector of Data Can Bog Down His Staffs," *Washington Post,* October 13, 2004, p. A1.

10. Paul Farhi, "In Kerry Campaign, Overlaps Chafe," *Washington Post,* October 9, 2003, p. A1.

11. VandeHei, "Old-School Team to Sell Kerry."

12. Anthony Corrado, "Party Finance in the Wake of BCRA: An Overview" (Washington: Campaign Finance Institute, January 14, 2005).

13. Jackson Dunn, "The Political Parties after BCRA," presentation at "The Election after Reform: Money and Politics and the Bipartisan Campaign Reform Act," Campaign Finance Institute conference, Campaign Finance Institute, Washington, D.C., January 14, 2005.

14. Corrado, "Party Finance."

15. Ibid.

16. Ibid.

17. Steven J. Rosenstone and John Mark Hansen, *Mobilization, Participation, and Democracy in America* (New York: Macmillan, 1993).

18. Donald P. Green and Alan S. Gerber, *Get Out the Vote! How to Increase Voter Turnout* (Brookings, 2004), p. 9.

19. Evelyn Nieves, "Unions Take Kerry Message Door to Door," *Washington Post,* June 21, 2004, p. A2.

20. Comments made at "The Election after Reform: Money and Politics and the Bipartisan Campaign Reform Act," Campaign Finance Institute conference, Campaign Finance Institute, Washington, D.C., January 14, 2005.

21. Quoted in E. J. Dionne, "The Democrats' Rove Envy," *Washington Post,* December 14, 2004, p. A27.

22. John F. Harris and Paul Farhi, "Taking the Campaign to the People, One Doorstep at a Time," *Washington Post,* April 18, 2004, p. A1.

23. Edsall and Grimaldi, "On Nov. 2, GOP Got More Bang for Its Billion."

24. Ibid.

25. Ibid.

26. Ron Hutcheson, "Poll: More Voters Following Race," *Detroit Free Press,* July 9, 2004 (www.freep.com/news/politics/pols9_20040709.htm) [accessed July 10, 2004]); Richard Morin and Dan Balz, "Bush Loses Advantage in War on Terror," *Washington Post,* June 22, 2004, p. A1.

27. Pew Research Center, "Voters More Engaged, but Campaign Gets Lukewarm Ratings," July 8, 2004 (http://people-press.org/reports/display.php3?ReportID= 218 [accessed July 12, 2004]).

28. Pew Research Center, "Kerry Support Rebounds, Race Again Even," September 16, 2004 (http://people-press.org/reports/display.php3?ReportID=224 [accessed December 16, 2004]).

29. Guy Gugliotta, "Politics In, Voter Apathy Out amid Heavy Turnout," *Washington Post,* November 3, 2004, p. A1.

30. Harris and Farhi, "Taking the Campaign to the People."

31. Rather, they are probably more likely to agree with the *London Daily Mirror* (November 4, 2004, p. 1), which, the morning after the election, ran the headline, "How Can 59,054,087 People Be So DUMB?"

32. Ceci Connolly and Jonathan Weisman, "The Choice for Voters: Health Care or Tax Cuts," *Washington Post*, June 28, p. A1; Dana Milbank, "All Politics Is Local as Ever, and so Are Issues," *Washington Post*, August 30, 2004, p. A6.

33. Twelve months later, however, in February 2005, Howard Dean was chosen to chair the Democratic National Committee.

34. Edsall and Grimaldi, "On Nov. 2, GOP Got More Bang for Its Billion."

35. In February 2005, in a letter to members of Congress, the chair and vice chair of the Federal Election Commission expressed their concerns about the future of the public financing system. Chairman Scott E. Thomas, a Democrat, and Vice Chairman Michael E. Toner, a Republican, stated that "if Congress does not act within the next two years, the system runs the risk of being totally irrelevant in the 2008 election and beyond" (Thomas B. Edsall, "Top FEC Officials Urge Higher Spending Limit," *Washington Post*, February 10, 2005, p. A5).

36. Stephen Weissman and Ruth Hansan, "Advocacy Groups: 527s and Soft Money," paper presented at "The Election after Reform: Money and Politics and the Bipartisan Campaign Reform Act," Campaign Finance Institute conference, Campaign Finance Institute, Washington, D.C., January 14, 2005.

37. Geoff Earle, "Multimillionaires Funding Expensive Pro-Bush 527 Ads," *The Hill*, October 27, 2004, p. 4.

38. Quoted in James V. Grimaldi and Thomas B. Edsall, "Super-Rich Step into Political Vacuum; McCain-Feingold Paved Way for 527s," *Washington Post*, October 17, 2004, p. A1.

39. Glen Justice, "McCain Calls for New Limits on Money to Political Groups," *New York Times*, February 3, 2005, p. A14.

40. *Jacobellis* v. *Ohio*, 378 U.S. 184 (1964), 197.

Index